endorsements

"There are many words that came to mind as I began to write an endorsement for this book (and its author!): remarkable, courageous, and honest are but a few! If you have ever found yourself in the middle of something that is life changing and mind blowing and didn't have a clue HOW to take the next step forward—**read this book**. Virginia Pillars beautifully conveys the grace-filled love of a mother for her mentally ill child as she lays it all on the line in pursuit of help for her daughter's increasing symptoms.

"You will be inspired and encouraged to read *Broken Brain, Fortified Faith*—a powerfully honest account of hope and trust in the midst of the despair of mental illness. I am grateful to the author for sharing this beautiful and hope-filled story with the world."

—*Wanda L. Sanchez, Executive Producer, "Lifeline with Craig Roberts," KFAX-AM1100, San Francisco Bay Area*

"Virginia Pillars tells the story of her adult daughter's descent into schizophrenia with unflinching honesty in *Broken Brain, Fortified Faith*. But Pillars does more than tell how family, friends, and mental health professionals rallied around one young woman, providing the treatment and support her daughter, Amber, needed to regain her mental health and learn to manage her condition; the author also educates readers about how the disease affects the brain, how it is treated, and what people must do financially and legally to protect loved ones until they recover from the disease. Best of all, Pillars shares her thoughts, doubts, and faith struggles, as well as the comfort and strength she found as she prayed for her daughter and saw those prayers answered in unexpected ways. *Broken Brain, Fortified Faith* is an approachable and highly readable book for anyone who wants to learn more about schizophrenia and how to support those dealing with it. I highly recommend it."

—*Jolene Philo, author of* Does My Child Have PTSD? What to Do When Your Child Is Hurting from the Inside Out

"A story of hope in a family that dealt with mental illness, infertility, and loss. Pillars has the ability to inject hope and light into what could otherwise have been a depressing and, for some, a devastating situation. Highly recommended for any family who is struggling with a diagnosis of mental illness or for readers who love a good memoir."

—*Mary Potter Kenyon, newspaper reporter, workshop presenter, and author of the award-winning* Refined By Fire

"From the first lines of *Broken Brain, Fortified Faith* . . . the reader is immediately pulled into the day-to-day life of a family discovering and then dealing with the nitty-gritty, raw emotions of mental illness. Pillars holds nothing back when she shares the reality of her daughter Amber's diagnosis of schizophrenia and its effect on her entire family and their friends. Her deep faith and sometimes brutal honesty will touch readers long after they've turned the last page."

—*Mary Jedlicka Humston, coauthor of* Mary & Me: A Lasting Link Through Ink

"Virginia Pillars has written an honest, no-holds-barred tale of her daughter's—and their family's—agonizing battle with schizophrenia. Yet along with the heartache, Virginia's story is one of hope and, ultimately, victory, achieved through earnest spiritual searching and openness to personal growth. If you are on a similar journey through the depths of mental illness with a loved one, you could have no better guide."

—*Nancy B. Kennedy, author of* Miracles & Moments of Grace: Inspiring Stories of Survival

"In *Broken Brain, Fortified Faith*, Virginia writes of an agony-filled journey complete with unpredictability, heartache, turmoil, and relentless grief. I know that journey well. It's called life with a mentally ill loved one. I appreciate her honesty as she invites readers into her world, and I'm grateful that she hasn't let what she's learned go to waste. Now, in her role as advocate and friend for others walking a similar path, she offers a gift of hope and help in this important book."

—*Twila Belk, speaker and author of* Raindrops from Heaven: Gentle Reminders of God's Power, Presence, and Purpose

"If schizophrenia has ever plagued the life of a loved one, then you will greatly appreciate this book by Virginia Pillars. She demonstrates how prayer, hope, encouragement, and endurance lead to fortified faith. Pillars is not a trained professional; however, her personal life journey taught her how to navigate through the mental health system in order to advocate for her daughter. A true story of love, hope, healing, and faith!"

—*Hope Huff, MA, LMHC, BCPC*

"*Broken Brain, Fortified Faith: Lessons of Hope through a Child's Mental Illness* is a must-read for those seeking insight into the struggles of families walking beside loved ones battling schizophrenia. Virginia Pillars writes with insight, transparency, and compassion about the realities of mental illness that forever changed the life of her twenty-four-year-old daughter Amber and the people who love her. The book honestly portrays the realities of the mental health system and its effects upon families. *Broken Brain, Fortified Faith* offers fresh hope both to those struggling with mental illness as well as to those who love and support them. Highly recommended."

"*Broken Brain, Fortified Faith* is an inspiring story of one family's journey through the fear and isolation of mental illness. This courageous memoir sends a powerful message: there is always hope."

broken
brain,
fortified
faith

Live in hope —
Live in faith —
Virginia Pillars

VIRGINIA PILLARS

broken brain, fortified faith

Lessons
of Hope
Through a
Child's
Mental
Illness

VIRGINIA PILLARS

Published by Familius LLC, www.familius.com

Familius books are available at special discounts for bulk purchases, whether for sales promotions or for family or corporate use. For more information, contact Familius Sales at 559-876-2170 or email orders@familius.com.

Library of Congress Cataloging-in-Publication Data

2016937548

Print ISBN 9781942934745
Ebook ISBN 9781944822170

Printed in the United States of America

Edited by Lindsay Sandberg
Cover design by David Miles
Book design by Maggie Wickes

10 9 8 7 6 5 4 3 2 1

First Edition

To my daughter, who taught me the true meaning of courage in the face of adversity, and whose faith and determination continues to inspires me. To my family, who stood together as we searched for answers. To our extended families and friends, whose loving and prayerful support upheld us during the hard years.

contents

introduction

"I can't change the past, nor can I predict the future. I can only promise to be here when life knocks you down. I may be scared, too, but I'll never leave your side."

This mirrors my mindset after I heard the devastating news: "Your daughter has schizophrenia. The next two years will be very hard," spoken to us by her psychiatrist. In *Broken Brain, Fortified Faith: Lessons of Hope Through a Child's Mental Illness*, I share my fears, thoughts, insecurities, and anger as I learned to cope with her diagnosis. I felt frightened, confused, and hurt, but our family clung to each other while we searched for help and answers as the brain disorder schizophrenia grabbed our daughter, Amber. Over the course of a few months, it unleashed all its nasty symptoms on her.

Mental illness affects one in five families in a given year, according to studies from the National Institute of Mental Health. It takes most families by surprise; it leaves them devastated and unsure where to turn for help. Often, the stigma associated with mental illness deters patients and families alike from seeking professional help. Studies show 50 percent of those suffering from mental illness never receive treatment. Those studies also indicate that early treatment may enable a better outcome for recovery and the return to a productive lifestyle.

On April 14, 2015, the Brain and Behavior Research Foundation presented a "Meet the Scientist" webinar. Doctors discussed RAISE, a research study launched by the National Institute of Mental Health in 2008. It studied a coordinated care treatment approach for first-time psychotic episodes in patients with schizophrenia. The study explored early intervention and a shared decision-making process for a treatment plan between the patient, the family, and the healthcare professionals. Components in the treatment plan include education for the family and retraining for the individual, along with medications tailored for the patient.

I found similarities between those techniques and the one we used ten years ago with Amber. In this book, I discuss our family's collective efforts. With the help of doctors, therapists, family, and friends, Amber regained her health and her independence.

Broken Brain, Fortified Faith begins on December 9, 2004 when I first learned Amber suffered from something more serious than depression. Uneducated, I didn't know what we faced or how to deal with it. My life felt chaotic, and I questioned everything, including my faith. I invite you to journey with me as I recount my struggle through many a crisis stage, toward finding acceptance, and finally moving into advocacy. I discuss the daily routines I used to keep my faith intact and my efforts to create a healing environment for Amber's brain. My faith and my prayer life may seem different than that of some of you, my readers, but I hope the process of turning to God for my help, using the tools I learned in my faith, will become the focus of my story rather than our discrepancies in doctrine.

Every day, scientists learn more about the brain. It is my hope that in time, the public's perception of mental illness will move into one of understanding and acceptance. I envision a day when society can discuss mental illness with the same openness we discuss diabetes or cancer.

At my family's request, I changed all the names and locations. They fear stigma will enter Amber's life if I reveal her identity. In a perfect world, she could share this with her employer and coworkers, but for now, this is not the case.

This story is about Amber, but it's also about me. It's our journey into the world of mental illness, through schizophrenia, as we faced crisis after crisis before she reached recovery. My purpose in writing this book is to help others to look past mental illness, to see the entire person, and to support those afflicted as well as their families. I write this in the hope that at least one person benefits by using a part of our story to improve their life.

Virginia M. Pillars

chapter one

December 9, 2004

I should have seen it coming. As I look back, the signs were all there. But honestly, I didn't know. I hadn't been told.

The day started as a typical one for me. My husband, Roy, worked in the field on our farm with his two brothers, and my embroidery machine stitched colorful thread in intricate patterns for my customers. The phone sang "Old McDonald Had a Farm," and I snatched the receiver from the cradle on the wall.

"Good day. This is Virginia. How may I help you?"

"Mrs. Pillars, my name is Judith. I work with your daughter. I am calling because I think something is wrong with Amber. She isn't acting like herself today. Would you call her?"

"What do you mean?" I asked.

"Well, she spent the morning shuffling papers, but she accomplished nothing. She started something, got distracted, and started it over again." She paused. "I've also noticed she is losing weight. Could you just call her?"

"Will do—immediately," I said. I disconnected with her and dialed Amber's cell phone.

"Hi, Amber," I said. I tried to sound nonchalant.

"Hi, Mom. I'm in the middle of something. Can we talk later? I'll be off work around four."

"Sure." But as I replaced the phone, my thoughts raced. *She sounded okay. Maybe she is just having a bad day.* Events of the last few weeks tumbled back to my mind in vivid, scrambled pictures.

I thought back to a recent conversation I had overheard with her older brother, Mitchell.

"You're gonna go to hell if you don't get God in your life," she had yelled at him.

That bothered me. Yes, she had always taken her faith more seriously than her brothers, but she had never confronted them like this before. Mitchell glared at her but didn't respond. And she dropped it.

That was a few weeks ago. She didn't say anything like that the last time she came home. Maybe it was a one-time thing.

My thoughts moved to Thanksgiving weekend. Our family came home to help celebrate. We filled the oval oak table in our farmhouse for dinner. The aroma of pumpkin pie tickled our senses as we dug into the traditional turkey feast. I could still picture our two sons and their families: Mitchell, his wife, Melinda, and their eighteen-month-old, Carter; Wesley, his wife, Suzanne, and Suzanne's mother, Tillie. Our third son, Clinton, and Amber sat next to Tillie. With Roy and me, we created an elbow-to-elbow seating arrangement.

Typically, Amber is bouncy and full of laughter around her brothers. Good-natured ribbing flies through the air, an obvious sign of their affection for each other. But things were different this time. Amber sat quietly through the entire meal. Her eyes looked vacant, as if lost in another time. She answered questions posed to her in a word or two, if at all. She picked at the food, leaving most of it on her plate. I also noticed she looked thinner. She had always been trim—barely filling out a size five on her five-foot-four-inch frame—but now her khaki corduroy pants hung on her.

"I'm tired," she said when I pressed her about her lack of enthusiasm.

I accepted that answer. That was Thursday, Thanksgiving day. On Saturday, we went to Roy's family gathering at his parents' home. Amber remained quiet, but she did hang out with her single female cousins. The girls disappeared to a back bedroom to watch a movie. A few hours later, the four of them came to the dining room, giggling and laughing—all of them except Amber. Her hazel eyes bulged round and wide as they darted from side to side.

"How was the movie?" I asked the group, but my eyes were on Amber.

"Great," one of the cousins replied. "It was really good."

Amber didn't look at me; instead, she stared at the floor.

"I need to go home now," she said flatly.

I tried to catch her eye, but she didn't look up. We retrieved our coats and left immediately for a silent ten-minute drive home. When we got home, she went to her old bedroom without even saying goodnight.

We attended Mass on Sunday morning. Again, Amber said very little. That afternoon, she packed her things to return to Boone, where she lived. Something seemed a bit off; she seemed exhausted and unusually quiet. Roy suggested she take an extra day off work.

"I can't, Dad. I work tomorrow," she said. "I have a lot to do and can't miss."

"She is dedicated to her job," Roy mentioned to me after she left. "But I wish she would have stayed home an extra day."

"Yeah. Me, too. That parish is lucky to have her. She's dedicated to their youth ministry program." I watched out the window as she drove away. *Make sure you talk to her this week*, I made a mental note to myself. *Check on her to see how she is.* Unfortunately, I got busy with orders in my business and forgot. It had been over a week since she left for Boone, and I had the chance to talk to her only once. And the conversation hadn't gone well.

"Virginia. Virginia, what should I do next?" I heard my employee Janelle call to me.

I looked up and shook my head. *Get back to work*, I chided myself when I realized I had been lost in a daydream. The month between Thanksgiving and Christmas is my business's busiest month of the year.

I had many custom orders to fill. It seemed all my customers ordered a personal item for gift giving, and I had many deadlines to meet. I needed to concentrate on my list of projects for the day.

I went through the motions, but I watched the clock as I embroidered designs on clothing for customers. Finally, the clock read four o'clock. I grabbed the phone and dialed her cell phone. "Amber?" I said.

"Mom," she whispered, then sniffled.

"What's wrong?"

"Mom," she started again, and then broke into a sob.

I wanted to reach through the receiver and wrap my arms around her.

"Do you want me to come?" I asked.

"Please."

"I'm on my way." I hung up and turned to Janelle. "Can you finish this order?"

She nodded.

"Then close up the shop. You're free to clock out, but go ahead and give yourself credit for the rest of the day. It's okay. We'll talk later."

Janelle smiled and stepped up to the machine.

"Go, go," she said as she waved me out the door.

I knew Roy was working installing drainage tile miles away for a neighboring farmer. *It will take too much time to call him and wait for him to get home. I have to go now. I'll call him once I get on the road.*

I backed out of the garage and steered my SUV onto the road. *Amber's not an emotional person. She's never done this before.* I inhaled sharply and stomped on the accelerator pedal. I drove the familiar route and thought back to her sobs. My right foot pressed down harder. I looked ahead and then glanced into the rearview mirror. I was the only one on the road.

The wheels gobbled up the gray pavement, and the fence posts became a blur.

How fast am I going? My eyes flitted to the speedometer. "Ninety!" I gasped.

I eased off the accelerator, but then I thought about Amber as she wept into the phone. I felt like a rock had landed in my stomach. I reached for my purse on the front seat, snagged the handle, and pulled it closer. My fingers explored the outside pocket until I found my cell phone. Balancing it on the steering wheel, I scrolled through my contact list until I came to Brooke, Amber's best friend. They had met in college, and the two girls had spent many weekends together with us.

"Brooke, I need you to do something for me. Can you call Amber? I think something's wrong." I took a short breath. "Keep her on the phone with you until you know I am there. I talked with her earlier today, and I'm really worried about her." I paused for a split second. "Can you do that?"

"Sure, I can do that. I talked with her the other day. I'm glad you're going to see her."

"Thanks so much. It will be another forty-five minutes before I get there. I really appreciate it." Next, I dialed Roy. *He should be finishing up the tiling job and heading home soon.*

"Hi. I'm on my way to Boone. Amber sounded really upset when we talked this afternoon."

"Should I come?" he asked.

"No, I'm already on the way. She sounded too upset to wait. I'm gonna see if she'll come home with me."

"Okay, keep in touch. Let me know if you need anything."

I flipped my phone shut and turned my attention back to my driving. In a minute, the white lines on the road blended into one long ribbon down the center. The utility poles smeared into a distorted streak. The monotony of the pavement set in, and I let my mind travel back to the events of the last week.

"You better call your daughter," Roy had said as I stepped in the door, my hands filled with bags of groceries. "I just talked with her, and she acted really scared. I could barely hear her. She said Carol, her coworker, was outside her apartment door, so she had to whisper."

"What?"

Questions raced through my head: *Why was she scared? What about Carol, and why was she there?*

"She was hiding in her closet as she talked with me. You'd better call her."

"Okay. Did she say anything else?"

Roy shook his head. "Just call her and talk to her. She sounded pretty upset."

I grabbed the phone from the wall unit. I dialed Amber's number then cradled the phone between my shoulder and my chin as I emptied the sacks of groceries. I listened to it ring over and over while I waited for her to answer.

"Hello?"

"Hi, Amber. It's Mom."

"Mom, Carol wants to get me fired. She talks about me behind my back to everyone."

Carol? Trying to get her fired? Why would she do that? Had Amber done something to her coworker to make her furious?

"Are you sure? What has she done?"

"She broke into my apartment and went through all my things. I know she's trying to find some evidence to use against me."

"She broke into your apartment? Did you call the police?"

"No," she answered.

I slipped the last box in the pantry, shut the door, and sank into a chair.

"Why not?" I said.

"I can't prove it was Carol, but I know she did it. She wants to get me fired."

"Did she do any damage? Or just go through your things?" I asked. *Why didn't she call the authorities? How does she know it's Carol?* "How do you know she's trying to get you fired? What else has she done?"

"This was the second time she came into my apartment when I wasn't home."

"What? When did she do that?"

"I already told you, Mom. I don't want to go over it all again."

She raised her voice, so I let it drop. I tried to remember the conversation; I couldn't. I talked with her for almost an hour as I tried to make sense of the things she told me. I listened, offered suggestions, and thought I had defused the situation. She seemed to calm down. But now, a few days later, I found myself in a mad dash to Boone. I hadn't helped at all. She had just told me Carol wanted her fired as she sobbed into the phone.

Deserted farm fields, blanketed in white from a recent snowfall, disappeared as the urban landscape came into view. A glance ahead alerted me to the speed limit sign. I slowed down, eased through the yield sign, and turned on a familiar street. A brown, four-story apartment complex came into view. I found it difficult to keep my speed under control.

Almost there. Don't get stopped for speeding now.

I pulled in next to Amber's car, shoved the car into park, locked the doors, and ran toward the apartment building door. The brass doorknob felt cold in my bare hand as I jerked the metal door open and bolted up the stairs, taking two steps at a time to apartment 312. My chest heaved up and down, and I gulped air as I knocked on the door. The murmur of her voice drifted through the wooden six-panel door before it flung open. Amber stood in the doorway, her phone to her ear.

"Brooke, Mom's here. I'll talk to you tomorrow," she said.

"Thank you, God, for Brooke," I whispered and raised my eyes.

Amber snapped her phone closed and set it on the round glass table near the door. She took one step before she collapsed into my arms, sobbing.

"What's going on?" I asked, but she only cried harder. "Do you have tomorrow off?"

She nodded.

"Do you want to come home with me for the weekend?"

She nodded again.

"Let's pack a suitcase."

"I can do it." She sniffled before she disappeared into her bedroom. I heard her soft cries mingle with the sound of scraping drawers as they opened and shut, so I went in her room.

"I said I'd do it," she spat at me. I backed out and looked around her apartment, confusion and concern fighting in my mind. The living room had haphazardly stacked piles of papers on the coffee table, with several more on the floor near the entertainment center and along the wall.

Are they important? If she thinks someone broke in, why would she leave these out?

I resisted the temptation to look through them. Instead I glanced at the picture window and noticed the aloe vera plant I had given her. The slender leaves looked wilted, brown, and curled as if life had drained out all of the healing gel contained within. I hurried to the kitchen to fill a glass with water and try to revive the poor plant. I noticed the kitchen sink held a pile of dishes. After I watered the forlorn-looking plant, I returned to her tiny hallway of a kitchen and kept myself busy by washing the dishes.

Squeak. Squeak. I stopped and looked for the source of the noise. I stepped through the doorway and spied Amber as she rolled a large green suitcase on the matted carpet. In a few steps, I stood beside her.

"Let me help with your suitcase," I said as I grabbed the handle. "Ugh, this thing is heavy. What's in here?"

"All my important papers . . . remember, I told you Carol broke into my apartment last week. I can't leave anything valuable here, even for a weekend."

"Did you pack any clothes?"

"Yeah, I have enough for the weekend."

"Well, let's hit the road then," I said as I grabbed the suitcase. Amber followed me, took her keys from her purse, and locked the door. *Bang, clunk. Bang, clunk.* The suitcase hit each step down the three flights of stairs. It provided a sharp contrast to Amber's shuffle as we made our way to my SUV.

"Help me put this in the back, will you?" I asked. I touched the button on the key fob. I grabbed the handle of the rear door and pulled it open. She stood and stared. "Can you help me?"

Together we lifted the bag and set it in the dark cavity. My hand slammed the door shut. As we slid into our seats, I heard Amber exhale a long, slow breath. I eased the car out of the parking lot, turned onto the street, and started for home.

I didn't know it then, but Amber would never return to her apartment.

chapter two

December 10

The sun hadn't risen yet when I woke up the next morning. I glanced at the alarm clock: 5:15 a.m.; time to start my day. I climbed out of bed, grabbed my robe, and tiptoed out to the kitchen to start the coffeepot. A few minutes later, I sat at my desk in my home office with a cup of steaming energy.

I worked on business for a couple of hours, but I kept an eye on the time in the right bottom corner of the computer as I worked. Would eight o'clock ever arrive? I planned to call the doctor as soon as the office opened. I paid a few bills while I waited.

Finally. Eight o'clock. I called my doctor's office. A receptionist answered with a cheerful greeting.

"Good morning," I replied. "Do you have anything available today? I think something is wrong with my daughter."

"How old is she? And what seems to be the problem?"

"She's twenty-four. She isn't acting like herself. And she's suspicious of things that I don't think are true." I took a deep breath. "Do you have any openings?"

"We had a cancellation. I have a 10:20 appointment. Is that okay?"

"Yes, we'll take it." I felt relieved and concerned at the same time. I had a sinking feeling in my stomach. Things seemed off with Amber, but I couldn't put my finger on it.

I walked to the hallway, stopped at the first door on the right—her old bedroom growing up—and knocked softly on the door.

"Amber, are you awake?" No response. I rapped my knuckles louder on the oak door. "Amber, can you get up? I need to talk with you right away." A few moments later, she emerged. The dark circles around her eyes resembled the pattern on a raccoon's fur.

Wow, those are dark. I wonder how much sleep she's had lately.

She didn't catch me staring at her. I felt grateful for that.

"I made an appointment for you today with a doctor," I said to Amber as she shuffled past me to the kitchen.

She ignored me and walked to the cupboard. She grabbed a bowl, opened the pantry, and pulled out a box of cereal before she walked to the table. I went to the refrigerator, grabbed the milk, and set it on the table next to her bowl.

"Did you hear me?" I said.

Almost mechanically, Amber poured milk on a bowl of cereal.

"You have a doctor's appointment this morning. We talked about that last night on the way home, remember?"

"Sort of." She glanced up and pushed the bowl away. It scraped across the table, spilling slightly, and knocked into a pile of unopened mail that fell to the floor. Her eyes stared at the scattered mail and drops of milk spilled from her bowl.

I bent down, gathered the letters, and stood up. Her expression remained the same; her eyes looked vacant, and her mouth was drawn in a slight frown.

"You haven't felt well lately. Let's go to the doctor and make sure you don't have something physical going on." I carried the milk back to the refrigerator as I talked. "It's been a long time since you had a physical. My doctor's office can get you in today. Why don't you hop in the shower when you're finished eating?"

"I'm not hungry," she said and pushed her chair back from the table. "I'll do it now." She ambled down the hallway and turned into her bedroom.

I stacked the breakfast dishes in the dishwasher, put away the cereal, and wiped the crumbs and milk from the table. I heard the sound of running water.

I retreated to the front room where I sank into my favorite chair, picked up a daily devotional book off the end table, and opened it to today's date. I tried to read the words, but couldn't concentrate.

What is happening to my girl? Amber just doesn't seem like herself. I hope they can figure it out this morning.

We left for her appointment shortly after she finished her shower. Neither of us spoke during the twenty-minute ride to the clinic.

As I drove, I thought back to another confusing time with Amber. I pictured us in the pediatrician's office for her two-week checkup. Her shrieks filled the tiny exam room.

"She cries almost all the time," I mentioned to the doctor.

He studied her chart.

"She hasn't gained very much. She's barely six pounds. I see her birth weight at six pounds, one ounce. Is that correct?"

I nodded.

"It's not unusual to lose a few ounces at first, but by two weeks, the baby has usually gained it back." He gently fingered her arms and then her legs. He frowned as he studied the red, bumpy rash around her elbows and knees and on the back of her neck. "Is she on formula or breast milk?"

"Breast milk."

"When did this rash start?"

"I think when she was three days old, about the same time she started crying."

He looked up. "Do you drink milk?"

I nodded.

"She may be allergic to cow's milk. Take all dairy out of your diet and see what happens."

I didn't know what I ate could affect her that much. I loved milk, cheese, ice cream, and butter, having grown up on a dairy farm. But I wanted to help Amber more than I wanted to drink milk and put butter on my potatoes. So I removed all dairy from my diet and noticed some improvement. She still cried most of the time, so I decided to watch her reactions when I ate other foods. The list of foods that caused her misery grew to include any spicy foods, carrots, squash, and anything with tomatoes. Before long, I lived on green beans, beef, and apples. Still she fussed.

The next clue for her health came one day at my parents' home.

"She is really upset," Mom said. "Her skin is bright red. Maybe it's the outfit she has on."

I hope not, I thought as I undressed Amber. The pink and white sweater dress and matching bloomers were a gift from Roy's mom.

Amber settled down almost immediately.

Add one more thing to the list—acrylic. I soon discovered other fabrics that irritated her; basically, she could wear cotton and nothing else.

I lost weight as a result of my limited diet. I tried to feed her various soy formulas which she vomited up almost immediately. Determined to help her, I continued to scrutinize every bite I consumed. Her distress continued.

She found some relief when I carried her in a baby sling, tummy to tummy. Each morning, I strapped her on my belly, taking her out only to feed her and change her diaper.

Exhausted, frustrated, and unsure what to try next, I threw my arms up in desperation.

"God, I don't know what else to do. I've tried everything. Show me what to do."

A few days later, I visited my great aunt.

"Have you tried goat milk?" she asked over Amber's wails. "I knew a family who gave their children goat's milk. They were the healthiest children I knew."

At her suggestion, I searched every store in our area and found a can of evaporated goat milk at the health food store. It cost four dollars a can, far beyond our meager budget. I mixed it in Amber's rice cereal, and she handled it well. Since we couldn't afford to use it full time, I used it sparingly. Again, I prayed, *God help us.*

A few months later in November, I corralled my young family as I stood in line to vote. A kind gentleman asked me about the sleeping infant tied to my tummy. In a matter of minutes, I poured out my problems with locating goat milk for her. His eyes twinkled.

"Don't you know who I am?"

I shook my head as I held on to the hood of Wesley's coat.

"I'm your neighbor. We have a herd of milking goats. Come by tomorrow and get a gallon."

As I drove home, I was overwhelmed with gratitude to have an abundant supply of milk for her. Her life changed at that point, and so did mine. She finally felt well.

God, you answered my prayer for her years ago. I glanced over at Amber. She stared out the window as I pulled into the family clinic parking lot. *Here we go again. This time she's twenty-four. God, something's wrong with her, and I don't know what to do. Help us find some answers for her.*

We parked, and I checked her in at the front desk while she took a chair.

"Can I go in with you?" I asked her softly after I took the chair next to her.

Amber shrugged. "I guess so."

I nodded but kept silent. I had to concentrate on silence; every part of me wanted to talk. She seemed so fragile, and I didn't want to upset her. After a nurse called her name, we followed her mutely to an exam room. After a few minutes, the door opened and a young-looking man in a shirt, tie, and white lab jacket entered.

He introduced himself to Amber and immediately questioned her as to why she came to see him.

I sat wordlessly in the corner of the exam room while Amber talked to the doctor. "I haven't been sleeping. And I don't have an appetite."

"Do you think you could be mildly depressed?" the doctor asked. I noted the name badge on his lab coat: DR. L. J. BANES, RESIDENT.

No, it's more than that. It's not mild, I wanted to interject.

Amber answered immediately. "Maybe, but I don't want to take any medicine. It will hurt my body."

"You may only need to take it for a while. This is probably tempo-rary," the doctor replied. "I'll make it the smallest dose possible to see if it helps."

I couldn't hold it in any longer. "Tell him about the way you think your coworker is trying to get you fired," I said.

"My coworker goes behind my back all the time. She makes up lies about me. She tells them to our boss. She wants to get me fired."

The doctor nodded. He didn't seem concerned.

"Let him know about the apartment break-in," I said.

Look deeper, Doc. Make sure it's not worse than depression.

Amber explained about the break-in, how there was no mess, but she was positive the person had rifled through her papers and drawers.

"Did you call the police?" he asked.

She shook her head.

Ask her why not. Come on, what are you waiting for? Doesn't that seem odd to you, Doc? UGH! Look, man, look! Open your eyes! That doesn't seem normal to me.

He continued to talk with Amber. "Sometimes things at our job get a bit stressful. Maybe a week off would help. I'll write a prescription for an antidepressant along with a work release for one week. You can go back to work in a week."

He grabbed his prescription pad and pulled a pen from his right breast pocket. The pen scratched as he scribbled on the paper. I cringed and rolled my eyes. He didn't see my anxiety.

I wanted to scream. *Don't you wonder why a twenty-four-year-old woman has her mother in the exam room? Why don't you look past what she said?*

I started to say something, but stopped when I saw the look in Amber's eyes. She had set her jaw and stared at the doctor. Afraid of her reaction if I spoke up, I clamped my mouth shut.

We left. Amber clutched the signed papers in her hand.

"I'm just a little depressed," Amber said once we were in the car. "I'll be fine in a week; the doctor said so."

I clenched my teeth, swallowing my frustration with the inexperienced doctor.

I hope so. Lord, I really hope so. I should have said more.

chapter three

We stopped, filled the prescription, and drove home. Amber took the first dose of medicine and went back to bed. I sank into my favorite chair in the front room to rest for a few minutes before my grandson, Carter, arrived for the afternoon for our daily Grammie Daycare.

Though the day progressed without mishap, I couldn't shake the feeling of unease that rested heavily on my heart.

December 13

A few days later, Roy and I sat in the front room, relaxing in our denim-colored rocker/recliners. Amber had retreated to her room; Roy watched a television show while I glanced through the headlines of our local newspaper. A shuffling sound interrupted my reading, so I looked to the hallway and saw Amber. Her eyes drooped, her wrinkled clothes looked unkempt, and her shoulder-length hair stuck out in all directions as she stood in the doorway.

"That show is about me," Amber stated as she pointed to the television.

"What?" Roy said. He turned to her but kept one eye on the television.

"That show. It's about me!" Amber barreled into the room with an energy I hadn't seen since before Thanksgiving.

Roy picked up the remote from the stack of newspapers on the end table. He clicked the power button and the screen went dark. "What?" he repeated.

"Turn it back on so I can show you."

Roy looked at me, then to Amber, and then back at me again. I tossed the newspaper onto the end table before I stood up. Roy pushed the power button. We all turned to the corner of the room as the set hummed awake. An old program, *My Three Sons*, filled the screen. All three sons, their father, and Uncle Charley appeared deep in a discussion.

"See, see what I mean?" Amber pointed to the set. Her voice sounded agitated. She looked from Roy to me, her eyes full of accusation. "That show has three brothers, and I have three brothers. One of those guys is Charley—I have an Uncle Charley."

Roy glanced in my direction before turning to her. "No, Amber, this is just a story," he said.

I really thought that would be the end of it.

"NO! It's about me!" Amber yelled. "Can't you see that? I told you, there are three brothers on that show. I have three brothers!" She paced around the room, her eyes downcast. "How did the writers know about me?" She lifted her head, looked straight at me, and then continued to walk in a circle in front of the television. Her rounded hazel eyes darted about the room then back to the screen. The muscles in her jaw twitched, and she breathed in short spurts. "How dare they write my private things for everyone in America to watch?"

She must have been in a deep sleep and had a bad dream. When she fully wakes up, she'll realize it.

I watched her pace, a stranger to me.

I often used the term *level headed* when describing Amber to people. We sailed through her high school years with only minor disagreements, usually over her clothing choices, but I rarely raised my voice with her. She focused on her studies to earn good grades. She worked hard to be an honor roll student and a National Honor Society member along with other activities. This unreasonable reaction left me feeling unsettled.

Roy pressed the power button again, and the screen went blank. Amber continued to pace the room, flinging her hands into the air. I crossed the room to her, thinking a hug from me would change her attitude. As I reached out to her, she pushed my arms away, so I stuffed my hands into the front pockets of my jeans. I moved back and headed to the sofa. With a stifled sigh, I yanked my hands out before I sank into the cushions and patted the spot beside me.

"Come, sit down by me," I said.

Instead, she spun around. "I wish people would just keep their nose out of my business." With that, she stormed back to her bedroom.

I looked over at Roy. He wrinkled his brow and shook his head. "What was that about? That didn't make any sense," he said in a hushed voice. Our eyes met, and we looked in unison to the hallway where Amber had disappeared.

We dropped the subject for the night but left the television off.

I had a hard time sleeping that night; Amber's outburst replayed over and over in my head all night long. Afraid my deep sighs and flopping from one side to the other would keep Roy awake, I picked up my pillow and carried it to the front room. I clicked the television remote to "On" and settled on the sofa. The drone of the television helped me relax.

I hope the medicine starts to work soon . . .

December 14

The next evening, Amber snatched a newspaper off the dining room table. She scanned the front page and threw it back down. I looked at Roy, seated in his chair, but he concentrated on her. He reached over and grabbed the paper. Amber spun around and snatched it from his hands, her mouth drawn in a straight line across her thin face. She rubbed her temple before she let a long breath escape. Her shoulders slumped as she plopped down in the nearest wooden chair.

"Even the newspapers . . ." she moaned.

"Huh?" Roy and I both said at the same time.

"The newspapers!" she yelled at us. "Even the papers are writing about me. Why can't everyone just leave me alone and let me be?"

"What do you mean? I didn't see your name in the paper when I read it," I said.

"Oh, Mom, it's right there! It says Omaha, right there!" she screamed at me as she hit the paper. "I'm moving to Omaha, so the newspapers think that they have to write and tell the entire world what I am doing with my life." She tossed the paper on the floor and jumped up from the chair. She stomped off to her room, as she had done the night before.

"Do you think this is more than depression? Should I call the doctor's office in the morning and see what they say?" I said to Roy.

"I dunno." He paused and looked toward her room again before he spoke. "Yeah, you'd better."

I didn't sleep well again and moved to the couch in the middle of the night. The light from the sunrise woke me as I lay in the front room. I tiptoed to the hallway, opened the door of Amber's room, and peeked in. She was sound asleep. *Maybe things will be better today.*

December 15

I phoned the doctor's office shortly after eight o'clock and talked with the triage nurse. "I think my daughter may have more than depression." I went on to explain her behavior last night. "Her father and I are concerned. Do you think she should be in a hospital?"

"Unless a patient checks into the hospital on their own, there really isn't much you can do. Do you think she is willing to do that?" The nurse spoke in a monotone.

How many times has she said that? I wondered. "I don't think she would do that," I replied. "But I'll see what she says," I continued and hung up the phone.

Amber got up around eleven that morning. She appeared to be moving in slow motion. I cooked lunch while she poured a bowl of cereal and dumped some milk on it. She didn't make eye contact with me or even acknowledge that I was in the same room.

"Amber, what did you mean the other night when you said the TV show was about you?" I asked as I continued to peel potatoes.

"Everybody knows about my life, Mom. Everyone in Boone knows everything about me. That's why I had to leave. A few weeks ago in the grocery store, the sales clerk knew about the flat tire I had the week before in Ames and said something. The other clerk laughed about it." Amber's voice got louder as she talked. "How did they know, Mom? I never told anyone about it. How did they know?" Her hands slapped the table, and she pushed herself away. Her sudden movement knocked the chair over. We both jumped.

"Are you sure she meant your flat tire?" I asked. "Maybe the two of them were talking about someone they knew that had one."

"No, Mom. It was about me. Don't you understand?!" Her voice had risen to just below a shout. "She looked right at me and made a comment about changing a flat tire myself, and then she laughed. It freaked me out that she knew when I hadn't told anyone about it." Amber began to pace the kitchen. "Why is what I'm doing everyone's business?"

"Maybe we should go back to the doctor?" I mentioned in a soft voice. "Maybe a different doctor could help us figure things out . . ."

"Dr. Banes said I have depression. I don't need to see anyone else. What can another doctor do about people talking about me, anyway?" she said as she stormed out of the kitchen.

I called the doctor's office again. After I explained Amber's recent outburst, I asked about hospitalization for her, for the second time.

The receptionist repeated, "She has to be a danger to herself or others . . ."

"What can we do?

She gave me the name of a psychiatrist in Waterloo. I called, and the receptionist in his office offered to make an appointment—for six weeks later.

"Can't you get her in sooner?" I pleaded.

"I'm sorry. I don't have anything sooner."

"What are we to do in the meantime? I don't think she can wait six weeks."

"You can take her to the emergency room if it gets too bad."

Less than a week had passed since I had taken Amber to see a doctor. She stayed home as I watched her state of mind deteriorate. I hoped the depression medication would kick in soon. I had read it could take up to four weeks to become effective. For me, it couldn't come soon enough.

December 16

Seven days after Amber left her apartment in Boone to come home, paranoia had taken over her thoughts. Convinced of a conspiracy against her, she couldn't relax. That night, sleep eluded us both. Filled with fear, the tears slid down her face in rapid succession.

She paced the floor or she stared out the window most of the night. Sometime during the early morning hours, I convinced her I could protect her by lying in her bed next to her. She finally fell asleep, while I allowed myself only to doze.

I noticed Amber's outbursts increased in intensity and frequency. They usually started as the result of a program on the television, a magazine, or a newspaper article. We thought we would help the situation if we hid the newspaper and magazines in the house and read them after she went to bed. The television remained off. I was grateful Amber didn't ask to turn it on. We kept our conversations to a minimum and free from talk about events outside our walls. We didn't know what would cause the next outburst from her.

Our efforts to protect her gave me the feeling of being a prisoner in my own home, as if I'd been sentenced to live in her world of paranoia without any means to bail either of us out.

chapter four

December 17

It had been eight days since I raced to Boone and brought Amber home. We didn't see any improvement in her state of mind. She insisted she was fine, but her actions told me differently. That evening, Mitchell invited her to attend a Christmas open house at Melinda's school. Naively, I thought it would be a nice change for her, so I encouraged her to go along. I watched Carter while they went. They were home before I expected them. Amber was quiet until after Mitchell and Carter left. Then she paced around the kitchen.

"Mom, the kids at the school were laughing at me tonight. Why would they do that? They don't know me."

"Are you sure they were laughing at you?" I said.

"Yes, I'm sure." Her volume increased as she paced around the kitchen.

I didn't disagree with her. I tried that before, and it got me nowhere. It only made Amber mad. "Maybe you should just go to bed. Things always look brighter in the morning."

Amber nodded and disappeared into her room. Later that evening, I noticed the light from her room streaming through the cold air return in the hallway. I opened the door of her room a crack and peeked in. She slept soundly, but her lamp and the ceiling light remained on.

Better leave them on; I don't want to upset her anymore tonight.

The uneasiness felt oppressive as I got ready for bed.

December 18

The next morning, I worked for a few hours. I watched the clock as I waited for her to rise. The restless feeling from the night before wouldn't go away, so I called the hospital to ask about my options. When I hung up, I knew the only way I could get Amber there was if she went willingly. Around ten o'clock, I moved to the kitchen, where I tinkered until she stumbled out of her room. I heard the shower turn on. When she finished, she walked to the front room. She plopped down on the sofa, a soft yellow bathrobe cinched tight around her tiny waist; her long, blond hair was wrapped in a towel, and her bare feet left a trail of drips. I followed her.

"Mom, they've found me; they know I'm here."

I sank into the soft cushion beside her. "Who has found you?"

"You know. They've found me, and they're trying to kill me. And now they know I am here." Her hands shook as she waved them around her head. "It's not safe here anymore."

I swallowed hard. "How do you know?"

"I saw the cameras in the bathroom. There's one above the shower and one above the sink. They're filming everything I do, even in the bathroom." She began to cry. "Why can't they just leave me alone? Why do they have to put my life on display for the entire world?" Tears flowed down her cheeks. "Everyone in America has seen me naked in the shower." She buried her face in her hands. Her shoulders shook, and the tears dripped through her fingers.

I wrapped my arms around her and held her. *Oh, God, help me to know what to say. I'm in way over my head here, and I'm scared.*

We sat on the couch in silence, my arms around her damp body. Her wet head rested on my shoulder. *God, please give me your words.*

"Amber, would you like me to take you somewhere safe?" I waited for her reaction. Silence. "I know a place where they can't find you and get to you."

Amber pulled her head off my shoulder, wiped the tears from her eyes, and turned to me. "Is there a place?"

I nodded. "I made some calls this morning. Will you let me take you there?" I held my breath for a moment. "Do you trust me?"

"Yes," she said, her voice just above a whisper.

"You get dressed. I'll tell Dad, and you and I can go right away. Okay?"

Her eyes searched my face for a moment, then she pulled away from me and stood up. "Okay." Her voice trailed off as she left the room. "Mom, they've found me; they know I'm here."

I called the hospital for the second time in a few hours and let them know to expect us within an hour. I explained the situation to the emergency room triage nurse.

I hung up and paced as I waited for Amber. Once she was dressed, we slipped into our winter coats and left. Twenty minutes later, we pulled into the parking lot of a local hospital.

"What are we doing here?" Amber said. Her shrill voice broke the silence. She gripped the door handle of the car with white knuckles.

I turned to her. "It's okay. You'll be safe here. I talked with them earlier today." I spoke quietly, and she glanced fleetingly at me. Her rounded eyes darted from side to side.

Words of a hymn from church played in my mind and gave me strength. *Be with me, Lord, when I am in trouble. Be with me, Lord, I pray.*

"Are you sure I'll be safe here?" Amber asked, the trust in her eyes battling with fear.

Thank you, God, that at least she still trusts me.

I nodded. We got out, and together we walked into the emergency room.

"Amber, let's go to the desk, and I'll check you in."

She nodded her head, and soon we stood at the reception desk. I explained our situation in a quiet voice. "I called earlier. This is Amber Pillars. She needs to be seen as soon as possible."

The white-clad gal behind the counter looked at her note, picked up the phone, and made a quick call.

"Please follow me," she said and escorted us to a cubicle of a room. "Have a seat."

Amber hopped onto the exam table; I stood nearby.

"Someone will be with you shortly."

She left, and I walked in circles in the tiny room. Every rotation, I stopped by Amber.

"You doing okay?"

She nodded mutely.

Within a few minutes, a middle-aged nurse with a clipboard in her hand came and joined us in the room. She fired question after question at us. Amber answered each one in the monotone voice that I had heard often over the past ten days. Finally, the nurse looked at me and then at Amber.

"Would you like to be admitted?" she asked Amber.

"I guess so." Amber shrugged her shoulders.

"I'll make the arrangements. Just wait here." The nurse turned, nodded to me, and left the room.

We waited in silence for the nurse to return. Amber stared at her hands while I read the boring posters that adorned the walls—the same things I had read in every hospital ER I'd ever stepped in. But I kept my attention fixed on Amber.

The sterile-looking door opened, followed by heavy footsteps. A police officer strode into our room; the gun in the holster on his wide black belt glared at me. My eyes darted to see Amber's reaction. She stared at him, her eyes round and her mouth open.

"I'm here to escort her to the ward," he said, his voice filled with authority. I shook my head as my anger simmered.

"Get out and send the nurse back in here," I demanded, probably louder than necessary. "I need to know what is going on."

He shrugged his shoulders, turned, and left. The nurse returned quickly.

"Ma'am, it's hospital policy for a police officer to escort patients from the ER to the psychiatric ward." She spoke to me as if I should have expected this.

"You should have explained that to us," I said. "Do you know how confusing this is?" I could hear the anger in my voice and willed myself to calm down. "You can tell him to come back in."

I turned to Amber. "The officer will take us to your room." A flash of inspiration struck me. "He'll help protect you. Okay?"

She nodded.

God, thank you for the idea to tell her he'll protect her. She's okay with the explanation.

Slowly, she slid off the exam table. Amber, the officer, and I left the emergency room. We walked and turned, walked and turned—the hallways felt endless. Finally, we stopped. I read the sign on the door: ADULT PSYCHIATRIC UNIT. The officer reached to his belt and removed his cluster of keys. They rattled as he found the one he needed. He unlocked a door, leading us into a small hallway. He produced another key, unlocked another door, and opened it. He motioned for us to go in ahead. We walked through, and the heavy metal door clanged shut behind us.

We were locked in.

A young-looking nurse dressed in white pants and a white top met us. "Follow me."

We followed her to a tiny room with a table and mismatched chairs. We sat down while she drilled Amber with the same questions she had just answered. The nurse looked up occasionally as she scribbled on some papers. Finally, she tucked everything into a manila folder and motioned us to follow her, and we were led into another hallway. "I'll give you a quick tour," she said.

She led us through a large lounge filled with institutional plastic chairs, several dilapidated sofas, and a table with a jigsaw puzzle in progress. Magazines with dog-eared edges lay strewn across a coffee table. Doors lined three walls, while an office area, encased in glass, filled the end wall.

Several men in sloppy sweatpants and wrinkled t-shirts sat in one corner, staring at a television. Their greasy hair looked matted, and their blank faces appeared rough with whisker stubble. A bed sat outside one door with a man tied to it. He yelled loudly, but no one looked in his direction. My stomach did a flip-flop.

What have I done to Amber? This place is scary, and I brought her here to feel safe. God, forgive me. What have I done?

"Patients are responsible for doing their laundry," she said as we stepped into a tiny, stuffy room with a washer and dryer. She turned briskly and pushed her way past us. "Let's get you settled. Follow me."

I followed her hesitantly. Amber shuffled beside me. The nurse paused by the door directly across the lounge from the screaming man in the bed.

"Here's your room. Each patient has their own room. You can put your things away in here," she said as she pointed to a lone dresser. "You need to remove your belt, your shoelaces, and the strings from your sweatshirt and turn them in. I will be back to get them in a few minutes."

She looked bored, as if she had recited that line thousands of times.

"We encourage patients to spend most of the time in the lounge, not in your room." She looked at Amber and then turned to me. "You can visit her from five to seven each evening." She started for the door and then turned back. "You're probably just depressed," she said to Amber. "You should be out of here in five days."

Shock and panic slammed into me when she offered her false placation. *Shut up. Don't tell her that! You don't know her—you can't know she will be okay in five days. Shut up, you stupid, stupid woman.*

chapter five

December 20

I found it difficult, no, impossible, to concentrate on my work that day. My thoughts centered on Amber in that terrible, scary hospital.

What is she doing? Is she scared? Did those guys do anything to her? How are they treating her? Is she safe?

"You're sure quiet today," Janelle remarked.

"Got a lot on my mind," I said and continued to program the machine. Usually, Janelle and I chat our way through the workday, but today I didn't feel like talking, so I gave instructions but said nothing more. I watched the clock, anxious for the end of my workday.

At four o'clock, I said, "You can leave early today. Roy and I need to leave before five."

Her eyebrows arched as she nodded. I could tell she was curious—this close to Christmas and we're closing early? I swallowed the explanation, too embarrassed to tell her where I was going. *How can I tell you my daughter is in a psychiatric ward at the hospital?*

Roy came in the house, showered, and shaved.

"You ready?" he asked when he finished.

I nodded. "Did you say anything to your brothers about why you left early today?"

"No. Did you tell Janelle?"

I shook my head and grabbed my coat and purse, and together we walked in silence to the car for the first of many visits.

For the next few days, I walked around as if in a daze. My mind refused to concentrate on business, but I put myself on autopilot so I could manage. Each day felt painful and much the same: work during the day; sneak off to the hospital during visiting hours; repeat. And Amber's state of mind didn't improve. We listened each evening as she lamented about the conspiracy at work to get her fired, the break-in to her apartment, and how everyone in Boone wanted to get her.

December 23

With all the customer's orders completed, Janelle and I worked in my shop finishing our personal items to give as gifts to our own families. The machines hummed as they stitched designs and provided the only sounds in the room. I couldn't bear to make small talk. It took all my concentration to keep my business productive.

The phone rang. With a sense of bone-deep exhaustion, I answered, praying that it wasn't a last-minute order for a Christmas gift.

"Hello, this is Virginia. How may I help you?"

"This is Sophia from the hospital psychiatric unit. The doctor wants to meet with you. Can you come immediately?"

A sense of dread washed over me. I sank into my office chair. I had no idea why the doctor wanted to see us. Had she gotten worse? Had she done something? Was she hurt? I took a deep breath before I answered.

"Of course. It will take us about half an hour before we can get there."

I hung up the phone and called Roy in the farm shop.

"You need to come in immediately. I just had a call from the hospital. The doctor wants to see us right away."

"Be right in," he said.

I turned to my employee. "Janelle, I have an emergency. Go ahead and finish your items. I'll do mine when I get back." She looked surprised.

I ignored her reaction. "Clock out when you are done. Make sure you record your hours."

Her questioning look asked, *What's going on?* I couldn't tell her. Instead, I gave her a quick hug. "Merry Christmas. See you after the holidays."

She nodded. "Merry Christmas to you, too. Thanks for letting me work on my own gifts on your time."

I smiled at her. "Thanks for all you do for me. Lock up when you're done. See you next year."

In a few minutes, Roy and I left the warmth of our home to go to the cold, impersonal mental health unit at the hospital.

What a way to spend the day before Christmas Eve . . . Once we went through security, a nurse escorted us to a small office.

"The doctor is waiting for you," she said as she motioned us in.

We shut the door and sat in two chairs in front of a large desk, opposite the doctor.

"Your daughter is very ill," he said. "She needs to stay in the hospital and be forced to take medication. You should sign papers today."

"I don't understand," Roy said, voicing my own confusion.

The doctor repeated himself, but there was no emotion in his voice. He didn't explain anything to us, just that she needed medication, that she refused to take anything more than the antidepressant prescribed, and that she was belligerent.

Belligerent? Our Amber? No, she doesn't act like that . . .

"Can you bring her in here? Perhaps we can help convince her." I asked.

Moments later, she burst into the room; a nurse scampered behind her and shut the door.

"Why did you bring my parents here?" she screamed at the doctor.

"You need to stay here. You are sick and you need medicine. They are here to help," he replied.

"I'm not staying here. You can't make me. I don't need any medicine." Amber's voice got louder with each statement. Her arms flailed as she paced around the room. "I'm depressed, that's all. The nurse said I could leave in five days—it's been five days, and I'm going home."

My thoughts turned to the nurse's final comment on the day Amber checked in. *That stupid nurse. I knew that was a dumb thing to tell a patient. I wish she had kept her mouth shut.*

"Amber, you need to listen to the doctor. It's best if you take the medicine he thinks will help you," Roy said.

I turned to look at my husband, surprised that he sounded so calm. Were I to open my mouth, I couldn't have kept my voice steady. *Keep your mouth shut, Virginia*, I thought. *Let him handle it.*

"What are you doing to my parents?" Amber continued to spew venom at the doctor. "You son of a bitch, why are you making them say that?"

I sat there, unable to speak as her language degraded even further to a level I had never heard from her mouth, ever. For a moment, we all were frozen in shock.

Make her stop, God, make her stop. Amber doesn't act this way. Her language is embarrassing. Make her stop.

"Amber, let's go for a walk," Roy said.

The doctor shook his head. "You need to sign."

Roy and I stood up at the same time. We didn't answer him—we turned and motioned for Amber to follow us.

Roy, Amber, and I left the cramped office without another word. We walked the hallways of the ward. For an hour, we made circles from one locked door to the other, up and down the short hallway. Amber continued to yell, swear, and scream, "I won't stay." Roy and I spoke with her in soft, reassuring voices letting her know we would be beside her.

"The doctor wants what is best for you," I said.

"He never listens to anything I say," Amber said and stomped her foot. "I hate him. I won't do anything he says. He's trying to poison me."

"Maybe a different doctor in a different hospital will listen to you," Roy said.

Amber stopped and turned to face him. "Do you think so?"

"I think we should try," Roy said, his voice low and soothing.

"Well, maybe I could do that."

"We'll be with you. We won't leave you there alone," I said.

Amber looked at me and nodded, finally calm again.

Thank you, God. Help us get her into a new hospital.

"We are leaving," Roy said to the nurse at the desk behind the glass window.

"You realize she will be discharged AMA, don't you?"

"What's that?" I asked.

"Against medical advice," she said. "The hospital is absolved of any responsibility if you leave AMA. You will have to sign a paper."

"Get the paper," Amber said, her eyes narrowing as she glared at the nurse.

After Amber signed it, Roy and I both signed as well. We left the hospital and drove across town to another one.

"I'm hungry; can we stop and eat something?" Amber asked.

Roy pulled into a fast food restaurant. The biting wind blew, and snow swirled around the car. In the warmth of the restaurant, we ordered hamburgers, fries, and sodas. Our trio sat at a table in a corner. Between bites of my burger, I glanced at Amber as she watched other patrons in the small, crowded space. Her eyes darted from person to person. At times, her eyes rounded and she looked away quickly.

What's going on in her mind? How sad; it's almost Christmas and we are in a fast food place and on our way to another hospital.

I wanted to cry.

Even as she watched the other patrons, Amber talked loudly about the doctors and nurses she had seen. "They are all part of the conspiracy against me. They tried to hurt me when I was there. I had to leave."

Roy and I looked at each other, gathered up the food, and stood to leave.

"Let's finish this while we drive," Roy said, and we hustled Amber back to the car.

"Drive faster," I whispered to Roy as he maneuvered the car to the quickest route to the next hospital. We pulled into the emergency parking lot. I turned to Amber. "Let's see what a different doctor has to say. Maybe they can help; a different opinion is always a good idea."

To my surprise, she agreed. The ER was empty, and we met with a triage nurse immediately. We answered her questions. She typed quietly and efficiently and pushed an insurance release form across the table.

"I need you to sign these papers," she said. "It's permission to treat and to file insurance." She handed Amber a pen.

Amber refused. "I'm not signing anything."

"We can't treat you if you refuse to sign," the nurse said. She looked at me. I saw sympathy in her eyes.

She's seen this before.

Roy talked in a soft, calm voice with Amber for the next five minutes. I don't know what he said, but she finally consented to allow the hospital to file for insurance. The nurse slipped the consent for treatment in front of Amber, and she signed it, too. We left the desk and quickly followed the nurse to the exam room.

A young doctor came in. He did a quick medical check and asked Amber many of the same questions I heard at the last hospital.

"Your daughter needs to be hospitalized," the doctor said.

We nodded. *We know that; that's why we're here.*

"Can we admit you?" the doctor turned and said to Amber.

"Will I be able to check out and go home for Christmas? I want to be home for Christmas."

"It doesn't work that way," he said gently. "You will need to stay until the doctor thinks you are ready to go home. Shall I get paperwork started and you can get settled?"

"No. I won't stay if I can't be home for Christmas with my family," Amber stated as she shook her head.

Roy and I tried to convince her to stay, but she became agitated again. Her eyes looked wild, and her voice got louder. The more we talked, the worse it got. The door on that discussion slammed shut. The attending doctor made a phone call to the psychiatrist on call and handed Roy a prescription for Geodon.

"This will help her get through the holidays. The psychiatrist wants you to make an appointment with his office for December 27. He will let his office receptionist know you will be calling. Here is the address of a twenty-four-hour pharmacy." He shook Roy's hand and then placed a hand on my shoulder. "Good luck, folks."

And he walked out the door. We were on our own, again.

chapter six

The Christmas Holiday

We came home with Amber late on the evening of December 23 with a prescription for Geodon, an antipsychotic. I gave her the single dose recommended by the psychiatrist. Amber took it willingly and fell asleep almost immediately.

The next morning, Amber looked wiped out. Her eyes looked glazed with dark crescent moons beneath them. She seemed to move even slower than before.

"I don't like how the medicine makes me feel," she stated when I handed her the morning pills as we ate breakfast. "I feel exhausted. I don't want to take it anymore."

"You need to, Amber, honey," I said. "The doctor feels it will help you. Maybe your body just needs to get adjusted to it."

I put the medicine in her hand and passed her a glass of orange juice. She shrugged, tossed the pill in her mouth, chased it down with a gulp of juice, and ate a blueberry muffin. Within an hour, she had returned to her room and quickly fell asleep once more. I continued with the dosage recommended throughout the day. As I gave her each pill, I truly believed I would see a change in her behavior. But she looked drugged, spoke little, and lumbered from bed to table and back again.

On Christmas morning, she balked when I mentioned taking her pill. I kept the encouragement flowing freely. She took it. I felt relieved. After attending Mass, Roy, Amber, and I spent the rest of the day relaxing.

Mitchell, Melinda, Carter, Wesley, Suzanne, and Clinton joined us for our annual Christmas gathering on Sunday, December 26. Suzanne took me aside when they first arrived.

"What's going on with Amber? Is she alright?"

I answered her questions as accurately as I could.

"The doctor thinks it's depression with psychosis. She's on medicine, but it hasn't kicked in yet." I assured her Amber loved being with her family. "I think this is good for her. Maybe she'll improve because her brothers are here."

We spent the day with no outbursts or accusations, but I noticed Amber's quiet demeanor. The celebration lacked our typical good-natured banter and silliness. I felt grateful for eighteen-month-old Carter, who provided a spark of glee for all of us as he delighted in each brightly decorated gift.

Amber did okay surrounded by her brothers and their families. She adored them, and it showed.

December 27

We met with a psychiatrist the next day, and Amber told him she would no longer take the medicine.

"It's hurting my body, and I don't like it," she said with a defiant toss of her of her shoulder-length hair. "No one can make me."

"Is there a history of alcoholism in your family?" the doctor asked Roy and me. We nodded simultaneously.

"Yes, my father and my brother," I said.

Roy added, "My uncle and grandfather. Why?"

"Some studies have shown the genetic disposition for alcoholism can manifest in female descendants as a mood disorder. It's important to keep her on this medication. It takes a while before it becomes effective." He folded his file shut. "I want to see her in a month. I recommend she see a counselor weekly until then. We have some on staff here. Stop at the front desk, and you can set up a time for both."

"Amber, would you like to try that?" I asked her. I remembered when she told me the last counselor didn't do anything and wondered how she would react.

She shrugged, so I took that as a yes and set a time for her to meet with the first available counselor for the following week.

"I don't like the doctor," Amber said once we were in the car. "I won't go see him again."

Neither Roy nor I commented. We made it through the next few days, but her reluctance to accept the medication increased with each dose.

"Let's just wait and see," I said, hoping her feelings would improve as the medication helped her.

"Keep a daily log," Roy suggested one day. "Record all the changes you see in her behavior. Make notes on things she does that seem odd."

"Good idea," I said, latching onto something I could do. I sat at the computer and began a document.

Her bizarre behavior continued. I heard her laugh when no one said anything funny. If I questioned, "What's so funny?" she replied, "You know."

I didn't.

If we took her anywhere with us, she sat mutely in a chair. On the way home, she complained about how everyone in the room talked about her and her situation. I hadn't heard anything. Later, I recorded the incident on the computer and saved it.

I felt helpless, inadequate. I called the doctor's office several times for advice but found no help.

"There's not much we can do unless she checks into a hospital," said an unsympathetic voice on the phone.

On Friday, the 31st, we took her to meet the counselor. It went okay, but honestly, I didn't see that it made any difference. Whenever we mentioned the doctor to Amber, she stated she would not go back to see him again.

January 1, 2005

By now, Amber refused to take anything but the antidepressant. Try as I might to persuade her that the Geodon would help, I couldn't convince her. Each time I brought it up, she became angry, so I eventually dropped it.

My extended family came to our home that day to celebrate Christmas and New Year's. I expected Mom, my brothers, my sisters, and their families—about sixty people—for meals, gifts, and games. This had been a family tradition since 1979, and I didn't want to disappoint them.

"What do you think about Amber being here for the party?" I asked Roy. "We don't know what could set her off, and there will be a lot of small children here. Do you think it would be too much commotion?"

Roy nodded. "It might be. I think it would be best for the two of us to be gone. I'll check with Mitchell to see if I can go to his house. Maybe she can rest while Mitchell, Melinda, and Carter are at our house. Since it's your family, I think you should stay."

He called Mitchell. A few minutes later, he confirmed it was okay. "I talked it over with Mitchell, and he agreed."

Our guests began arriving around noon, and before long, they filled our entire basement, eating oyster stew and chili. Sweets overflowed the dessert table, and cousins sat in clusters as they chatted about events from the last year. Roy and Amber ate and mingled for a few minutes, and then he suggested to her to go somewhere quiet. Surprisingly, she didn't object, and without any fanfare, they snuck out.

"Where's Amber?" someone asked.

"She wasn't feeling well, so Roy took her over to Mitchell's house to rest," I said and changed the subject. Embarrassed, I didn't want them to know about her fragile state of mind.

The party went on as it did every year. Plates of food adorned every flat surface; adults visited or played games; small children bugged the adults about gift opening; lots of cookies and candies disappeared from the treat table. Laughter and chatter filled the rooms.

The sun dropped in the west, and daylight slowly disappeared. The crowd thinned as those who had to travel left for home. We still had about thirty people meandering around the house when Roy and Amber came home. Mom, several of my brothers and their families, and our immediate family lounged in various rooms of the house. I had my hands in a sink of soapy water when they walked in. I looked at Roy, my eyes wide with surprise. I probed his eyes for the answer to the unspoken question: *What are you doing back so soon?*

He moved close to me. "She started acting really strange at their house. She took a nap, and when she woke up, she tore around the entire house, looking in every room and in every closet. The more rooms she went in, the more upset she got." Roy whispered to me but looked troubled. "I decided I had to get her out of there." He rubbed the whiskers on his chin. "Who is Craig?"

"I've never heard of him. Why do you ask?"

"She kept saying, 'Where's Craig? What did they do with him?'" He shook his head. "When I asked Amber who he was, she exploded and started shrieking at me. I thought it best to get her out of the house."

"Yikes. I don't know who is he, but I hope she settles down."

Instead, Amber charged past me into the front room where a cluster of women relaxed as they chatted.

I dropped the pan in my hands back into the sink. Hot water and bubbles splashed in all directions. I quickly followed Amber to the living room.

Melinda sat on the sofa, engrossed in a conversation.

"What did you do with Craig?" Amber hurled her words at Melinda. "You better not hurt him!"

Melinda's face turned pale as she quietly rose from couch. She maneuvered her way past Amber and calmly made her way out of the room. Mitchell had Carter with him in the basement, and Melinda hurried in that direction, her lips tightly sealed and her eyes downcast.

"If you hurt Craig, you're gonna pay. Where is he?" Amber shrieked at Melinda as she hustled away from her.

I stepped toward Amber and wrapped my still-wet hand around her shoulder as I tried to steer her to her bedroom. She grabbed my arm and pushed it away. And the pacing began.

"They're dead, they're all dead, and it's my fault," she wailed as she circled from the front room to the dining room.

"Who's dead?" I asked.

My heart sunk in my chest like a rock. The joy I felt with my family at my house was sucked out of me as I fell in step beside her.

"Lydia and Suzanne—they're dead! It's all my fault."

Lydia, her first cousin and closest to Amber in age, had always been more of a friend, and Suzanne, Wesley's wife, had been unable to attend the party. Amber now had them involved in her other world.

"They're not dead, Amber. They're just not here," I tried to reason with her.

"No, they're dead!" she screamed at me. She pushed past me and continued to rant as she walked the path from the kitchen into the living room and back again.

My relatives backed away from her with downcast eyes and furrowed brows. When I tried to catch their eyes, they looked quickly to the floor.

I heard hurried footsteps coming up the basement steps. I glanced toward the open door and saw Melinda and Carter bundled up in their winter coats. I caught Melinda's eye. "Mitchell is going to stay," she mouthed to me as they made a beeline to the garage door.

I gave a quick wave goodbye as I moved my arm through Amber's and turned her around. I didn't want her to see them leave for fear she would verbally attack Melinda again.

It didn't work. Amber saw them.

"What did you do with Craig?" she screamed. "You're gonna pay for what you did to him!"

Melinda kept her eyes toward the door, moving quickly through it. I heard a light swish and a gentle thud as they disappeared into the garage. She never looked back. My heart plunged from my chest to the floor.

Amber continued to pace, throwing her hands in the air, slapping her sides, and shouting names of people who were dead. Names of friends from high school, family members absent from the party, people I had never heard of—all pronounced killed because of her. I felt so helpless, unable to stop this freight train of jumbled words from tumbling in her brain and spewing out for all our guests to hear.

The room soon cleared. My relatives gathered their belongings, threw on heavy coats, and made a hasty exit from our home. A few of them caught my eye as they hurried past Amber and me, but many of them looked away. I'm guessing they just didn't know what to say.

"She needs to be in a hospital," Ann, my brother's wife, said in my ear as she gave me a quick hug goodbye.

"I know. We have tried to convince her, but we can't force it. Unless she is a danger to herself or others, our hands are tied. I have talked to doctor's offices and the hospital several times, and each time, I'm told the same thing." I whispered back. "It is so frustrating. I don't know what else to do."

"Is she on medicine?"

"She's supposed to be. She refuses to take it."

Mom stood next to the sink. As Amber passed by, she opened her arms and held them out to her raging granddaughter. Amber paused.

"Put your warm face on my ear like you always do," she whispered loud enough for me to hear. Amber reached in and for a brief moment rested her head against Mom's head. I watched as grandmother and granddaughter embraced while Mom whispered, "I love you."

I had a short reprieve from the pain exploding in my chest. *That's what Amber always does with Mom.*

Mom gave me a timid look. I felt her love pass to me before she slipped out the door. The rest of the relatives left, quickly and quietly. Amber's agitated state continued while we marched together. I quit trying to convince her that no one had died. Instead, I linked my arm through hers and just walked beside her. I don't know how long we strolled in circles.

"Amber, we can't change anything. It's late. Let's just go to bed," I finally suggested. I spied her medicine bottle and snatched it off the counter as we passed by. "Here, it's time to take the medicine the doctor gave us."

She pushed it away, so I steered her to her room.

"It's late. Everyone has gone home now. Let's go to bed."

She allowed me to guide her into her bedroom. Without a word, she slid into bed without changing into her pajamas. I covered her with her blankets and softly touched her shoulder. I saw her relax and listened for a moment to her soft, rhythmic breathing. I slipped out of her room and left the door slightly open so I could hear her if she became upset again.

Not yet able to seek my own bed, I scurried to the basement to check if all the perishable food had found the safety of the refrigerator. I noticed wrapping paper shreds that created gold, red, and green patterns on the carpet; scattered dishes mingled with the bottles and cans that filled the card tables nestled in the basement; trash overflowed from the plastic bin. In my family's haste to leave the uncomfortable situation, no one took time to clean up.

What a mess, I thought, referring not just to the basement.

chapter seven

January 2

The following morning, I opened the drapes in the living room. The sky looked gray, overcast, and gloomy, echoing my own feelings. The night before had been a nightmare. I stepped over toys strewn on the floor, made my way to the kitchen, and started my coffee before I ambled into my office. After a quick punch to the power button, my computer hummed awake. I returned to the kitchen, poured myself a steaming cup of joe, and made my way back to my office desk. The thought of sharing Amber's illness and our struggles terrified me, but I knew what I must do, so I opened up my email account and composed a letter.

Dear family,

I feel I owe you an explanation and an apology for last night. Some of you had already gone last night when an incident happened here involving Amber. Some of you saw her ranting, pacing, and hurling accusations. I am truly sorry. Roy and I really thought she would be okay, but we were wrong. We moved her home with us three weeks ago. We've had her meet with several doctors. At this time, her diagnosis is depression with psychosis. Last night got out of hand, and she had a meltdown. Please know we are doing the best we can to help her through this time. We will keep you up to date if you want. Until then, please keep our family in your prayers.

Love, Virginia

I hit send and felt a bit of relief that I had finally shared the truth with them. Roy's family still did not know, but I didn't want to write another painful note.

I'll send them an email later, I promised myself. *There's no need to tell them yet. Maybe I won't have to.*

I would spend the next ten days jumping back and forth between frustration, fear, and heartbreak.

January 3

I had a new companion: the box. Invisible, I carried it with me everywhere. It grew heavier with each outburst, accusation, bout of raucous laughter, or crying session. It resided beneath my rib cage, tightening around my heart with compounding strength: an unseen, unwavering, relentless box. Was it trying to shatter my heart or merely hold it together as my daughter descended further into madness?

As the circle of trust Amber drew around herself tightened, the box grew.

"What if she quits trusting us?" Roy asked. We spoke in hushed voices over breakfast while Amber slept in her bedroom down the hall.

"I'm afraid she will run away if that happens," I replied. Roy crushed his cereal in a bowl, poured on the milk, and paused. Our eyes locked.

"We need to be prepared for that. If she runs, we may never find her. She could end up homeless, on the streets . . ." He gulped. "Or worse."

I chewed the inside of my cheek. The thought of her roaming the streets, alone and scared, filled me with fear. I held my breath and blinked back the hot tears threatening to escape at any moment. "We can't let that happen."

"We need to make sure she is never left alone, even for a minute. I think we should take turns sleeping so one of us is aware of where she is and what she is doing at all times," Roy said. His hazel eyes clouded over, his brow furrowed.

"Mmm-hmm," I nodded. "We can't let her know what we are doing, though. She may think we are against her, too."

"Yeah. Once she is in bed for the night, one of us can spend the night in the chair in the living room. That way, if she gets up, we will hear it."

We finished our breakfast; the crunching of cereal provided the only sound. When he finished, Roy stepped through the back door to the garage, locked our cars, and brought the keys in the house. "I'm gonna hide the keys so she can't find them," he mentioned as he strode into his office.

I followed him and watched him stash them out of sight. I returned to the kitchen, refilled my coffee cup, and carried it to the living room. I fell into my rocker/recliner and reached for my devotional.

I sure don't feel like praying today, God. How can you do this to our family? Haven't we been faithful to you? We work retreats, go to church, sing in the choir . . . I ticked off a list of church activities in my head. *And how could you do this to Amber? She was doing your work! She loves you! How can you do this to us?* My heart raced and my breaths came fast as my anger boiled over. I closed my book, threw it onto the end table, left the room, and started my workday. *I just can't pray. It feels so hollow, like no one is listening.*

I wanted God to quiet Amber's mind, to give her peace. I wanted him to take away our heartbreak. I wanted him to quiet my mind, too—to give me peace—but I was too overwrought to say the words.

I worked on autopilot but continually walked to the personal side of our house and checked on Amber. Mostly, she sat and stared at the television, had her Bible open on her lap, or slept. I'm not sure if she even knew I walked into the room.

Later that day, Mitchell dropped by.

"Here's a number for you, Mom," he said as he showed me a slip of paper. "It's for an organization called NAMI."

"What's that?"

"It's an organization for people who are dealing with the same issues you and Dad are now. Melinda's mom gave it to her to give to you. She knows about a chapter near her town," he said as he pinned it to the refrigerator with a magnet. "Just call them. I think they can help."

I noticed his jaw twitch, his mouth slightly curved down.

"I know you are concerned, and I appreciate your help. Tell Melinda's mom thank you, too." I gave him a quick hug. "I will call the number the first chance I get." I took the number off the refrigerator—a.k.a. our bulletin board—and stuffed it in my pocket. "Thanks again." I knew I'd have to call when Amber was sleeping. She'd freak out if she thought I was talking to someone about her.

Later that day, I talked on the phone with a kind woman named Katherine and poured out my heart to her. She listened as I paced the floor and rambled on. Every once in a while, she interjected a comment.

"I understand. My mother is mentally ill. I've experienced something similar."

I'm not the only one who deals with this. She understands. My heart leapt. "What should we do?" I asked after we had talked for about fifteen minutes.

"You're in a tough spot," she said. "It doesn't sound like the medicine she agrees to take helps her at all. It sounds like she is getting worse."

"I think so, too."

"We have a class on mental illness in children starting tomorrow evening. I understand your daughter is not a child, but I think the information will be helpful for your family. There is room if you wish to join us."

That's the most encouraging news yet. Finally, some direction.

"Yes, sign me up. I'll check with my husband and see if he wants to come, too. Is there room for both of us?"

She said she had room for us both, and I felt a glimmer of hope—the first in a long time.

"I want to go, too," Roy said when I shared Katherine's comments with him.

"I don't think it's a good idea to leave Amber home by herself. Do you?" He shook his head. "No, I don't think we should."

"I'll call Brooke; maybe she can come and spend time with her those nights."

Brooke willingly agreed to come each Tuesday evening. "I usually have Bible study on those evenings, but I will let them know I won't be there. I'm happy to come."

For the second time in a few weeks, she answered my call for help.

Now that's living your faith. She's willing to change her plans for us in our need. Thank you, God, for Brooke. Maybe things will be okay after all.

January 4

The NAMI (National Alliance on Mental Illness) class began. We met in a church basement, huddling around a table in the corner. Each person introduced themselves and offered a short reason why they came. Everyone in the room had a child with mental illness. Even though we didn't have a young child with mental illness, I felt welcome. We each shared our story during introductions.

I'm not alone. These people understand. Their lives are different, but they understand.

Katherine, the friendly voice on the phone, was one of our instructors, mentioned a book she found very helpful, *The Broken Brain*.[1]

"It gives an insight into how the brain works in addition to what doesn't work during mental illness. I've read it at least three times," she continued. "I highly recommend it."

I jotted the name down in my notes and continued to listen.

"Some studies have indicated that traumas in the womb change the brain structure during development. These changes may make it susceptible to disorders such schizophrenia or bipolar later in life," she said.

I inhaled a sharp breath.

It's my fault! My pregnancy with Amber was harder than with the boys. I'm responsible. I zoned out as my mind traveled twenty-five years earlier to my pregnancy with Amber: the pains in my abdomen, the spotting, the fear of a miscarriage all tumbled together in one word: guilty. An unseen hand reached in and twisted my heart. But a calming voice of peace struggled against my anguish.

Breathe. You didn't do anything wrong.

I should have gone to the doctor.

What could he do?

I should have taken better care of myself.

You did the best you could. It's not your fault.

It happened when I carried her.

The internal argument deafened me and made it hard to concentrate on the rest of the lesson.

Lord, take these thoughts away. They don't help me at all. I can't change the past; I need help now for the future.

I did my best to listen, but guilt continued to assault me.

"You can't know what no one has told you," Katherine announced, cutting through my internal diatribe. "You can't be expected to know the things you will learn in this class." She paused.

The message started to take root, calming some of my guilt.

"You can't know what no one has told you," she repeated. "Don't beat yourself up about things you didn't know."

It was just what I needed to hear.

When feelings of guilt tried to invade, I fought it with the prayer: *Lord, help me remember: It's not my fault. I need to learn more so I can face this.*

January 5

My hope was short lived. Amber slipped further away from our world into one I didn't understand. Her eyes darted around continually. Her comments about the danger surrounding her life and ours came regularly. Her conversations, when she did speak, made little sense, and she spent even more time sleeping. Mitchell stopped by daily and strongly encouraged us to get her into a hospital. After Amber's accusations against Melinda, he also brought discouraging news.

"We've moved Carter to a daycare. We think it's best for him and you."

Amber's threats to Melinda made them both uneasy. I felt a sharp pain in my chest. Her shrieks of "You're gonna pay if you hurt Craig" reverberated in my head.

"I understand."

"We are really worried about you. Remember Melinda and I studied behavioral science in college? We think it is more serious than depression with psychosis." Grimacing, he shifted from one foot to the other. He glanced to the hallway; he winced when his eyes flitted near Amber's bedroom door. He turned back to me and rested his hand on my shoulder. "We think it is schizophrenia."

"Schizophrenia?" I said. "People end up living on the streets with that."

He nodded. "Her circle of trust is getting smaller and smaller. If she stops trusting you and Dad, you both could be in danger. There's no telling what her brain might tell her to do." He looked uneasy as he shifted from one foot to the other. "Please get some help for you two. And you have to get her into a hospital."

Long after Mitchell left, I paced. I felt confused and helpless. I couldn't get her into a hospital, even though I could see the rapid decline in her mental state. *Lord, how do we do that? She won't agree to go to the hospital. Katherine told me the criteria the state says we have to meet. She's not a danger to herself or others—at least not yet. Do we wait until that happens? What if we're too late?*

I felt hopeless, as if I had just watched Amber slip off a cliff. I jerked out to catch her but missed. She hung on to a small twig. I sprawled on my belly as I hung over the edge, groped for Amber's hands, and grabbed them. I barely held on. My hands grew sweaty, tired. My grip slowly loosened as she slipped closer to her death. Every fiber of my being tried desperately to hold on. But my hands cramped and I winced in pain. I felt her fingers letting go of mine.

This was my child; I couldn't watch her world spiral into madness without doing everything in my power to help her.

January 6

God, are you listening? Help us, please; help me. I don't know what to do.

Call Elaine. Call Elaine. Words popped into my head. *Talk to David. He's a doctor, and he knows Amber.*

I pulled the Rolodex off the shelf above Roy's desk and twirled it until I found their number. Elaine, my cousin, and I shared a deep friendship. I knew David, her husband, as a straight shooter. He didn't mince words. I knew his truthful, respectful, but sometimes brutally honest manner. But maybe he could give me some direction.

My fingers trembled as I punched the numbers on the phone.

"Elaine, I need advice. Is David around? Things are really bad here."

"What's going on?"

I quickly explained the situation and Amber's bizarre behavior the past few weeks.

"I agree; you need to talk to David. I should have put him on right away. I'm sorry."

Once I explained everything to David, he spoke gently but firmly to me.

"She needs hospitalization, Virginia. She won't get better without medicine. She will get worse. It's the only way."

"She won't go. We've tried."

"Then you will have to force it. Commit her."

Silence. I'm guessing he waited for me to speak. But I couldn't; it hurt too much.

"Virginia, it's the only way. I know the laws here, but you need to check your state and county procedure. It may differ from place to place."

Silent tears slid down my face. "Okay, thanks. Can I talk to Elaine again?"

"Sure. Call again. Keep in touch. Let me know if I can help you in any way."

"Oh, Virginia," Elaine said when she came back on the line. "I wish we were closer."

"David said we need to force her into a hospital. We've checked on that. It's so hard to do. Our state has strict criteria for us to commit her. I don't think we can meet it. What should we do?" I gulped hard to swallow the sobs.

"You will have to do it. It's the only way."

"How will I know when it will work? When she's so bad that it will work?"

"When that time comes, you will know. I know you; you—will—know," Elaine spoke softly. "You are strong. You can do this."

"What does that mean? I don't feel strong. I feel weak and helpless and totally confused."

"You are, Virginia. You just can't feel it. But I know you are strong."

I twirled the cord but said nothing. Elaine continued.

"I love you. Call anytime. I mean it, anytime."

We hung up. I sat quietly at my desk for a few moments. The conversation sunk deep into my heart.

I don't know what Elaine sees. I'm not strong. What now, God; what now? How am I supposed to get through this?

I thought about Carter. I hadn't seen him in over a week. I knew Mitchell and Melinda did the right thing in moving him to a daycare, but it still hurt. I missed Carter immensely, and I missed my time with Melinda, too. I enjoyed our conversations when she stopped each day to pick him up. As I watched Amber descend into darkness at an alarming rate, I could have used a friend to lift some of my pain. I couldn't see past it.

God, where are you? Are you even listening?

I turned back to my embroidery machine just to give my hands something to do as my heart wept. As I worked, I thought back to my conversation with Elaine. "You're strong; you can do this." Her words repeated over and over in my head, and a new thought emerged.

Where's that book of prayers Elaine gave me?

I went directly to the bookcase and riffled through the stacks of books, finding it wedged between two larger books.

I pulled out the pocket-size book. I studied the maroon cover, ran my thumb over the gold embossed lettering, and read the title aloud—*Illuminata: A Return to Prayer* by Marianne Williamson—and opened the front cover.

"To Virginia, from Elaine, 1999—Enjoy."

The sight of Elaine's handwriting brought times we shared to mind: the joint family trip we took in 1997, her visit to our home with her children the following year, all the chats on the phone. My heart lightened. The book fell open to a bookmark. I prayed the Morning Prayer on page seventy-eight.

"Please enter where you already abide . . . I surrender to You my doings . . . Direct my footsteps, and show me what You would have me do . . ."[2]

Words of a familiar song, based on Isaiah 45:22, sung in church popped into my head. *Turn to me, oh turn and be saved.*

I tried to concentrate on turning to God, but my heartache hijacked my thoughts.

I will never forget you, my people. Another song from church, based on Isaiah 49:15, resonated in my head. Words I had sung so many times played softly and gave me some comfort. *I have carved you in the palm of my hand. I will never forget you; I will not leave you orphaned. I will never forget my own.* In this difficulty, I knew I couldn't forget the Lord, no matter how hard it got—and God would not forget me. I vowed to think about the verses every time fear crowded my mood. I would cling to hope even though I couldn't see any change in Amber, in her mental state, or in the prison I called home.

I closed the book to start supper when the melodic sound of "Old McDonald" drifted into the room. I snatched the phone from the cradle. "Hello, this is Virginia. How may I help you?"

"Virginia, this is your Aunt Josephine. Elaine called me, and I just had to call you to let you know I'm praying for you."

"Thanks; we sure need it. I'm so confused; I don't know what to do."

"I know, Elaine explained everything. How are you doing, really?"

"Do you want me to be honest or give the expected answer?"

"The truth."

"Exhausted, and I can't seem to help being really mad at God. I feel betrayed. I have spent my entire adult life trying to do the right thing. I took my kids to church every week, read them Bible stories, and prayed with them each night."

"I know."

"Not only that, Roy and I did retreats for years, both attending and working on them. We've been active in what we thought was God's work. And Amber has been faithful—she was a youth minister for him."

I heard the anger in my voice. I paused for a breath. Silent outrage met me head on.

"And this is the thanks I get. I feel like I just got kicked in the stomach."

"I know it doesn't make any sense. And you are really hurting," Aunt Josephine said. She continued in a soft voice, "I'd like to offer you a suggestion."

"Sure." I felt a special connection with Aunt Josephine and would take all the advice I could get.

"Read."

"Read?"

"Yes, go get a book called *When Bad Things Happen to Good People.*"

"I've never heard of it."

"It's been around quite a while. It's written by a Jewish rabbi. I think it might help you."

"Okay, I will go to the library and get it the first chance I get."

"One more thing; are you praying to St. Dymphna?"

"Who? I've never heard of her."

"St. Dymphna is the patron saint for mental illness," Aunt Josephine said. "I know things are hard for you. Just know others are praying for your family and we love you. You will get through this."

Within a few hours, I went online to do research to find the book and to learn of St. Dymphna. I found the book first, wrote down the author, and then found St. Dymphna. I read the history of her life and the reason some Catholics pray for her intervention with mental illnesses. I clicked a link to a prayer site and found a specific prayer to her. I hit print. As it printed, I explored more links.

I continued to read, print, and pray, not only for our situation but for other people in their painful situations who came to mind that day. Prayers for mothers and families; prayers for the sick; a prayer for the seven gifts of the Holy Spirit. I hit the print button and the printer spit out page after page of prayers that spoke to me. I found a small three-ring binder, inserted the pages, and added blank pages opposite each prayer.

I can write in the names of people I want to remember in prayer, people who asked me to remember them. I snapped the rings shut. Then came the admonition.

You've just made your own prayer book. Now use it.

chapter eight

January 7

I visited the library and found *When Bad Things Happen to Good People* by Harold Kushner, *The Broken Brain*, and another book, *Surviving Schizophrenia*.[3] I checked out the stack of books and started with Kushner's book. I read whenever I had a few spare moments. The words he wrote made sense to me.

> When a person is dying of cancer, I do not hold God responsible for the cancer or for the pain he feels. They have other causes. But I have seen God give such people the strength to take each day as it comes, to be grateful for a day full of sunshine or one in which they are relatively free of pain.[4]

Will I ever feel that—a day free from heartache?

> When people who were never particularly strong become strong in the face of adversity, when people who tended to think only of themselves became unselfish and heroic in an emergency, I have to ask myself where they got these qualities which they freely admit they did not have before. My answer is that this is one of the ways in which God helps us when we suffer beyond the limits of our own strength.[5]

Is this the strength Elaine meant? Am I strong?

Life is not fair. The wrong people get sick [*tell me about it*] and the wrong people get robbed and the wrong people get killed in wars and in accidents. Some people see life's unfairness and decide, "There is no God; the world is nothing but chaos."[6]

I'm seeing chaos . . .

Others see the same unfairness and ask themselves, "Where do I get my sense of what is fair and what is unfair? Where do I get my sense of outrage and indignation, my instinctive response of sympathy when I read in the paper about a total stranger who has been hurt by life?"[7]

Okay, yeah, I do feel this sometimes.

"Don't I get these things from God? Doesn't He plant in me a little bit of His own divine outrage at injustice and oppression, just as He did for the prophets of the Bible? Isn't my feeling of compassion for the afflicted just a reflection of the compassion He feels when He sees the suffering of His creatures?" Our responding to life's unfairness with sympathy and with righteous indignation, God's compassion and God's anger working through us, may be the surest proof of all of God's reality.[8]

I found words that sounded so much like my own thoughts. *How many times have I cried, "It's not fair?" How many times have I said that, believed that, felt that?* Reading thoughts from Harold Kushner made me question my attitude.

Is God saddened by Amber's illness, even more than me? Was her illness a result of our imperfect world, not part of his plan?

I flipped back through the pages to find a passage that had struck me earlier as I continued to study the rabbi's thoughts.

God does not cause our misfortunes. Some are caused by bad luck, some are caused by bad people, and some are simply an inevitable consequence of our being human and being mortal, living in a world of inflexible natural laws.[9]

This isn't from you, God? Is that what this means?

The painful things that happen to us are not punishments for our misbehavior, nor are they in any way part of some grand design on God's part. Because the tragedy is not God's will, we need not feel hurt or betrayed by God when tragedy strikes. We can turn to Him for help in overcoming it, precisely because we can tell ourselves that God is as outraged by it as we are.[10]

God, show me the way. I can't do this on my own.

My attitude changed gradually—it didn't happen immediately. I once asked a friend, an ordained deacon in the Catholic faith, "If I'm supposed to praise God when things go right, why I can't be mad at him when things go wrong?" He gently assured me that I would discover the answer for myself. The more I read about the brain and my faith, the more I gradually found the answer and accepted the mental illness that had invaded my daughter.

Helpful people tried to give me comfort: "It's God's will." I wanted to scream at them, "SHUT UP! It is NOT God's will that Amber suffers this way." I dismissed their well-intended attempts at wisdom; instead, I delved deeper into the book.

We could bear any burden if we thought there was a meaning to what we were doing.[11]

Had I made it harder for people to accept their illnesses, their misfortunes, their family tragedies by telling them that they are sent by God as part of some master plan of his?

I don't think it could be harder than it is now.

Let me suggest that the bad things that happen to us in our lives do not have a meaning when they happen to us. They do not happen for any good reason which would cause us to accept them willingly. But we can give them a meaning. We can redeem these tragedies from senselessness by imposing meaning on them.[12]

I don't have control over Amber's illness, but I do have control over my attitude. Will I ever find meaning in this?

We too need to get over the questions that focus on the past and on the pain—"Why did this happen to me?"—and ask instead the question which opens doors to the future: "Now that this has happened, what shall I do about it?"[13]

What can I do about this? I let the concept simmer. *I can learn about this invader called mental illness. I can change me.*

I finished the book with a new determination and a feeble sense of peace. Somehow I needed to quit feeling sorry for myself and let go of my anger. I began to realize Amber's illness was not sent by God. Rather, it came from our imperfect world. Finally, I asked myself, "What can I do about our situation? Can I help her? If so, how?" Then I challenged myself to learn about the brain and how it worked. I resolved to do what I could to change the future for Amber.

I picked up the next book on my self-imposed course of learning, *The Broken Brain* by Nancy Andreasen, MD. I found the beginning of it fascinating as I read about the different mental illnesses and reactions to them. However, the explanations on the biology of the brain were complicated. I understood the basic principle of the connections for the thought process: what happened during mental illness and how medication helped those afflicted overcome some of the problems associated with the different illnesses. But I couldn't remember the correct names for the parts of the brain and the processes that occurred millions of times per second. Discouraged, I stopped reading the book.

Try it again later, I thought. We still had five weeks left of the six-week

NAMI class. We studied brain biology together, and it gave me lessons on the brain at a pace I could absorb. The technical terminology didn't come easily to me, but I grasped the concepts.

Of course, my basic knowledge did not alter Amber's situation. All that changed, outwardly, was that I spent more time in the front room, studying my situation and watching Amber sit in a chair. She stared at nothing or laughed at an unspoken joke. Roy and I both knew we couldn't continue like this. She spent less time in our reality and more time in a place we couldn't reach.

January 8

The following night, the three of us sat at the table, sharing an evening meal.

"Amber, here's your medicine," I said as I handed her a pill.

She threw it on the floor. I picked it up.

"Please take it."

"No!" She ran to the bathroom, slammed the door, and locked it.

We followed. "Amber, open the door. Please?" Roy pleaded as the two of us stood in the hallway.

"Leave me alone," she yelled. "I'm not taking the pills."

We stood outside the door. Every few minutes, we knocked and called to her softly. No answer.

A carbon/sulfur smell wafted from under the door. Roy and I looked at each other, eyes wide and eyebrows arched. "She has matches . . ." Roy mouthed to me.

"Amber, what are you burning?" he called through the wood.

"I'm lighting candles. What's the big deal?" she yelled.

"Come out, Amber," Roy said gently.

"No, you will make me take the medicine. I won't take it."

I hurried to the kitchen, opened a drawer, found a narrow nail, and hurried back. I poked the slim end into the hole in the doorknob and heard the click as it unlocked. Roy tried to open the door, but it wouldn't open. "She's blocking the door. Just leave her; trying to force our way in will only agitate her more."

"Blow out the candles, Amber," I said, willing my voice to not sound as scared as I felt.

No answer.

"Amber, blow out the candles. Please?"

The doorbell rang. Roy stayed in the hallway while I hurried to the front door and opened it cautiously.

"Brooke!" I reached out and embraced her. "Your timing is incredible," I said. "Amber has locked herself in the bathroom and has matches."

"God's timing is amazing," she replied. "I had a feeling I should come tonight." She smiled at me.

We both hurried to the bathroom door.

"Amber, it's me, Brooke. Can I come in?"

The doorknob turned slowly, the door cracked open just wide enough for Brooke to slip in. The door closed as quickly while I sent a silent prayer of thanks heavenward. Brooke—just who we needed. Amber would be safe with Brooke in there. She still trusted her best friend.

About a half hour later, Brooke came out. "Can I take some blankets and pillows in the bathroom? I think she'll be okay, but I will stay with her in there."

After I gathered pillows and blankets for her, Brooke slipped back in the bathroom. I heard the lock click, but I relaxed. I knew Brooke could handle it. Exhausted, I plopped on the couch and eventually fell asleep. Roy disappeared into our bedroom, a few steps away from the bathroom door.

Sometime during the night while I slept, the two young women emerged from the bathroom and made their way to Amber's bedroom. An averted crisis, thanks to Brooke, who listened to the voice of God with instructions for action.

Roy and I stopped trying to force the medicine on Amber. We understood now—it didn't work.

January 9

The following evening after supper, Roy, Amber, and I sat in the front room. Roy read a book as he relaxed in his chair, and I did the same in mine. The television rested silently in the corner. The only sound in the room came from Roy or me turning the page in our book.

"Mom, will you and Dad pray the rosary with me?" Amber broke the silence. We had just finished eating, and she had changed in to her pajamas. "Prayers help me feel better. A friend from college, Cliff, always prayed the rosary to feel better. Maybe I will feel better, too. Can we?"

My hope soared for a moment. Her request made sense.

Maybe she will be okay after all.

I went to the prayer corner, reached on the shelf, and chose three rosaries. I handed one to Amber and one to Roy. I plopped onto the sofa and patted the spot next to me. Amber moved next to me, snuggling up, and we began. We said the Our Father together, our voices mingled. I concentrated on the words as I spoke. "Thy will be done on earth as it is in heaven." *Oh, God, what is your will?*

We recited the next prayer together. "Hail Mary, full of grace, the Lord is with thee. Blessed art thou among women, and blessed is the fruit of thy womb, Jesus. Holy Mary, Mother of God, pray for us sinners now and at the hour of our death. Amen."

Amber closed her eyes and rested her head on my shoulder as Roy and I recited the five Sorrowful Mysteries of the Rosary, decades that concentrated on the suffering of Jesus. I concentrated on his life as we spent the next fifteen minutes in prayer. Words I repeated thousands of times became alive. I thought about Christ's passion and about Mary, his mother.

Thoughts of her witnessing his suffering, her feelings as he hung on the cross dying, and her sorrow at his death settled deep in me as I prayed.

I felt a sudden connection with Mary. She understood my feelings. She had watched Jesus, her son, suffer through a brutal, excruciating death. She knew about extreme sorrow. I knew she understood my pain as I watched Amber suffer from the fear and pain of paranoia, the terror of feeling someone wanted to kill her. I realized my pain didn't come close to her suffering, but suddenly, I knew, Mary understood.

Praying the rosary became a nightly routine. Every evening, Amber curled up next to me on the couch, Roy sat in the recliner, and we recited the Sorrowful Mysteries. Rather, Roy and I prayed aloud; Amber rested her head on my shoulder with her eyes closed.

The prayers took on new meaning for me. I recited the memorized words but had a running commentary in my mind.

"Hail Mary, *Hey, Mary,* full of grace, *God chose you to be his mother,* the Lord is with thee. *You are in heaven now.* Blessed art thou among women, *You are holy, you listened to the Lord,* and blessed is the fruit of thy womb, Jesus. *You bore the Son of God.* Holy Mary, mother of God, *You're Jesus's mother; he'll listen to you,* pray for us sinners now, *take my prayer for Amber to him,* and at the hour of our death. *Please hurry 'cause we're dying down here.* Amen." *I believe my prayer will be heard.*

My heart sent my pleas for wisdom and understanding heavenward, as I hoped against hope we could pray the pain away.

chapter nine

January 11

At the next class, I sat with both feet on the seat of my chair, my knees up to my chin, my arms wrapped around my legs with my head bowed through most of the lecture. At times, I rocked back and forth. I wanted all of this to stop, but felt powerless as I watched our world as we knew it slip further and further away.

Katherine came up to Roy and me after class finished. "Things are pretty tough, huh?" she asked kindly.

I couldn't speak, afraid that if I opened my mouth, the dam I fought to keep from leaking would burst. I nodded. Roy explained the situation and how it had worsened. Katherine had been through the committal process with a family member—her mother—and understood my heartsick feeling. She agreed with David, Elaine, Mitchell, and Melinda: we needed to commit Amber for treatment.

"When the time comes, you will need three things: a doctor's statement declaring she needs hospitalization, two witnesses, plus proof she is a danger to herself or others," she instructed. "If she refuses to go, you can call the sheriff's department. They will come and force her to go." I pictured a sheriff putting handcuffs on Amber. I felt the contents of my stomach lurch up. I tasted the bile, swallowed hard, and forced it back down.

"Let's hope it won't come to that," Roy said as he placed his hand on the small of my back. "Thank you, Katherine."

We returned home. Brooke left shortly after we arrived.

Roy, Amber, and I lounged in the front room. As was our nightly routine now, before we prayed, Roy and I read a book as Amber sat and stared into her own world. An occasional paper rustle as a page turned provided the only sound. Suddenly, the back door slammed with a bang. Mitchell strode quickly into the room and marched up to Amber.

"You're going to the hospital tonight," Mitchell said.

"No, I'm not," Amber replied and got up from the sofa. She tried to walk past Mitchell, but he reached out and grabbed her arm.

"Oh, yes, you are. I'm gonna make you."

She pushed his arm away. "Get away from me. You can't make me do anything."

"I'm gonna make you go tonight," he repeated.

"Mitchell. Stop," I said. "This isn't helping. What's going on?"

My eldest son turned to me; a mixture of worry, exhaustion, and anger glared at me. "Melinda and I have been telling you for weeks to get her into the hospital. Amber's gotten worse—her trust circle dwindles every day. What happens when she doesn't trust you anymore?"

He stared at me. I froze.

"We're concerned what she might do to you—and to us. She's already threatened Melinda once."

I glanced at Roy, still in his chair. His knuckles were white as he gripped the arms.

"Melinda said she is moving home with her parents until Amber gets some help. And she's taking Carter," he said. His thumbed jerked toward his sister. "I won't let her illness wreck my family."

Mitchell's eyes narrowed. He glared at Amber, then at Roy, and then turned toward me, but not with the same look; it was more of a please-back-me-up expression.

"I won't let my wife move four hours away. Amber has to go to the hospital tonight."

Mitchell reached out to grab Amber, but she wriggled away from his hands. She dashed past him, ran to her room, and slammed the door.

Roy jumped up and hurried after her. Mitchell followed him with me right behind. Roy pushed the door open and entered her room first. Amber rushed to him and gave him a shove.

"You are not taking me anywhere," she yelled.

I stepped in the room directly behind Mitchell. "Stop!" I shouted. "This is not the way." I turned to Mitchell.

"Go home. I will take care of this in the morning," I said firmly.

I know he is really hurting. Elaine said I would know when the time was right—when I had no other choice. The time is now. I have to do this.

"You've tried before. It didn't work. Now I'm gonna make sure it happens." Mitchell's shoulders rounded, but his face was hard and determined. "I won't lose my family."

"I won't let that happen, Mitchell." I gently touched him on the shoulder. "I will take her in the morning, one way or another. It's our job; we're her parents." I looked at Roy; his eyes looked exhausted. "You go home to your family. She will be in the hospital tomorrow morning." I breathed deeply. "I promise. We'll let her calm down tonight and take her in the morning."

Mitchell nodded. "Just make sure it happens." He stormed out the door, turned, and glared at Amber one last time before leaving us. A few moments later, I heard the back door shut.

"I'm not going to the hospital tomorrow," Amber said. She narrowed her eyes, crossed her arms across her chest, and set her jaw in a hard line.

"We'll talk about it in the morning," I said. "Let's just all go to bed and get a good night's sleep."

She crawled into bed and threw the covers over herself. She burrowed beneath them, completely hidden. Roy and I quietly left her room.

"What if she tries to run during the night?" Roy asked me in a hushed voice.

"I've thought of that. What should we do?"

"I'm going to rig up something so we can hear if any of the doors to the outside open," Roy said.

Together, we worked to stack cans in front of each exterior door until we felt satisfied any door movement would create a loud clatter of cans. He took his place in a chair in the front room. I went to bed, but I didn't sleep much. I listened with one ear all night long for any sound from Amber. I watched the numbers flip slowly on my alarm clock.

January 12

Finally, the clock said five o'clock. I crept into the bathroom, showered, and padded silently to my office. I kept my hands busy until I heard movement in the personal side of the house. I felt relieved that Amber hadn't tried to run in the night, but at the same time, my anxiety level soared off the charts. I dreaded what awaited me once Amber got up.

Roy woke, showered, dressed, and ate breakfast. I couldn't eat the cardboard-tasting food. It seemed like hours before Amber stirred. Finally, I heard the shower start. I waited until I thought she would be dressed and made myself walk slowly to her room.

Lord, give me strength for this. Be with me, 'cause I'm so scared.

I knocked on her door. "Come in," she said.

I inhaled deeply and forced myself to walk through the door.

"Pack a bag. Dad and I are taking you to the hospital," I said firmly.

Amber plopped on her bed. "I'm not going."

"Yes, you are."

She stood and faced me. "No, I can't. I won't. They'll hurt my baby."

"What baby? You don't have a baby."

"I'm pregnant, Mom. I'm pregnant."

"I don't think so, Amber." I sighed.

Oh, God, not this. Where did this come from? She can't be pregnant, can she?

"You haven't had sex with someone, have you?"

She shook her head. "Of course not. Geez, Mom."

"Well, then you can't be."

"I am, Mom. I am. It's the second Immaculate Conception. I'm carrying the new Christ child." Her eyes bored into mine. "The doctors will make me take medicine. It will hurt my baby."

Ugh, not this now, God. Now she thinks she has a mission from you? Will this ever stop? Help us, Lord; show me what to do.

For a few minutes, I tried to reason with her. I might as well have saved my breath. I should have heeded the prompting in my heart to be quiet. Nothing I said changed her mind. I shook my head. "Amber, you will go to the hospital today. Here's your choice: either you go willingly with us," I stopped and took a long, deep breath, "or I will call a sheriff so he can come to take you."

God, did I just say that to my daughter? That I would call the sheriff on her? Please, God, don't let it come to that. I can't handle it if she gets hauled out of here in a squad car. Lord, help her. Help us.

Amber stomped over to the dresser. She threw items into a duffel bag. I handed her a pair of pajamas.

"I don't need those. I'm not staying."

"Just put them in. They don't take up much space. It won't hurt to have them."

"They better not hurt my baby." Silently, I picked up the bag and motioned to her.

"Let's go." And we walked out.

Roy had the car running in the garage. After Amber climbed into the backseat, I set the bag beside her. Then I slid into the other backseat.

"I set the childproof locks," Roy mouthed to me. "She can't open the door from the inside."

I nodded, grateful that Roy always thought of everything.

We rode in silence until we pulled up to the emergency room entrance of the hospital. We chose to go back to the second hospital, the one we had taken her to on December 23, instead of the one Amber had left AMA. She disliked the doctor she saw there, and I remembered her anger when she left. Roy and I both hoped a new hospital would be better for her.

"We'll be here with you, Amber," Roy said as we escorted her to the desk. Roy explained our plans to the nurse. She nodded and took us to a room immediately. A doctor arrived within minutes. He asked Amber several questions. Amber acted belligerently, repeating her unwillingness to stay, but no one argued. He turned to Roy and me with more questions concerning her state of mind.

After a few minutes, he turned to Roy. "I think she needs hospitalization and to be forced to take medicine. Do you have someone who will go with you to the courthouse and sign papers for us to keep her?"

Roy nodded. "My son." He looked at me. "Our son."

The doctor turned to me. "Will you be okay if you stay here with her? It may take a couple of hours."

I nodded. Amber and I sat silently in the small exam room. Someone brought some water for Amber and a coffee for me, but mostly everyone left us alone. She stared at the floor. I watched her as I chewed on my lip.

About an hour later, Roy and Mitchell returned from the courthouse with the legal papers. Earlier in the week, they had gone to the courthouse to start the preliminary paperwork. Roy learned then the criteria needed, which helped speed things up as they initiated the process to force Amber into the hospital for observation with a possible committal. They requested immediate custody for her, afraid she may disappear once she realized our intentions.

The doctor informed Amber of her rights.

"The county is required to have a hearing within five days. At that time, a judge will determine if you need forced medication for your welfare or for the welfare of others. An attorney has been appointed to represent you."

Amber scowled at Roy, then Mitchell, and finally me. No one spoke for a few moments.

"Well, if that's all you need right now, I'm gonna go," Mitchell said, breaking the oppressing silence. "Unless you need me to stay longer?"

"No, you need to get back to work." Roy said. "Thanks for everything."

Mitchell gave me a quick hug and then turned to Roy, who reached out and hugged him first. Mitchell glanced toward Amber, but she stared silently down at her hands. I caught his eyes and saw in them pain mixed with relief. He nodded and then left. The doctor and the nurse stepped out of the room. Roy, Amber, and I sat in the room alone for only a minute or so before a no-nonsense looking nurse entered.

"Here's a hospital gown," she said as she handed it to Amber. "You'll need to change, and we will take you to the ward."

Roy stepped out of the tiny exam room.

"I'm not changing." Amber slid off the exam table, folded her arms across her chest, and backed into a corner.

"You need to change. It's policy."

Amber shook her head, her jaw set.

"Either you change clothes or I will have some strong men come in. They'll do it for you."

"Amber, they're gonna make you change. Just do it. If you fight, it will just make it harder for you," I said quietly.

Amber grabbed the gown from the nurse as she glowered at her. "Get out of here—and shut the door. I'll do it myself."

I sat in the chair quietly while she changed. After she put on the gown, I folded her clothes in a neat pile and opened the door. Roy came back in. Amber paced the eight-by-six-foot room while we sat, each of us in our private misery, watching her make tiny circles in the cramped space.

A quiet knock on the door interrupted our distraught trio. We all looked at the door. "Come in," I said.

An officer strode into the room. "I'm here to accompany you to the ward."

This time, we expected it. I had prepared Roy and reminded Amber of the hospital policy for an armed escort. We followed him mutely down a winding corridor. Within a few minutes, we stood behind a locked door. We followed a nurse to a small room. The three of us took a spot on the vinyl-covered couch, while a nurse with a clipboard fired question after question at us.

"I just answered those questions. Look on the chart," Amber said as she folded her arms across her chest. Her jaw twitched.

"Just answer them, okay?" Roy said.

She obliged. That was one good thing about Amber: even as a teenager, she obeyed, even if she didn't agree. I sighed, relieved for the parts of her personality still visible.

Thank you, God. She still does some of the things we ask. It makes this a bit easier. Shortly after the nurse acted satisfied with the answers, she took Amber to her room. The small square space had two beds and a bathroom off to the side.

"All of our rooms are doubles," she stated. "For now, you have it to yourself, but if someone else comes in, you will share your room."

Amber tossed her bag on the bed.

"We will let you folks know when the hearing will take place," the nurse told us after Amber sprawled on her bed. "Visiting hours are from one to three and from six to seven each day. You can stay for as long as you like today, but after that, it's only during visiting hours."

We stayed most of the day, spending some of our time together in the lounge. When it grew dark, Amber announced, "I'm tired and want to sleep. You and Mom can go home."

She disappeared down the hall into her room. For the second time, I felt like I abandoned my daughter in a scary place, but this time, it was against her will. As we walked in silence to our car, the bitter, cold wind blew relentlessly in my face.

Is this freezing wind a punishment for what we did? Oh, God, forgive us if this was the wrong thing to do. Help me stay focused, God, on you and what I should do next.

chapter ten

January 14

The hearing date arrived. Our court-appointed attorney for us suggested we meet an hour early so he could familiarize himself with our situation. Before we left, I printed off the daily log I had recorded for the last few weeks. At ten pages, longer than I remembered writing, it detailed every change we observed: Amber's paranoia, her verbal outbursts, etc. Roy's suggestion to keep a daily journal weeks before produced a timeline for her break with reality. I handed it to the attorney.

Lord, why do I feel like I am betraying her?

Roy had told Mitchell the time, so he met us at the hospital, where the hearing would take place. The lawyer interviewed Mitchell, read my diary, and pronounced that this wouldn't take very long. "It appears this is an open-and-shut case."

An important-looking woman marched through the waiting area where we sat. She wore a navy business suit, her gray hair pulled into a tight bun, and she clutched a silver clipboard in one hand and a black leather satchel in the other.

"That's the magistrate. We meet here in a room. Your daughter will have a court-appointed advocate to protect her rights, along with her own attorney," the lawyer explained. He turned to me. "The judge allows only those involved in the hearing in the room. You will need to wait here."

"I can't be in there? I want Amber to know I care and am there for her. Will you ask the judge if I can come in?"

He returned a few moments later. "You have permission, but you are not allowed to say anything."

"I can do that." *Lord, help me to be quiet. Help Amber know we love her.* He shook our hands. "Let's go, folks."

We gathered our things and followed him to the room. The magistrate sat at the head of the table. Amber sat on one side with her attorney beside her. Our lawyer was to sit opposite them. A middle-aged woman with long brown hair sat on the far side of the table with a yellow legal pad and pen. She looked ready to record everything said. Lastly, a blonde woman with perfect makeup sat on a chair away from the table in a corner.

"That's Amber's court-appointed advocate. She is here to look out for Amber's best interests," our lawyer explained.

"May I sit behind you so Amber can see me?" I asked him. He looked to the judge. She nodded, and I took my seat as Roy and Mitchell took theirs beside our lawyer.

The hearing began. It seemed to go on and on and on. First, our attorney presented the doctor's report. Next, he asked Roy to explain each item as he used the timeline we had provided to illustrate Amber's bizarre behaviors over the past month. Then Amber's court-appointed lawyer cross-examined him but couldn't disprove any of his statements. Next, our attorney questioned Mitchell.

"Amber threatened my wife recently. As a result, she no longer feels safe in our home. I also saw Amber push my Dad. I'm concerned for the safety of my family and that of my parents." Mitchell's professionalism kept a calm atmosphere in the room.

Amber's attorney questioned Mitchell but found little to dispute. He turned to Amber. "Is this true?"

She nodded. He continued to talk to Amber.

"Tell me what's going on with you," he said.

"Everyone in Boone is out to get me. The whole town is trying to get me killed."

"How do you know this?"

"Someone installed video equipment in my car. They know everywhere I go. Someone broke into my apartment and went through all my things." Amber paused.

"Go on."

"They tried to run me off the road several times when I was driving."

"What did you do?"

"I stopped in the middle of the intersection so they wouldn't hit me."

God, I've never heard this before. This is new.

I looked at the judge; her eyebrows raised, and she scratched something on her legal pad. Amber's attorney snatched the papers I had supplied before he read anything aloud. He asked Amber about each incident I had recorded as if he wanted Amber to deny it. She didn't. Instead, she elaborated on most items with her own confused version. The judge continued to write on her legal pad.

Everything that comes out of her mouth sounds like she needs help. Nothing she says makes any sense. Am I a horrible person because I'm happy about this? Am I a bad mother because I'm glad? Will the judge see what I see?

"I see there is a paper here about a movie. What does that mean?" Her attorney continued with his questions for Amber. Earlier, Mitchell had printed an internet page with a movie synopsis after Amber repeatedly referred to it. Our attorney included it in the paperwork he gave the judge.

"I saw it at Thanksgiving with my cousins. That movie is about me. My friend wrote it—it's about me. Everyone knows that."

"This paper says the movie is about a young man who kills a child."

"Yup, it's about my life," Amber stated before she folded her arms and slouched in her chair. Her eyes squinted shut.

"Can you explain it further?"

"It's my life. Just watch the movie."

Amber's lawyer looked at Roy and Mitchell and then at the judge.

"I've heard enough to make my decision," she said.

Finally! Oh, God, I hope the judge sees it as clearly as I do.

"It is my determination that Amber is a danger to herself and to others. This was demonstrated by her driving, her threats against her sister-in-law, and her own statement that the movie about the killing of a child is about her."

The room remained silent except for the judge. All eyes remained on her, except for Amber's. She looked around the room, almost as if she didn't understand that the decision the judge would soon make affected her life.

"I will order her to receive medication and to remain under the jurisdiction of the court. In addition, she will remain under a doctor's care and medication until further notice."

She stood up, put her paperwork in her briefcase, nodded to each person in the room, and left. When I realized I had been holding my breath, I released it slowly, blowing it out my mouth.

Our attorney turned to Roy. "I have never seen a hearing take two hours before. Usually, it lasts twenty minutes and it's decided. But then I have never had a family present documentation like yours. It seemed clear the direction this would go, but she had to hear all the evidence before she could rule." He shook Roy's hand. "I will file the paperwork today."

Everyone prepared to leave. Roy turned to me, and I saw a deep pain in his eyes mixed with relief. He had just testified against his own flesh and blood. I glanced at Mitchell. His eyes held the same look. Roy and I both hugged Mitchell as I thanked him. "I know it this hasn't been easy for you. Thank you for your help."

"I'm just glad she's finally in here. Now she can get some help."

I felt optimism creep into my thoughts. *Now she will get better.*

"May I speak to Amber?" I asked her attorney.

He turned to Amber. She shrugged. I went to her and put my arms around her.

"It's gonna be okay. I will come and see you every day. I love you."

Amber pulled back, looked at me with hollow eyes, and turned to her court-appointed advocate. "I don't like that doctor. He made up lies about me."

"You have the right to request a different doctor," the advocate replied.

Shut up! That will not fix anything. We will have to start over again. Again, I was exasperated by the unthinking comments people felt like they could offer Amber. I felt like clamping my hand over the woman's mouth.

Amber looked at us. "I need to meet with my advocate and make a plan. She said I can change doctors. You can go now."

I groaned inwardly. I clenched my teeth and turned to the woman. *Choose your words carefully.*

"Do you have a business card?" I asked. "I'd like to talk with you as well. Let's work together. We both want what's best for Amber."

She handed me her card without a word. Roy and I walked to the nurse's station.

"When will she get her medication? Will it be today?" I asked the nurse who escorted us to the exit.

"As soon as the lawyer files the paperwork, we can start. It usually takes a few hours. I imagine it will be sometime this evening," the nurse said. She spoke softly.

"Should we be here?" Roy asked.

"No, I don't recommend it. She will probably fight us, and we'll have to hold her down. I think it would be too hard for you folks to watch that." Her eyes filled with kindness. "She's probably angry with you. Take a day away. We'll take good care of her. We will."

I turned and looked back to the room we had just left where Amber spoke with the advocate. As I watched, both of them walked out and headed toward Amber's room. Roy and I both walked back to Amber and gave her another hug. She stood there as we wrapped our arms around her and looked at us. "Dad and I will be back. You will be safe here. No one can get to you in here. We will see you soon. I love you."

She looked at me but didn't speak.

We walked out. I felt relieved and sad, but I also had with a glimmer of hope. Roy looked at me. "I'm exhausted. Amber is safe and will get her medication today. We need a break from everything that has happened. Let's just leave town."

"Okay," I muttered. Suddenly, it felt like every muscle in my body turned to jelly, and I just wanted to go to sleep. "Amber's safe. That's all I care about."

chapter eleven

After a brief stop at home to pack an overnight bag, we drove to a nearby town and checked into a motel. Once in our room, we tossed our bags in a corner and collapsed on the bed. The next thing I knew, it was morning.

"Let's go see a funny movie," Roy suggested after breakfast. "I looked at the paper and saw *Meet the Fockers* is playing down the street. I think we both need a good laugh."

I don't think either of us had laughed since I brought Amber home that day over a month ago. The movie struck us both as utter nonsense, and we belly laughed until it hurt. It felt great to relax and release some of the pent-up emotions. That night, I slept well for the second night in a row.

January 16

On Sunday morning, we searched the phone book and found a church, where we attended Mass. I hoped we wouldn't see anyone we knew there. I didn't feel like talking to anyone except God. I didn't think I wanted to share my sorrow with an acquaintance. Thankfully, we didn't see anyone we knew.

"I'm ready to go see Amber and see how she is doing," I said to Roy as we drove out of the church parking lot. "Can we go after we eat?"

He understood. We quickly ate lunch and headed to the hospital, arriving at the beginning of visiting hours. We rang the buzzer for admittance and once again, we stood behind the locked door on the psychiatric ward. I scanned the lounge area but didn't see Amber, so we found the head nurse.

"Where's Amber? How's she doing?" I hoped I would see some improvement. She should have been on medicine for two days by now.

"She refused to take any medication when we tried to give it to her," she answered.

"What?" Roy hissed loudly. "She's under court order to take it." He ran his hands through his hair. "Why wasn't she given it?"

"I didn't get any paperwork for that. If I don't have it, we can't force her to take it."

I heard Roy's moan, so I turned and saw his face deepen to a dark scarlet.

"Go look through the paperwork. The hearing was two days ago," Roy instructed her. I heard anger riding just below his words, but he stayed outwardly calm.

She went to the nurse's station and rummaged through a stack of papers.

"Here it is. It wasn't put in her file. We'll get it started when we do meds tonight."

I can't believe it. Two more days without medicine. Two more days wasted. Ugh, people—I'm so sick of inept people. God, why do we keep hitting roadblocks?

We asked the nurse to call Amber to the lounge. She shuffled out to the table where we sat. Her hair looked like it hadn't been combed or washed since we left her. Her slacks hung on her, wrinkled and baggy with no belt to hold them up. Her shoes flopped as a result of no laces in them.

We sat at the table together and made sparse conversation with her. It wounded my broken spirit to see her unkempt appearance, to hear her anger because she was stuck in there but still frightened from the plot she imagined.

"Mom, will you call my counselor? Will you ask her to come visit me here?"

"Sure. I'll call her tomorrow, first thing in the morning."

When visiting hours ended, we left for home. I didn't want to witness the battle Amber would face in a few minutes and felt relieved that I had to leave. I couldn't bear to watch someone hold her down while they injected her with medicine. My imagination handled that for me as I pictured the scenario. I felt the tears threaten to spill out at any moment. I hugged her tightly. "I love you, and I'll be back tomorrow."

The air felt cold and crisp as we made our way to our car. I inhaled deeply as if the fresh air would erase the heaviness in my chest. We climbed in, and the engine roared to life.

"Let's pray the rosary as we drive," I suggested.

Roy turned and dipped his chin. "You lead."

I began, "In the name of the Father . . ." We recited the rosary as he drove home, and I concentrated on the torture Christ endured. I envisioned Him as he suffered through the night at the hands of the soldiers. I pictured Him as he trudged under the weight of the wooden cross on the walk to Calvary. *Lord, help me to carry this cross.* We said the last "Amen" as Roy pulled into the garage.

January 17

The next morning, I dialed the office number for Amber's counselor and informed her of Amber's hospitalization and her request to talk to her.

"No, I can't do that," her counselor replied immediately. "I don't visit patients in the hospital; they have to come to the office."

"She's in the hospital; she can't come to you. She asked for you," I said. "Your office is affiliated with the hospital. The doctor who treats her works with you at the same office," I continued. "Can't you come?"

"I'm sorry, no. I can't do that. I don't make hospital visits."

"Thanks for nothing!" I yelled, slamming the phone down. "Thanks for absolutely nothing! You'll not see us again. You just lost a client, honey."

I stewed about her reaction for the rest of the morning. *What a worthless system.*

I told Amber her counselor would not be coming when I visited the hospital that afternoon.

"Oh, that's great," she said. Her eyes rolled, and she clenched her teeth.

"It made me mad, too," I said. Then I changed the subject. "How'd you sleep last night?"

"They gave me a shot after you left last night. I tried to fight them, but they made me take it."

"That must have been hard for you."

"What's the difference? I have to stay here. They force me to take medicine. I have no say in my life anymore."

I didn't know how to respond, so I said nothing. We spent most of the hour just sitting side by side, saying and doing nothing.

January 18–22

One week passed. The routine for each day never varied. I visited Amber during afternoon visiting hours then went home and worked until it was time for evening hours. Roy worked during the day, and we went together after supper. She always greeted us when we came. Sometimes, we walked the hallways together; sometimes, we sat and played a game of Yahtzee or Uno. But I didn't see any improvement in her mental state. Most days when I arrived, she sat in front of the television staring straight ahead. Every so often, she laughed, although I never saw anything humorous on the TV. When we played a game, she played for a few minutes and then quit concentrating.

After our visit one evening, I called the number on the business card of Amber's court-appointed advocate. We discussed our plans for Amber's care with her.

"I think your family can do more for her than I can," the young woman stated. "I'm going to back off and let you handle it."

"Thank you," I replied, feeling more determined than ever to get Amber the best care I could.

One afternoon after my visit with Amber, as I waited to leave by the locked exit door, a nurse slipped beside me.

"I'm not supposed to talk with you about your daughter because of the HIPAA law," she whispered. "But I feel I must tell you—she's refused to eat any meals since yesterday. Could you bring in something for her to eat when you come back tonight?" Her eyes darted back to the nurse's desk behind the large glass window. "She is so thin already; I hate to see her lose any more weight."

"I appreciate you sharing this with me," I said quietly. "Yes, I will do that. And thank you."

She opened the door for me, and I turned to her before I stepped through it into the open hallway. "Thank you."

I heard the door shut and the lock click. I wagged my head as I walked to the elevator.

Another thing, God? Now she won't eat? Will she ever get well?

That evening as we ate our meal at home, I relayed the conversation with the nurse to Roy. After we finished, we left for the hospital and stopped at a fast food restaurant on the way. We purchased a burger and fries for Amber. After a quick hello once we arrived at the hospital, the three of us sat at a table, and she took quick bites. Roy and I smiled at each other.

"How was your day?" Roy asked.

She stopped chewing, wadded up the burger and fries in the paper, and walked to the trash can; I heard a thud as it landed in the metal can. She went to a sofa, plopped down, and stared ahead. "Aren't you hungry?" I asked her.

She turned and looked at me, but her eyes looked far away, blank. There was no more conversation or games that evening. We just sat. Our conversation became one sided. When visiting hours ended, we hugged her goodbye and headed home.

We prayed as Roy drove.

"She's not getting any better," I said to Roy after we finished the prayers of the rosary.

"No, but maybe the medication hasn't kicked in yet. Give it time. It will," he replied.

"I really thought once she had the proper medicine, we would see an improvement. Instead, she's worse."

He nodded.

Mitchell dropped by the next morning after breakfast. "How's Amber doing? Any improvement?" he asked.

I bowed my head. "No, none. I think she's worse."

"I'll drop by later today during visiting hours. I'm not sure how she will react to me, but I will stop by anyway," he said. "You won't need to go twice today that way."

"No, I want to go. It would bother me not to go see her," I said.

"Did you know some studies suggest she won't remember very much while she is in this state of mind?" Mitchell said tenderly.

"I'll remember," I replied. "She's my daughter, and I want to see her as much as I can."

"I understand. But I'm concerned about you. I can see how tired you look."

"I appreciate that, but I feel better going to see her." I looked directly into Mitchell's eyes. "I'd worry if I didn't go."

"Okay. I'm still gonna stop by."

Mitchell gave me a hug before he left.

Before I left one afternoon, I composed an email explaining our family's situation, the hospital, and visiting hours. I hit the send button and shared it with both Roy's family and mine. I also included my friends. My fingers shook as I hit send. *How will everyone react? Will they blame us? Or worse, blame her?*

Later, I checked my account. To my surprise, I found dozens of replies. Every response assured me of their prayers and support both for Amber and for us. Many of them promised they would stop by the hospital to see Amber, followed by *Can we take her anything?*

I wrote back, *She enjoys Snickers bars.* Soon Amber had more candy than she could want or eat—and she loved candy. She began to hand it to Roy each evening when we arrived for our evening visit. I also noticed new stuffed animals in her room.

"Somebody gave it to me," she usually said if I asked her about them. Sometimes she could remember who brought it and sometimes not. The fact she couldn't recall their names bothered me, so I concentrated on the generous reaction of our family and friends.

I also received a few faxes and letters from acquaintances who had heard about Amber. Every note sent encouragement: *It will get better; It's hard now; We've had similar things; We are praying for your family.* I filed the snippets of hope in my heart.

January 23

One week turned into two. Amber's condition worsened as time passed. My hopes fell along with my spirits.

Lord, I'm asking for some change soon.

One afternoon as I made my way through the hospital lounge to visit Amber, I noticed two of Roy's brothers and their wives seated in a small cluster.

"Hi," I said as I paused by the group.

"We went to visit Amber, and she kicked us out," Frank, Roy's brother, said, shocking me.

"What happened?"

"We had been there for a few minutes, and out of the blue, she accused us of stealing the farm from you and Roy. She didn't make any sense; she got really upset and then yelled at us to get out and not come back."

I felt my lunch lurch in my stomach. I swallowed before I spoke. "I'm so sorry. Please don't take it personally. It's the illness talking, not Amber.

She has no basis for saying that. Her thoughts are a jumbled mess."

The four of them looked at me, then at each other, and back at me again.

This is awkward. Do they wonder if Roy and I talked about something similar and that's why she said that?

"I'm really sorry she reacted to you that way. Her circle of trust has evidently gotten smaller. I'm so sorry."

They all nodded.

"It's probably best if you don't go visit her for a while," I said. "I appreciate you coming to see her. I do. Thank you." I shifted from one foot to the other. "I guess I'd better get up there to see her. Thanks again."

They were still sitting there when I left.

Amber mentioned when I saw her that they had stopped by and then proceeded to tell me her latest delusion. She added other family members and how they all were in a conspiracy against her. I made a mental note to send a new email to everyone.

The following morning, I picked up my daily book of devotions and the binder of prayers I had printed days earlier. I opened to a page with prayers for the seven gifts of the Holy Spirit. I reread the prayer for wisdom and understanding several times. With some semblance of composure, I closed the books and strode to my office. My computer screen came to life, and I opened my email account. The words jumped from my mind through my fingers to the keyboard and materialized on the screen.

Amber needs lots of prayers. Please check with us before stopping to see Amber. Her world is getting smaller and smaller. If she turns against you, PLEASE don't take it personally. The medicine is not working, and instead of getting better, she is getting worse. Please keep the prayers coming. I ask you to please pray for these specific things:

- *For the doctors to find the correct medication Amber needs;*
- *for her to understand her illness and the need for medicine; and*

- *for wisdom and understanding for me.*
  Thank you in advance.

Love, Virginia

I hit send. I knew I couldn't do this by myself any longer.

chapter twelve

Before Amber became ill, I watched Carter, our grandson, five afternoons a week. I looked forward to spending time each day with him, our only grandchild, while Mitchell and Melinda worked at their jobs. At eighteen months, he learned a new skill every day. He added dozens of new words to his vocabulary while he entertained himself in the play corner of my work room. I embroidered, folded, and shipped out customer orders in between hugs, snacks, and story time. I experienced joy mingled with excitement each day he spent with me. His mind, like a little sponge, seemed to absorb everything around him. I surprised myself with the amount of patience I discovered, something lacking as I raised my own children. His absence the past few weeks left a hole I hadn't imagined. I understood, but it didn't take away the sadness. I missed Carter.

Now the house seemed abandoned. Amber was in the hospital, and Carter still didn't come for daycare, which left the house an empty shell— pretty much like I felt. My concern about Amber overtook my other emotions. I lost excitement for my business. I made a sign and hung it on my shop door: DUE TO FAMILY ILLNESS, I AM CUTTING BACK ON REGULAR HOURS. PLEASE CALL FOR AN APPOINTMENT. THANK YOU FOR YOUR PATIENCE AND UNDERSTANDING.

I told Janelle I wouldn't need her in the afternoon for a while, just in the morning.

For almost two weeks, I had the same routine: coffee; prayer/devotional time; business; eat my lunch; stop to buy fast food for Amber's lunch; sit quietly while she consumes her meal (we had learned any conversation from either of us caused her to stop eating); sit with her for an hour; return home; work on orders; force down some supper; get Roy, take food, and visit Amber together; sit quietly while she ate; return home after visiting hours ended.

As the days turned into weeks, I found it increasingly difficult to stay positive. I saw no improvement; in fact, her mental state worsened. I saw her slow descent into a world I couldn't enter. The calm and focus I tried so hard to achieve, all the lessons I was learning from my study and prayer, felt far away and immaterial. My head tried to speak to my heart, to remind me of the things I had vowed to practice, but discouragement won out. Instead, I felt helpless and angry at the entire situation.

Amber continued her refusal of hospital food, or anything other than chicken nuggets, and resigned herself to the injection of medicine, but communication with her was dwindling to practically nothing. Most days when I arrived, she sat in the lounge staring at the television. She didn't respond to my conversation and laughed without speaking. I looked around but never saw anything funny. She looked at us only if we shouted her name repeatedly, but she rarely spoke.

The worse she got, the more depressed I became. I lost my appetite. I took a couple of bites at each meal before I just couldn't eat any more. It tasted like cardboard—dry, tasteless, and an effort to chew. It became easier to not eat at all. My clothes began to hang on me, but I felt powerless to change.

One evening, as we left the hospital, Roy turned to me.

"Virginia, I don't know how to tell you this, but your breath is awful."

"Really? I'm sorry. I floss and brush. Why would it be bad?"

"I think it's because you don't eat. Do you think it could be the stomach acid? Maybe you should eat more. See if that helps." Roy spoke gently. "I'm worried about you . . ."

"OK, I'll try. I don't want to knock people over with my breath. But it won't be easy. I can't stand food right now."

"I know. Just try."

So I tried. Food still had no taste, but I managed to choke down more than a few bites.

January 24

That afternoon during my visit, Amber's mood switched from indifference to raging anger. She hurled insults and swore at the staff as she paced the lounge. She bellowed about their role in Craig's disappearance. This disturbed me—I still didn't even know how he fit into her life.

I positioned myself on the green linoleum tile floor beneath a window. "Amber, come sit by me," I said calmly and patted the floor. She continued to stomp and curse at the nurses.

"Amber, please come sit by me for a few minutes," I repeated as I tapped the cold floor.

I breathed a sigh of relief when she stopped marching in circles and plopped down next to me. We sat quietly for a few minutes before the swearing returned. I reached over, touched her leg gently, and looked at the staff with a grimace of apology.

Bang. Clang. The heavy steel door opened and shut. I glanced over as Brooke walked into the lounge carrying a stuffed animal. My heart jumped a little, and I felt a glimmer of happiness. She came to the corner immediately, handed a soft brown puppy to Amber, and sat on the other side of my screaming daughter. Amber hugged the puppy as Brooke encircled her arm around Amber's shoulder and whispered, "Hey, sweetie." Amber stopped yelling and leaned on Brooke's shoulder. She rested her head in silence, relaxed. *Thank you, God, for Brooke. She acts as your hands.*

The three of us sat on the hard, cold floor for the rest of the visiting hour. In the deafening silence, the drone of the nearby television provided a welcome sound. When visiting hours ended, Brooke and I reluctantly left Amber sitting in the lounge. I turned one last time before I walked through the outside door. I felt a glimmer of relief; we had at least convinced her to move to a chair.

January 25

The next day, things reached a breaking point. Amber had been in the ward for two weeks. When I arrived for visiting hours, she sat alone on a green plastic couch. A young nurse approached me immediately.

"She is not responding to the medicine. She's worse. Last night, she dumped the entire pot of coffee into the wastebasket. She kept saying that we had poisoned the coffee and she had to protect all the patients." She shook her head. "It was a fresh pot with fifty cups. She could have been seriously burned."

My heart sank. "Oh, my." I wanted the floor to swallow me up. *I don't know how to do this, Lord!*

"Someone has to watch her all the time. And another thing—she started hanging with the male patients, getting very friendly, if you know what I mean." Her brow furrowed. "Once, I caught her under a blanket with one of them." She looked around. "I'm concerned, and so is the doctor. He wants to meet with you and your husband."

"OK," I nodded but kept my eyes downcast. "I'll call him to come up right away."

I asked her to let me back out, stepped out into the hallway, and called Roy on my cell. "You need to come to the hospital. The doctor needs to talk with us."

After we hung up, I leaned against the wall in the hallway. I closed my eyes.

It can get worse. God, it can get worse. Are you there? Are you even listening? Please let me know how to handle this! I've tried everything—it's not working. I need your help now more than ever.

Within an hour, Roy and I sat opposite the doctor in his office on the ward.

"Your daughter is resistant to all the medicines I've tried. She refuses to speak to me; instead, she stares at the floor. I don't feel I can help her any longer at this hospital," he said.

I glanced at Roy and then back to the doctor. "I know she won't speak to you. What do you recommend?" I asked.

"Sometimes patients respond to ECT. I think it is a good option for her."

"What's ECT?" I asked.

"Electroconvulsive therapy. The hospital in Iowa City does a better job with this treatment. Would you consider a transfer for her to the university hospital?"

By this time, Roy and I had already discussed another hospital for Amber. We could see she hadn't responded to treatment here. The doctor's words made our decision easier.

"Yes. What do we need to do?" Roy asked.

"I will start the process for transfer. We need her permission to send her medical records, permission from the county to transfer her case out of county, and a bed in Iowa City to open up," he stated. "We will let you know when we have the arrangements made."

Roy and I left. We walked to our cars in silence, parted ways, and each drove home.

As I drove, a face came into my mind: Stephen, an old classmate of mine from high school who had studied psychiatry. If I remembered right, he was on staff at the university. After I arrived home, I hurried to my computer, connected to the Internet, and navigated to the hospital website. I clicked link after link and finally found his contact information.

I quickly typed an email and hit send. In it, I explained our situation and gave him my phone number, asking him to call me any time. Stephen called me within a few hours. I explained the rapid decline in Amber's mental health and her initial diagnosis of severe depression with psychosis, with a strong possibility of schizophrenia.

"Did it really come on that suddenly?" he asked. "Schizophrenia is an insidious illness."

"What's that mean?"

"It comes so gradually the signs are often missed. As a result, the symptoms become well established before others notice them."

"Oh, but it sure seemed sudden," I said.

"As I said, it is an insidious illness."

We went on to discuss ECT. "It's been effective for many patients with severe depression." He shared a case he had observed, careful not to use any names. "The success blew me away. She went from catatonic to responsive quite quickly." He continued with a promise of his help and support. "Call me anytime," Stephen said as our conversation ended.

I had a glimmer of hope again.

January 26

It was short lived. When I visited Amber the next afternoon, the same young nurse pulled me aside immediately after I arrived.

"The paperwork is ready to transfer Amber, but she refuses to sign it. Without her signature, we can't send her records," she said. "And there's another problem: the beds are all full. The university hospital put her on a waiting list."

I groaned and rubbed my forehead. "Any idea how long it will be for an available bed?" I said.

"It's really hard to tell. I have no idea."

Great; that's just great. Now what, God? Now what? We've hit another roadblock.

To top it off that day, Amber acted violently. I don't know what triggered her— maybe the paperwork. I had never seen her like this before.

She stomped up and down the hallway, hitting the wall, kicking the doors, and swearing loudly. I fell in step beside her.

"Amber, what's upsetting you?" I asked.

No reaction from her at all. In her world, I don't think I existed anymore.

"Amber, stop hitting things," a voice called from the nurse's station.

She stopped hitting the wall briefly but continued to pace. Within a few steps, she screamed more curse words at the staff, kicked doors, and pounded the wall every few steps. I felt helpless. I wanted to cry. Instead, I continued to walk beside my raging daughter.

A nurse jumped up from the desk, caught up to Amber, gently wrapped her arm around her, and guided her to a sofa. I made a point to sit beside her, hoping she would feel less threatened than if I faced her.

"Amber, what's wrong?" I said.

Amber stared at the floor, oblivious to my presence.

"Amber, it's Mom," I repeated several times. No response. I placed my hands on her face, one on each cheek. I gently turned her head until our noses almost touched. I tried to look into her eyes.

"Amber?" Nothing. "Amber." She pulled away and stared at the floor. I turned her face back.

Where are you, Amber? Are you still in there? Don't cry, Virginia; don't cry. It won't help.

"Amber." My voice echoed in the room.

Her eyes lifted; she looked at me. "Mom? What?" she said but turned her head toward the floor again.

I tried once more, but she remained unresponsive and silent. I sat next to her quietly, holding her hand, as she allowed it. Visiting hours ended. I turned to hug her, but again, she didn't react. It felt like I had just embraced a wooden statue. I passed the nurse's station on my way out. The nurse looked up as I passed, and we locked eyes. I saw sympathy in hers; I'm guessing she saw a broken heart in mine.

I sped through the doors, hallways, lobby, and parking lot until I reached my car and slid in. Finally alone, I bowed my head, buried it in my gloved hands, and gave in to the sobs I had swallowed for the last hour.

Once I was composed, I wiped my eyes with the back of my glove and drove home. I went about rest of the afternoon on autopilot, doing what I needed to do but without any enthusiasm. The phone rang at about five p.m. I didn't want to talk to anyone, but forced myself to pick it up.

"Hello," I said flatly.

"Yeah, it's Claudia."

Claudia, Roy's mother, never said hello. Every phone conversation began with "Yeah," so this wasn't out of the ordinary. "Virginia, there is a special Mass tonight. Would you want to go with me?" she asked.

"I don't know . . . it's been a hard day," I replied.

"Ivan, one of the visionaries from Medjugorje, is in town; he'll be at the Mass. I think you would like it."

I knew about Medjugorje, a town in the Herzegovina region of Bosnia in southern Europe. I knew many people believed six young villagers saw a vision of Mary, the mother of Jesus. Pilgrims now flock to the region by the millions. Claudia and Phillip, my in-laws, made a pilgrimage visit there some years ago. She later shared with me how the people believe Mary continues to appear and deliver messages of encouragement to pray to Jesus.

"Oh, I really appreciate you thinking of me and asking me to go along, but I'm going to pass. I go see Amber every night," I said. "But thank you."

"I'm going to say an extra prayer for Amber tonight, and for you, too," Claudia said. "Let me know if you change your mind." We said goodbye and hung up.

I knew she would follow through with her promise of prayers. *That is so Claudia. She signs every card, every letter, with the identical line:* love and prayers. Right now, I counted on the prayers of others. I felt too beaten down to do it on my own.

"Are you about ready to go?" Roy said later after we ate supper. "It's almost time for visiting hours."

"She was really bad this afternoon; it broke my heart to see her that way," I said. "I don't think I can do it again tonight. Do you mind going alone?"

"I'll call Mitchell. Maybe you could go spend some time with Carter, and he could go with me," Roy suggested. "You haven't seen Carter in a few weeks. I think that would be good for you."

"That's a great idea, Roy," I said. His thoughtfulness brought a brief smile in spite of my exhaustion and defeated feelings.

Roy dialed Mitchell. After speaking a few sentences, he turned to me and smiled. "He said that would be great. Melinda had to work late, and he wants to go with me. I'll drop you off and pick up Mitchell."

I smiled inside and out. "Can we go now?"

Excited to see Carter, I practically ran into Mitchell and Melinda's home. Carter toddled over to me with his pudgy arms stretched up to me. I bent over and swept him up, bringing him close. He threw his arms around my neck and squealed, "Grammie!" For the first time in many weeks, my heart swelled from happiness instead of sorrow.

For the next two hours, I watched Carter build towers with red, yellow, and blue chunky plastic blocks. He assembled puzzles, and we read stories. I marveled at how much he had changed since I had last been with him. Periodically, he would stop playing and climb into my lap. We sat there doing nothing at all until his curious mind prodded him to do the next activity.

The two hours passed quickly. I felt joy for the first time in weeks.

Roy and Mitchell returned. Roy's words raced as soon as he stepped into the house. "Amber signed the papers tonight!"

Mitchell smiled at Carter and me.

"It was pretty amazing," he said. "She sat and stared, pretty much out of it. Dad and I were just sitting there with her when, all of a sudden, she acted like she knew what was going on."

"I think I hurdled over chairs to get to the nurse's station for the paper-work to give permission to transfer her health records to Iowa City." Roy said. "I quickly told her what she was signing, and she signed them." He pumped his fist in the air.

"It only lasted about thirty seconds, and then she was gone again. But you can transfer her now and send her records!" Mitchell added. He sighed and smiled.

"I also scribbled down a note that gave me permission to let her apart-ment lease go," Roy said, still excited. "She signed that, too." He waved a paper.

"Thirty seconds? How did you get the papers and her signature in thirty seconds?" I asked, baffled at how they accomplished all that in such a short time.

"When we first arrived, I had asked the nurse at the desk to get the paperwork ready. I remembered the last few visits when I almost got her to sign one and I missed my chance. It had taken too long by the time I explained everything to a nurse and she got me the paper." Roy said.

I nodded.

"The paperwork was sitting on the desk ready to go, and when the nurse saw Dad leaping over the chairs, she had it in her hand ready to pass it to him," Mitchell added.

"And we were only a few feet away from the desk," Roy added.

"Really, it only lasted about thirty seconds," Mitchell said. "After that, she didn't even acknowledge us. But in those few moments, we got what we needed."

We talked for a little while longer, elated; then I hugged and kissed Carter goodnight, Mitchell gave me a hug, and we went home. I think my steps felt lighter than they had been for a month.

January 27

The next morning, Roy and I took our customary places at the breakfast table. As he ate the last of his cereal and I finished the last of my coffee, he paused briefly. "I'm gonna go to Boone today. Since Amber signed the paperwork, I'm gonna go talk to her landlord and get her out of her lease."

"Good idea. I'll stay around here and go visit Amber."

"Yeah, sounds good."

He left, and a few hours later, Claudia called.

"The Mass last night was wonderful; I wish you could have been there," she said. "They had a box in the back as we walked into church. It said SPECIAL INTENTIONS, so I put Amber's name in it."

"Thank you," I said.

"I was with Aunt Germaine. She put Amber's name in, too."

"What time did you say Mass was again?" I asked, an inkling stirring in my heart.

"It started at 7:00. Why?"

"Last night, Amber came out of her unresponsive state for just a moment while Roy and Mitchell were there. She signed some important paperwork at about 7:15."

"That's about the time we prayed for the special intentions in the box."

Thank you, God, thank you!

After lunch, I stood at the nurse's station. "Have you contacted the university hospital today? What's the status on Amber's transfer?"

"Not good news, I'm afraid," she said. "There are no beds available. They told me it could be three weeks or longer before one is open."

"Three weeks," I said. I looked at the floor and swallowed hard before I looked at her. "Three more weeks of her getting worse by the day . . ."

"I'm sorry. I wish I had better news."

I scanned the lounge and spied Amber on the couch in front of the television. I went to her and said hello. She didn't look at me. I stood, catching snatches of the talk show blaring from the set; Amber sat transfixed on the screen. I moved quietly in front of her and spoke her name. She ignored me and continued to stare at the TV. I sat next to her on the couch.

Amber continued to watch the program; I watched Amber.

Every few moments, she laughed loudly. I wanted to cry. I heard nothing funny in the show.

She doesn't even know I'm here. She isn't watching the show; she is in her own private world. Oh, God, please help us.

I went home and flopped on the sofa. I covered myself with a knit afghan. I wanted to pull it over my head—to hide away from it all, to escape this nightmare.

When Roy got home from Boone a few hours later, he found me still there.

I sat up. "How'd it go?"

"Pretty good," he said. "I talked with the landlord, and he reacted with understanding. He let her out of her lease."

"Oh, that's good. One less bill for her to pay each month."

"I also stopped by the church and talked to the office manager. I gave them Amber's key to her office and explained she was still hospitalized."

"How'd she react? She didn't act very nice on the phone the last time she talked to Amber."

"She seemed okay, like she understood."

"That's good."

I shared what I had learned that afternoon: the lack of beds and the wait list. A large part of me wanted to call Stephen again to see if he knew how we might get Amber there sooner, but Roy expressed his doubts.

"It's lucky you know Stephen, but I'm not sure how much help it will be," he said.

I heard something in his voice. "Is something else wrong?"

He sighed loudly. "When I saw the landlord today, I stopped in Amber's apartment first. I didn't expect it would be as hard as it was."

"Oh." I wanted him to keep talking, but all my strength evaporated, and I reflexively curled back under the blanket.

"Looking at her things, at how disordered everything was, I thought of how scared she must have been before we got her home. I should have gone and got her right away. I'm supposed to protect her." I heard him choke on emotion. "I didn't protect her."

Roy lifted the blanket and slid in beside me. Feeling him, sharing his pain, my tears flowed again.

"I just want my daughter back. I just want my daughter back," I sobbed.

"Me, too."

And we cried together.

chapter thirteen

After our evening meal, we went to see Amber. No change. When we got home, I dialed my old classmate, Stephen, at the university hospital, praying that he could do something to help Amber.

"The hospital told me this afternoon it could be three weeks before they can transfer her to Iowa City. There are no beds available."

"Let me see what I can do," he said. "I know the chief resident pretty well. Maybe I can pull a few strings for you."

"That would be great. Thanks so much, Stephen; I really appreciate it."

"I'll get back to you when I know something."

He called me back the next morning.

"I talked to the chief resident. He moved her to the top of the list. When a bed becomes available, she will be first to get it."

"Oh, my. That's wonderful."

"Yes and no," Stephen said. "There are two lists, an A list and a B list. She is on the top of the B list."

"What does that mean?"

"The A list is for patients still at home. The hospital figures they are ones that need immediate help. The B list is for people already in a facility. He moved Amber to the top of the B list. It could still be a couple of weeks before she gets a bed. The A list will always get first priority."

"That makes sense. If I knew someone had no help or treatment, I would want them to have first priority, too." I spoke those words, but I really wished it was different. *God, I want Amber to have help now.*

"Let me know if I can do anything else," Stephen said. "I did my best."

We talked a few more minutes and hung up.

January 29

Saturday night, just two days later, Roy and I decided to attend a dance to celebrate the recent marriage of a neighbor's daughter. Friends and neighbors packed the hall, people we had known for many years. We made our way around the room as we talked for a few minutes with a neighbor and moved on. The noisy room had a spirit of festivity as everyone laughed and partied—everyone but me. I didn't want to talk to anyone. I wondered if anyone could see the weight on my shoulders, if I looked as depressed as I felt.

We stood at the bar, surrounded by relatives of the bride. Sam, a business acquaintance, squeezed through the group and stood before me.

"How's your family?"

I gave him a quick summary of the happenings in the boys' lives, where they lived, their jobs, etc.

"Don't you have a daughter?" he asked.

"Um, hmm—Amber. Uh, um, she's in the hospital."

"Those mental problems, they can be tough," he said.

I froze in shock.

"How did you know that was the problem?" I finally asked, bewildered. "I never said anything about it."

"I just guessed. If it had been something else, you probably would have mentioned it."

Did you just do that, God? Lead me to the one person here who might understand?

Once Sam opened the door for the discussion, I charged right through. I told him everything in a matter of a few minutes: her mental state, the medicine that didn't work, and our struggle to get her transferred to a different hospital.

"Now I know the prayer . . ." he said. His eyes looked contemplative but determined.

"What do you mean?" I asked. After telling him so much, I had an uneasy feeling.

"My dad is a very good friend of Ivan, the visionary from Medjugorje. Ivan called him today and asked for our special prayer request. Dad said he didn't know of one, so he asked me if I had one. I didn't at the time," he spoke with confidence. "Now I know what it is. I will get the word to Ivan that your daughter is the person who needs the intercessory prayer." Again, shock flooded my mind, but this time, it was joined with relief and joy.

"Thank you, thank you."

Suddenly, I felt exhausted, weak in the knees, on the verge of collapse. I turned to Roy. "I'm really tired. Can we go home now?"

We said our goodbyes, made our way to the door, and left.

January 30

The next day, Sunday, we went to the hospital after Mass and a fast food meal. We purchased the usual chicken nuggets to go for Amber. All too soon, we stood at the mental health unit and rang the bell for admittance.

"Who are you here to see?" a voice echoed through the speaker.

"Amber Pillars," Roy said.

The door swung open, and we stepped through into a small hallway. A familiar nurse met us in the hallway between the locked doors. She gave me an understanding smile as we stood waiting for the second door to open.

"Your daughter is a very sick young woman. None of the new medicines helped her, so the doctor started her on Haldol yesterday."

"What's Haldol?"

"It's an old medicine. It has lots of bad side effects, but sometimes it works when nothing else does."

She quickly finished as we stepped through the second door into the open room filled with tables, chairs, couches, and patients. Unexpectedly, Amber came to meet us, and Roy handed her the greasy sack. We found an empty table and sat down.

We sat in silence as Amber ate, finishing the entire meal.

"I'm tired," Amber said, pushing away the paper wrappings. I couldn't believe it. For the first time in weeks, we saw a tiny bit of improvement in Amber.

Oh, Father. Thank you for this blessing. Please, please help her to continue to improve.

January 31

Monday morning, the phone rang at about eight. It was a nurse from the hospital.

"I just had a call from Iowa City. They have one bed available, and they are saving it for Amber. If you can have her there by one o'clock, they will save it for her."

I hung up the phone and wanted to jump in the air, but suddenly my knees felt weak, and I slid into a nearby chair instead. My hand flew to my neck, and then moved down over my heart. It was then I realized I had been holding my breath since the nurse had said goodbye. I inhaled sharply and released it slowly, shaking my head in disbelief. Gratitude still filled my heart for the miniscule change in Amber the day before. Now, this answer to the prayer to get her into the university hospital in Iowa City was overwhelming. As I sat alone in my kitchen, my spirit soared. I felt safe, warm, and loved as my thoughts turned to God's grace.

Ivan took our prayer for Amber to the Blessed Mother sometime after Saturday night. Now, there is a bed for her when we had been told it would be weeks. I felt like Elizabeth in the gospels when Mary came to visit her.

Her words "Who am I that the mother of our Lord should come to me?" reverberated in my head.

I felt as though heaven had touched our lives. I whispered "Thank you" over and over as I dialed Roy. "They have a bed! Iowa City has a bed. But we have to leave immediately."

"I'll be right in."

After I hung up, my thoughts turned to the last conversation with Stephen.

"You will need to have her committal transferred. Petition the judge. Ask for permission for you and Roy to drive her there yourself. Otherwise, a sheriff will take her," Stephen explained. "You don't want that for her. They will treat her like a criminal. They will put her in shackles during the drive from one place to the other."

When he'd described it, my mind had shuddered. Amber in chains— that felt barbaric. An unknown force had reached into my chest, seized my heart, and squeezed. Amber was already convinced there was a conspiracy to kill her. What would criminal treatment do to her? She would be so scared. I couldn't let that happen to her.

We had immediately followed Stephen's advice and petitioned the court for permission. The judge granted it on one condition: two men accompanied Amber. She had agreed one of them could be Roy but stipulated that we needed a second man. Concern for our safety had to be top priority.

"She could turn on you, and it would take two men to restrain her," the judge had cautioned us. I guess my five-foot-four, 130-pound frame didn't appear strong to them. We assured them we would have two men. Roy had already made arrangements with Eddie, a good friend, to ride along.

After I called Roy, he called Eddie, but Eddie couldn't get away on such short notice.

"What are we gonna do?" I asked.

"Nothing." Roy's face was set with determination.

"But what about the stipulation for two men?"

"We won't tell 'em. If they find out, we'll figure it out then." Roy grabbed his coat off the hook. "We'll just take the chance they won't find out. I don't think Amber will fight us. I really don't."

Roy switched on the childproof locks on the car doors for a second time in three weeks, and we hurried to the mental health unit. The staff had prepared for our arrival. While Roy gathered the paperwork from the nurse, I helped Amber with her bag. We didn't mention to the nurse that we would be the only two driving her there, and she didn't ask. Roy helped Amber into the car and tossed her bag in the back. In less than a month, we drove our daughter to yet another hospital.

Roy had understood Amber's trust in us correctly. She rode peacefully; silent, but peaceful. Neither of us spoke, either.

An hour and a half later, we sat in the University of Iowa Hospital's mental health admissions unit. Chairs lined the waiting area. A few people sat in a corner. No one made eye contact or small talk, for which I was grateful. I wanted to stay secluded in my own painful world, not join someone else in theirs. We waited in the little room. A man sat at a desk behind a glass window with a small rounded opening to the waiting area.

Finally, he called for Amber, and the three of us moved to sit near the glass mousehole. He fired question after question, pausing to type in between. We let Amber answer some, but before long, she glared at him and refused to answer, so Roy answered for her. The worker's fingers tapped the computer keyboard, recording the answers, but he rarely looked up. Amber sat slouched in her chair, arms crossed, and stared at the floor as Roy talked. Finally, the man behind the glass pushed a paper and a pen through the hole.

He leaned forward and spoke through the hole. "I need your signature, and we can get you to your room."

Amber shook her head and re-crossed her arms. No surprise there. She had refused every place else, so I didn't expect anything different.

He asked again. "Just draw a line through anything you don't agree to."

Amber took the paper, scratched a line through every item, and pushed it back to him as she yelled at him. "You're part of it. I won't sign anything for you. You just want to control me."

She crossed her arms again, her jaw set so hard I saw her muscles twitch.

Finally, the man looked up and met my eye. "We'll do this later," he said as he pulled back the paper and pen. "I'll call the floor for an escort for you." I heard kindness in his voice.

He's seen this before.

We returned to the waiting area in silence. I clicked my thumbnails back and forth but kept an eye on Amber. And then I heard a loud, rattling, clanking sound in the hallway and looked toward the outside door. A tall, muscular man strode in, his black boots clunking with each step. My heart lurched as I saw the dark green slacks with the khaki stripe, his well-pressed, khaki shirt with a starred patch, his black belt with a holster, and his pistol. He held the elbow of a young woman in shackles. Her wrists had cuffs attached to chains that draped around her hips. She shuffled as she walked, the chains on her ankles clanging as they struck the floor.

I turned to Roy; he looked at me. Our eyes locked for a few seconds. I saw the pain in his eyes as the unspoken words passed between us: *That could have been Amber.*

Thank you, God, for Stephen and his advice.

The officer and the young woman sat down in front of the glass window. I heard them murmur to the man behind the glass. Our escort arrived, and we followed him to the elevators, rode to the mental health unit, and watched him unlock the door. Internally, I struggled to find peace as we entered the mental health unit.

Amber's gonna see a team of doctors here, I told myself. *This place is one of the best—they do research here. God, let this be the place. Let us finally get some answers and help. Please, God, send her some help.*

The door clanged shut, and I heard the lock click as the nurse relocked the large steel door. She strolled down the carpeted hallway, doors on the right, glassed-in office on the left. At the end of the corridor, I spied a television surrounded by sofas, chairs, and tables with puzzles, magazines, and books.

"Follow me," the nurse said over her shoulder when we failed to keep up.

We passed the doorways, the nurse's station, and the lounge, all with assorted patients and personnel engaged in various activities. The sight was so similar to the other hospitals, I realized that it didn't shock me.

We rounded a corner and entered a darkened room.

"This is the dining area," the nurse explained as she flipped the light switch. "But it's not meal time, so we can use for it now and won't be disturbed." She motioned to empty green plastic chairs. "Have a seat." She produced a packet of papers filled with questions.

"Where do you live?" she asked Amber.

"Here," she said. Her eyes bored into the nurse.

I glanced at Roy. The corners of his mouth curved up a bit.

"I know you live here," the nurse replied. "Where did you live before you came here?"

"A different hospital," Amber said as she looked up, crossed her arms, and leaned back in the chair. She tossed back her unkempt hair.

At this, Roy burst out laughing and grinned at the nurse. "She still has her sense of humor," he said. "She doesn't trust anyone, so she won't tell you her address."

With a hint of a smile, the young woman in her neatly pressed white tunic turned to Roy. "Where did she live before she entered the hospital?"

"Boone."

She recorded and gently directed her intake questions to either Roy or me. Amber slouched in her chair, arms crossed, eyes fixed on something I couldn't see, and scowled. The nurse snapped her metal clipboard shut, stood up, and motioned to the door.

"That should do it. I'll show you your room."

We followed her silently to Amber's room. Amber lumbered along beside us.

We stepped into a small room with two beds covered by white chenille spreads. I scanned her new surroundings. A simple nightstand stood beside each bed, along with two chairs, a closet, a door to the bathroom, and two windows. It looked clean and warm; sunlight from the good-sized windows made it feel brighter, almost cheerful. I looked around and thought it seemed more welcoming than the two previous rooms she had in the other hospitals.

"You have a roommate. She is quiet and shouldn't disturb you. She's gone to an activity now," the nurse said, motioning to the bed closest to the door. Though there were few personal items, there were small touches—a blanket, an imperfect turn-down of the bedspread—that claimed that bed. "You should meet with a doctor sometime this afternoon. Until then, you are free to rest or watch television in the lounge."

Amber plopped onto the unclaimed bed and closed her eyes. Roy and I squirmed in the uncomfortable chairs and waited. Finally, the nurse knocked softly on the doorjamb and poked her head in the room.

"Miss Pillars, the doctor wants to see you now. Follow me." Then she turned to Roy and me. "Mom and Dad, you can wait here."

Amber swung her feet to the side of the bed and slid off. She shrugged and followed her out.

"She's gotten used to orders, whether she likes them or not," Roy said, reaching over to take my hand.

I nodded, not knowing what to say.

Time crawled as we waited for Amber to return. I didn't feel like talking, and I'm guessing Roy didn't either, because we sat in silence while I stared at our hands. I refused to watch the clock. Finally, the door swung open. Without a word, Amber climbed back on her bed and her eyes slid shut. Roy and I resumed our somber stakeout.

Amber's deep, slow, rhythmic breathing provided the only sound. A soft knock, followed by a swish of the door, interrupted the stillness.

The young woman saw Amber sleeping and whispered, "The doctor would like to see you now. Please follow me."

I glanced at my dozing child then tiptoed out and accompanied Roy and the nurse. As we passed by the lounge, hollow-eyed patients in the hallway stared at us. A middle-aged man stood in front of a tired-looking armchair, watching the television screen. The television blared, and he rocked in place. He pointed at the television and shook his finger. Rock, wag his finger, rock, wag . . . I looked away.

On the other side of the lounge, I saw the door to an office. I noticed a name plaque next to it. Our escort opened it and swung her arm toward the room. "Have a seat."

A dark-haired, middle-aged man sat behind the desk in the corner. He stood up and shook our hands as he introduced himself.

"I'm Dr. Masterson. I will be your daughter's doctor while she's here." He smiled as he gestured for us to take the chairs arranged in front of his desk. "I've had a chance to talk with her. I still want to run some tests, but after visiting with her, I believe she has schizophrenia."

I looked at Roy, but he had focused on the doctor.

I had known it could be schizophrenia, but I fervently hoped it wasn't. My heart sank and my shoulders slumped as feelings of dread washed over me.

Oh, God, I didn't want it to be this. Please let this be the doctor that can help her.

"Each individual responds differently to medication," Dr. Masterson continued. "I see from her chart the doctor in Waterloo tried the newer antipsychotics, but they were ineffective." He stopped.

I nodded as I acknowledged what he said. *Don't we know it!*

"The last doctor started her on Haldol, but I've ordered a higher dose for her. It's one of the oldest antipsychotics and can sometimes work when the newer ones fail."

Roy and I nodded simultaneously. Our NAMI class had taught us that, and we saw a tiny improvement after they gave her that in Waterloo.

"I must warn you, Haldol can have some pretty nasty side effects. We will watch for those," he said. "Tomorrow, she will have tests most of the day. I've ordered brain scans, an MRI, and X-rays. I need to rule out any tumors, even if all her symptoms point to schizophrenia."

Schizophrenia. God, I really hoped it wouldn't be that. Not that.

"You folks look exhausted," Dr. Masterson said after he explained his intended course of treatment. "I want you to go home and get some rest, doctor's orders. You look like you haven't slept in weeks." His blue eyes glistened as he articulated delicate but deliberate words. "She is in good hands; we'll take good care of her. You need to go home and take care of yourself."

I wasn't sure that I could do that. Every fiber in my body wanted to see her, to continue seeing her every day. Yet I felt a tiny bit of relief. The doctor didn't mention using the ECT recommended by the previous doctor. I wasn't sure if I really wanted Amber to receive those treatments, even if Stephen had assured me they were safe and effective.

"I'm in charge of the research for schizophrenia here at the hospital," he continued. "We'll be giving her the additional medication tonight. We want to get the delusions under control. She'll probably sleep a lot at first." He looked from Roy to me, making firm eye contact. "I promise we'll take good care of her. Give us two days and then give us a call. Go home and take care of yourselves. You've earned it."

My eyes met Roy's. The pain and weariness in his hazel eyes made me choke up. I glanced to the floor and blinked my own tears away. I stood, reached out to Dr. Masterson's outstretched hand, shook it, and gave him a weak smile. "OK," I managed to say.

"Thank you, Doctor," Roy said. "We want to say goodnight to Amber before we leave. Is that okay?"

"Certainly."

Amber was still sprawled on her bed, but she sat up when we entered her room.

"We're going home now. The doctor says you will have tests all day tomorrow," Roy said. Amber sat there, mute. "He said we wouldn't be able to see you, but we'll be down the next day. Okay?"

Amber shrugged and curled up in a ball on the bed. I pulled out my book of prayers—which was always in my purse these days—and read the parent's prayer for a child.

"Dear God, there are no words for the depth of my love for this child. I pray for her care and for her protection. I surrender her into your hands. Please God, send your angels . . ." I looked at Amber and continued. "Make me the parent you want me to be. Show me how to love most patiently, to be there for her most fully." I took a deep breath and began again, struggling to get the words out. "To understand . . . what she needs."[14]

I finished the rest of the prayer. Amber's eyes had closed, and she breathed deeply by the time I said "Amen," so I patted her shoulder, kissed her softly, and left.

We stepped into the carpeted hallway. A nurse escorted us back to the outside heavy steel door. The jingling of the keys on her lanyard clinked as our trio ambled in silence. We paused and watched her unlock the heavy door. A buzzer rang out as the door swung open. We strode through the small passage and into an adjoining hallway. The door slammed shut behind us, and again I heard the click of the lock. I turned around, rose up on the balls of my feet, and peered through the tiny square window back into the wing. I glanced at the sign by the door. "3 East, Adult Psychiatry," I read aloud. My stomach cramped, and I stretched higher for another look. Roy took my hand.

Neither of us spoke as we sauntered to the elevator, when he pushed the down button, or as the doors slid open and then shut. I had no words as we found our car in the parking garage, paid the fee, and drove the ninety minutes home.

"She'll be okay," Roy said, breaking the long silence as he turned the key and the car shut off in our garage. "In a few days, we'll call her. We have to trust the doctor. We have no choice."

"Mmm-hmmm," I agreed, too exhausted to add anything.

I slept fitfully that night.

chapter fourteen

February 1

"I want to call her," I said to Roy as we ate breakfast. "They gave us a number for the desk."

"The doctor said to give them a couple of days."

I lowered my head and spread peanut butter on my toast. "You're right. I don't like it, though; I really don't like it."

I ate a few bites and found it had a bit of flavor. In early January, suffering from the effects of stress and anxiety, I had visited our family doctor. While I sat on the exam table in my doctor's office, Roy stayed home with Amber. I had explained Amber's bizarre behavior to him and shared my concerns.

"I think you can use some help. This is very stressful for your family," he said, his voice reassuring. "I'd like to prescribe a small dose of an antidepressant for you. This is probably temporary. In a year, we will revisit how you are feeling and decide at that time if you need to continue it."

I filled the prescription and started on it immediately. I learned it could take up to four weeks before I saw any results, so I wasn't surprised I continued to feel depressed through the end of January.

Roy cleared his throat before he took a bite of cereal. I looked up and came back to the present. He ate another bite of cereal. I bit a corner off the piece of toast and took another sip of coffee. Between the antidepressant and knowing that Amber was safely in the university hospital, I was feeling a little better about things.

We finished breakfast. Before Roy left to work in his shop, he reminded me to not call the hospital, no matter how much I wanted to. I held off as I worked on an order, but my thoughts stayed with Amber.

What's she doing now? Have they finished the tests? Is she scared? How is she? God, I know you are there with her. Protect her. Send your angels to surround her.

The morning dragged, and I welcomed the break to make lunch. I watched the clock as I chewed the cardboard called "food." I ate because I knew I needed it. Just as I finished stacking the lunch dishes in the dishwasher, the phone rang.

"Mom."

I strained to hear the timid, hesitant voice. *It's Amber . . .* Instantly, my stomach rolled.

"Amber, what's wrong? I can barely hear you."

"Can you come? I don't feel right," she said. Her voice shook. "I don't know what's wrong."

"I'll get Dad, and we'll leave right away," I said. "It's over an hour's drive, so it will be a while before we get there."

"Thanks, Mom," Amber said. "Hurry."

I heard a click. *Oh, God, what is happening to her? Be with her.*

I ran to Roy's shop.

"Something's terribly wrong," I blurted out. "Amber just called and she sounded really scared."

He dropped his tools; we bolted to the car and raced down the highway to the hospital. Roy pushed the accelerator hard, traveling well past speed limit. I sat in the passenger seat wringing my gloved hands together.

"I'm going as fast as I dare," he looked over at me.

"I know." I bit my lip.

He slammed the car into park once we arrived at the hospital. We dashed to the ward, and Roy buzzed for admittance while I paced the hallway.

It seemed to take forever for a nurse to come and let us in, but in reality, only a few minutes passed. We took giant steps past the nurse's station, past the television lounge to the last room on the far hall—Amber's room.

After a quick knock, we stepped inside. She had sprawled across her bed, but when she heard us, she sat up, swung her legs over the edge, and stood up.

"What's wrong?" Roy and I asked at the same time.

"I don't know. I just don't feel right. My neck feels weird."

"Let's walk and see if that helps," Roy said.

He linked his arm through Amber's right one, and I did the same on her left. We strolled down one way and back again. We had just turned at the halfway point of lap two when Amber paused.

"I'm tired; can we sit for a while?"

We found a row of hard, wooden chairs in the hallway directly across from the nurses' station.

Amber slumped down on one. Roy and I sandwiched her between us.

"Rub my neck?" Amber asked. "It feels stiff."

Roy reached over and massaged her neck.

"Does that help?"

"Sort of . . ." She paused. "They're giving me shots, you know."

"Do they hurt?" I asked softly.

"Not too bad," she said. "As long as I lay still and don't fight." She glanced up as another two young women walked by. "They walk all day long. They have to stay here, too." She sighed loudly. "I don't need the medicine. But I have to take it."

Roy and I dipped our chins simultaneously but said nothing.

A nurse passed by, opened a door, and entered the nurse's station. I saw several of the staff sitting at the long, narrow desk. They stacked papers, wrote on them, and moved to the next stack.

"Rub my neck again, Dad. It's getting worse."

Roy placed his large, calloused hand on her neck. He positioned his thumb near her left ear, his middle finger by the right. He lightly rotated them in a rhythmic motion.

"Harder," Amber said. "It's getting worse."

"I don't want to press too hard."

"Harder."

I saw him increase pressure, his fingers turning white as he pushed down on her neck muscles.

Suddenly, her head jerked to the side and she threw her hands in the air. She fell on my lap.

"Dad!" Amber screamed. "My neck!"

Her hands stiffened in gnarled, crooked, unnatural angles. Her head jerked farther to the side; her face tilted up as her entire body contorted. Amber cried out. She tried to straighten her neck.

"Dad!"

Her head twitched further to the side, an unknown force pulled her chin straight up, and her mouth gaped in a crooked grimace. Amber's hazel eyes rolled back in her head—rounded and glaring open. Her skin turned pale as the spasms took over her entire body. She tried to talk but could only grunt.

Oh, God! Oh, God! What's happening?

Her eyes filled with terror. I hung on to her, but she kept slipping as she twisted into unnatural positions.

"Help!" I yelled to the nurses behind the desk. They didn't hear me through the glass or the closed door. I grabbed at her shoulders, then her waist, trying to keep her from falling to the floor.

Roy reached over and grabbed the belt loop of her jeans. His grip tightened, and we both held on.

God, what is happening? Help us, God, help us. She was fine seconds ago.

"Help us!" Roy shouted at the glass-enclosed nurse's station.

I felt my grip loosen around Amber's waist as her body stiffened and distorted even more. I grabbed at her, trying to find a solid hold on her to keep her on my lap. She rolled toward the floor. Roy and I struggled to hold on as she writhed and jerked. My eyes pleaded with the nurse who looked up from her desk.

"Help us!" Roy yelled for a second time.

Her eyes widened, and she sprung from her chair. "We need help, STAT!" she shrieked. Everyone behind the glass jumped into action. They bolted through the door and clustered around our distraught trio. Hands reached out to keep Amber from tumbling on to the hard floor.

A young woman with a small cup in her hand appeared.

"Open your mouth, Amber," she instructed. "Open your mouth. This will help."

She held the clear plastic cup near Amber's face. I watched my daughter open her mouth and the nurse lift the cup to her lips. She gently shook the white circular pill into Amber's mouth. Another nurse handed her a small cup with water, and she lifted that to Amber's still open mouth as well. Amber took a small swallow and her head jerked into another spasm. As one, the nurses grabbed Amber from our arms and called instructions to each other as they hurried down the hall.

"Get her to her room."

Every cell in my body screamed silently. My chest heaved as I watched them whisk her efficiently through the hallway. My heart wanted to jump out of my throat. Roy and I ran behind them. Other patients stepped to the side or backed up to the walls. Once we were in Amber's room, we shot to a corner as they placed her on her bed, unbuttoned her jeans, and tugged them down.

Stay out of their way; let them work, I told myself. *God, help her. Help her.*

One nurse rubbed a cotton ball on Amber's thin hip. Another nurse with a syringe stepped forward, poked the needle into Amber's flesh, and pushed the plunger.

"This will counteract the reaction. It usually works pretty quickly," she said to us as she gently rubbed the spot after she pulled out the needle. She looked up and met my eyes. "We've seen this before. I know it is really scary." She continued to explain as Amber's muscles began to relax. "It isn't life threatening, but it is extremely frightening for the patient." She massaged Amber's hip for a little longer, then pulled up Amber's panties and jeans. "This medicine will probably make her extremely tired for the next few hours. She'll sleep."

Within a few minutes, the nightmare was over. Amber looked completely wiped out. Her eyelids slid shut. Roy and I stood to one side of her bed. She opened them briefly and looked up to us. "I needed that medicine tonight. I think I should take the medicine." She drifted off to sleep.

Did I hear that right? Did she say she needs medicine? Oh, God, let it be so.

"The medicine I gave her knocked her out," the nurse said to us. "She will sleep until morning, folks. You might as well go home."

"What happened to her? What made her get stiff like that?" I wasn't ready to leave Amber, asleep or not, without answers.

"It's called a dystonic reaction. It sometimes happens with high doses of Haldol, the antipsychotic medication the doctor ordered for Amber. Dr. Masterson put her on a pretty large dose in order to slow down her delusions. I know it was scary for you, but her life was never in danger," she explained.

"Will it happen again?" I asked.

"It's possible. Sometimes, it does happen a second time. Dr. Masterson typically orders a medication that helps prevent it when one of his patients has one. The medicine we injected to calm the spasms also comes in a pill."

"Is there a warning that one is coming?" I asked.

Her head bobbed. "Usually it's a stiffness of the neck, just like you witnessed tonight. I know it scared you, but she's okay," she said. She waved her hand toward the door. "You folks should go home and get some rest. I'm here until seven o'clock tomorrow morning. I will keep a close eye on her tonight, but I promise she'll sleep 'til morning."

Her chocolate eyes glistened and dimples creased her smooth, pink cheeks. I watched as she pulled the blankets around Amber and tucked her in. *She is as gentle with her as if it were her own daughter. Thank you, Lord, for a nurse willing to be your hands.*

I leaned over Amber's bed and whispered one more prayer aloud. "Dear God, please watch over her until I come tomorrow. Keep her safe from harm. I pray for a quiet night and peaceful rest for her. Amen."

Straightening, I reached over to clutch Roy's outstretched hand; together, we left her room. I turned and glanced one more time at Amber, sleeping soundly, needing reassurance that the nightmare was over. One of the nurses, instrumental in getting Amber to her room, walked us to the door. She unlocked it. I hesitated again, turned, and looked back to the hallway.

Can anyone else hear the thumping in my chest? I don't want to leave her. What if it happens again tonight?

The nurse touched my shoulder. "She'll be okay."

My hands and knees shook the entire ninety-minute ride home. I climbed into bed with the image of Amber writhing, the muscle-stiffening spasms, and her screams all churning in my head. My chest squeezed in a tight, heavy vise.

God, I'm so thankful we were there for Amber tonight. I can't imagine how she might have reacted if she had been alone. God, thank you that we had the phone call and made it there before it happened. And please, God, please let her be safe and comfortable tonight. Please don't let her react like that again.

I felt my eyelids start to droop.

But she is willing to take medicine. God, I don't like the method, but thank you that she knows she needs it.

chapter fifteen

February 2

"We can't discuss her with you because of privacy laws."

Roy and I heard this statement time after time when we tried to talk with Amber's doctors and therapists, as well as all the places Amber owed money. All her bills, letters, and even her junk mail now came to our address. But by now, she was too ill to deal with the everyday things in life. The pile of bills grew, but the laws to protect her also prevented us from doing anything for her.

"It's bad enough she's in the hospital, but I don't want the bills to follow her for the rest of her life because of it," Roy remarked to Mitchell and me when Mitchell had stopped for a morning visit.

"Have you thought about conservatorship?" Mitchell asked. "That would allow you to handle her money and pay her bills. In other words, you would make all her financial decisions."

"I hadn't thought of that," I replied.

"I think you should get guardianship, too," Mitchell said. "That way you can talk to anyone on her behalf. I would start the application immediately," he continued. "It may take a while to get approved."

"Good point," Roy said. "Thanks. We'll call and start the process."

That same day, before lunch, Roy picked up the mail. He dumped it on the kitchen table, and I sifted through the stack and saw one from the church that employed Amber.

"Should I open it?" I asked Roy.

"Yeah, maybe it's about their plans. The day I cancelled Amber's apartment lease, they assured me they would keep her on the employee list so she still had insurance until she recovered from this." He opened his hand, so I handed it to him.

I watched his eyes as he scanned the letter. He scowled as he read and then threw the letter on the table. "I can't believe it," he muttered.

I grabbed the letter and quickly skimmed the first three paragraphs. "What? Unbelievable. Unbelievable!"

"Let me see it again." Roy reached out to take it.

"They fired her. She's in a hospital, and they fired her. That's real Christian of them, isn't it?" I spewed the words toward the letter as I handed it to him. "Way to live your faith, folks. Kick someone while they're down."

"You know this means she doesn't have insurance anymore. And they even told me they would keep her on their policy until she got out of the hospital." Roy threw the letter down again. "They disgust me. They really disgust me."

A new thought gripped me. "Should we tell Amber about this or wait?"

Roy met my worried expression. We'd seen some progress in her, but neither of us wanted to jeopardize that. "We'll see how she is when we get there today."

In the end, we decided to wait to tell her. When we went to the hospital to visit her, Amber's minor improvements didn't give us confidence that she could handle the stress of finances.

The following Monday, we met with Carl, our lawyer, to begin the process for guardianship and conservatorship. While I knew it was for Amber's benefit, it made me sad. Our daughter's independence was slowly oozing away like the weeping of an open wound. Her lifeblood trickled out as her illness cut deeper without mercy. No job, no insurance, and now we wanted to take control of her money and her healthcare decisions.

"I'm sorry, folks," Carl said to us after we explained the situation. His brow furrowed as he wrote on his tablet. "It's tough. I'll get the paperwork started immediately. Just so you know, she may fight you on this." He paused for a moment. "It's not unusual for the family member to protest it. I want you to know this before you start."

"We'll take that chance," Roy said. "Go ahead and start the paperwork. How long do you think it will take?"

"I can have the papers drawn up today. Once I file them with the court, they will appoint an attorney to represent Amber and set a court date for the hearing. The hearing probably won't take place while she's staying in the hospital. Once everything is filed, a sheriff will serve Amber notice of your intent."

He strode out of the office, spoke to his assistant, and returned with the forms.

"Can you give us a day or two before the papers are served to Amber?" Roy asked. "We want to tell her ourselves and explain everything to her. She may get really upset if she has no warning."

"When can you get to the university hospital next so I can put the date on the form?" he asked.

"We'll go tomorrow."

The following day, Roy and I went to see Amber in the hospital in Iowa City.

"An officer came to see me here this morning," Amber said the moment we walked into her room.

Roy groaned. I rolled my eyes.

Amber walked to the nightstand, opened the drawer, and handed the papers to Roy. "What does this mean?"

"I want to pay your bills and help with all your financial things," Roy said. "That way you don't have to worry about anything but taking care of yourself. Once you are feeling like your old self, I will let it go."

Amber stared at Roy. There was no anger or distrust in her expression, just confusion.

Roy continued. "We asked them to wait until we talked with you today before they served you. We aren't trying to do things behind your back."

She took the papers from Roy and placed them back in the drawer before she turned toward us. "Do you want to go for a walk in the hallway?"

I was startled by how easily she took his answer. Could she still trust us so completely? Was she saving her reaction for later?

As we walked, I spied a room in the corner, just past the TV lounge, that I'd never noticed before. It had a large glass window facing the hallway. Through it, I could see that the inside of the room had a thick, gray cloud. It settled over the entire room, and in the fog, I could see people as they paced around the room.

"Is that smoke?" I asked.

No answer from Amber.

I caught Amber's eye. "What's with all the smoke?"

"It's the smoking room. It's the only place they can smoke cigarettes in here," she said. Bits and pieces of the NAMI class came back to me. Katherine had explained that nicotine helps lessens some of the effects of schizophrenia. For that reason, often people with schizophrenia are chain smokers. Katherine's words made sense of why the hospital would have a smoking room in a psychiatric unit. "I see."

"That guy that just came out," she nodded to a man who'd just emerged, "he spends most of his time in there."

I watched him saunter down the hall in his neatly pressed dress slacks and shirt. His professional attire and authoritative stride reminded me of the doctors, so different from how I expected a patient to look.

I watched him turn into one of the rooms and chastised myself. *Knock it off, Virginia. Don't judge. It just goes to show, you can't tell if someone is ill by their appearance.*

We ambled up and down the hallway.

"So what's that paperwork about?" Amber asked for the second time.

Patiently, Roy again explained. "Mom and I want pay your bills and talk the doctors on your behalf, but because of the law, we can't. If the courts approve our petition, we will be able to do it for you. That way, you can relax and not be concerned about bills and money," Roy spoke slowly. "There will be a court hearing for you to object if you don't want this to happen."

"Oh, when will that be?"

"Not until you are out of the hospital."

Amber looked up from the floor and gazed at him. She looked at him, but her eyes had returned to the vacant expression I had begun to expect. The conversation ended, so we walked for another half an hour quietly. Her reaction, or rather her lack of reaction, made me question if she understood what Roy had just told her.

I asked her about the food. "I eat what they give me. Not the greatest, but I eat it." I noticed her clothes looked tighter on her, far faster than I would have expected from just eating normally.

I read Haldol can cause weight gain. I never dreamt it would be so quickly and so noticeable.

Over the next few days, our visits resembled every other visit. We walked the hallways with her, mostly in silence. We sat with her quietly or in a largely one-sided conversation. Still, I could see improvement in her mental state since her arrival here at the university hospital. Her tirades happened with less frequency and intensity. Sometimes, Amber relayed a list of the people who had stopped to visit her. Other days, we heard about things that happened in the ward. Each time, I had a surge of hopefulness. I glimpsed a bit of her personality from before this monster, schizophrenia, had invaded.

February 3

Our lawyer called. "Be at the county courthouse tomorrow morning at ten. You will meet with a judge. He will check the case to see if you meet the criteria for conservator and guardianship."

"We will be there," I said. "What happens there?"

"The judge will look at proof you have for Amber's incompetency. He will look for three things: Can she make her own decisions? Is she impaired by physical or mental illness? And can she handle life on her own?"

"I see."

"Don't worry. I think it will be approved," he said. "I will meet you at the courthouse in the morning."

All that night and the following day, I couldn't stop wringing my hands. My stomach twisted in a knot and tugged while the pressure started in my chest again. For the second time in less than six weeks, we would stand in front of a judge to testify that our twenty-four-year-old daughter couldn't take care of herself. Yes, I knew it was the truth, but it still hurt to testify about it. I felt like I betrayed Amber every time I did it. But at the same time, I knew I had no choice. I wanted to give her a chance for recovery. I hoped the stress would transfer from her shoulders to ours if we got guardianship.

Just put on your big girl panties and go do it, I told myself as we stood at the courthouse, waiting for our appointment.

Roy took my hand, and together we walked into the courtroom. Clusters of people stood or sat around the room. One young man stood before the judge. We slipped into a row of wooden seats to wait our turn. Finally, the bailiff called our name. My knees shook as I stood to approach the bench.

The judge sat behind a large oak desk. I noticed a wooden gavel on his right, a stack of papers centered in front, and his bald, shiny head, fringed by gray hair. He seemed efficient, ready to go through each case and on to the next one. The bailiff stood nearby.

"I've read your petition," he said. "What can you tell me about this?"

Roy spoke first. "In early December, our daughter moved home with us. She had lived on her own since her graduation from college in May 2003."

I glanced over and saw him rub his temples.

"But in November, she began to fear there was a conspiracy against her and her life was in danger. Her mental state deteriorated further, and last month, we committed her to force her to take medication."

"I see," the judge replied. "Where is she now?"

"At this time, she is at the University of Iowa Hospital in the psychiatric ward. This is her third hospital since December," I added. "Her attending doctor recently diagnosed her with schizophrenia."

"Folks, I'm really sorry your family has to go through this." The judge set down his pen before he looked at Roy and then turned his compassionate gaze toward me. "I'm sure this is tough on you. If you don't mind, I'd like to share with you something my father said to me when I was a boy. I once asked him, 'Dad, why's our family so screwed up?' My dad looked at me and said, 'Son, every family's screwed up. Ours is the one you know about.' I've never forgotten that."

He paused as he looked from Roy to me.

"I'm sorry you have to do this. I will schedule a hearing. Good luck, folks."

"Thank you, sir," Roy and I spoke in unison.

We left the room quietly and returned to Carl, who waited in an adjacent room.

"He was very kind to us," I blurted out as we walked in. "He treated us with compassion as he told us there would be a hearing."

Carl bobbed his head. "He is a good judge. I'm glad you had him."

The three of us went to another office, where we filed the proper forms in the courthouse.

I'm glad that part is over. It went better than I had hoped. Thank you, God.

We left and returned home. As we walked through the door, the phone rang.

I answered it quickly only to hear Amber's court-appointed lawyer ask to speak to her. I explained to him why he couldn't talk to her.

"She's in the hospital. We will let you know when she is home. Is that soon enough?" I asked.

He agreed it would be, and the conversation ended.

February 6

Over the next week of her treatment at the hospital, we made the trip to Iowa City at least every other day, sometimes every day. I just felt better seeing Amber often. We saw baby steps of improvement with each visit. A week or so after our court appearance, she was given a short pass from the ward, and we took her out to eat. It was an exceptionally warm day for February with bright sunshine and a balmy breeze, so we strolled outside around the hospital for a few minutes before we returned to the hospital. It almost felt normal, and I allowed hope for recovery to enter my bruised heart again.

Maybe now that she takes her medicine, things can go back to normal, I thought.

That day, we had parked in the rooftop parking lot. After we returned Amber to her room and visited for a few hours more, we moseyed our way back to the parking area. We stepped into the sunshine, using our hands as a visor as we looked for our car.

Roy nudged me. "There's Dr. Masterson," he said as the doctor walked out of the glass door toward us. We both stopped and waited for him.

"Hi, folks," he said as we approached him. "Nice day, isn't it?"

We both nodded. "So how do you think Amber's doing? Is she making progress?" Roy asked. After a successful outing with Amber, I was sure that her condition was improving, but we both wanted to hear the doctor's confident assurance. That wasn't what we got.

"Your daughter has schizophrenia," the doctor said. "The next two years will be very hard." He spoke in a gentle and kind voice, but he might as well have kicked me in the stomach.

Two years? I wanted to scream at him as my hopeful attitude blew away on the light breeze. *Like the last two months haven't been hard?* Instead, I swallowed my disappointment, nodded, and forced myself to listen to his words.

"It takes a long time for some to find the right medicines," he continued. "A lot will depend on the correct medicine, therapist, and care." He kept his voice quiet and soothing, and his eyes acknowledged all the pain that my heart was screaming.

When I saw that silent message, I no longer wanted to clamp my hand over his mouth. *He cares about our family. He's taking time to visit with us and offers guidance in our distress. Thank you, God. Thank you that Amber is here under his care.*

February 11

A few days later, Dr. Masterson asked us to come into his office when we visited.

"I plan to release Amber tomorrow. She's made enough progress, and we've done as much for her here as we can. She doesn't need to be an inpatient any longer."

My apprehensive heart, though grateful that she was improving, was scared to take Amber out of the hospital.

No, I'm not ready. She's not ready. Keep her here. Keep her here, my mind drummed relentlessly.

"We will set up appointments in Waterloo with a psychiatrist and a counselor," he added. "Where shall I send the referral?"

"Can't we keep her appointments with a psychiatrist here?" I asked, desperate to not lose all contact with this place that had provided hope for us. "She doesn't like any of the doctors she saw back home. I think she'll do better here."

"Yes. If that's what you want, we can refer her to the outpatient clinic in the hospital. I won't see her there, but we have great doctors that staff it. I can make an appointment for her, but I recommend she see her therapists near you."

I nodded. "Okay; that sounds okay."

On February 12, we brought Amber home with appointment reminders for the outpatient clinic at the hospital and a counselor at a local clinic in hand.

Now that Amber had been released, we couldn't put off the hearing for conservatorship. We called the county office and within a day, four people sat around our wooden table in the kitchen: Amber, her court-appointed attorney, Roy, and me. The attorney explained the process to Amber and then asked her if she understood what it meant.

"My dad can to make my decisions for me, take care of my money, pay my bills, and speak to people for me?" she asked him. "Is that right?"

I felt pride and gratitude swell in my chest. *Two weeks ago, she couldn't put a full sentence together. She has come a long way already. Thank you, God.*

Her lawyer nodded.

Amber continued. "Then I have one question."

"Yes?"

"Can you add my mom? I only see my dad's name, and I want them both on it."

"You want me to add your mom? You don't want to fight them on this?" He looked puzzled. "This is not what I usually hear."

"My parents wouldn't do anything to hurt me. I want Mom to handle things for me, too."

"Okay, if that's what you want." Her lawyer gathered up the paperwork as he shook his head. He tucked everything in his briefcase and stood up. "Thank you, folks," he said and left.

It took several weeks, but finally, March 12, the day of the hearing for conservator and guardianship arrived. Roy and I met Carl at the courthouse.

"Amber didn't come?" he asked.

"No, she doesn't want to contest it and said she didn't need to come." I said. "She's home with a friend."

"Wait here," he said and ducked into the judge's office.

He returned a few minutes later with a signed paper. "The judge approved it without the hearing. He commented about how unusual this is; he said it's rare to have it uncontested. I'll file this, and you're finished. You can go home."

He smiled as he shook our hands. I wanted to rejoice. The court approved our petition for conservator and guardianship for Amber, yes; but more importantly, Amber wanted it, too.

Thank you! That was easier than I ever imagined. Thank you, God, for another answer to my prayers.

I hadn't specifically asked for Amber to agree with the petition, but I knew others kept our family in their hearts and prayers. Cards, phone calls, and conversations reassured me of this over and over.

It shall come to pass that before they call, I will answer; and while they are yet speaking, I will hear.[15] The verse from Isaiah I had recently read popped into my head.

chapter sixteen

After Amber's release from the hospital on February 12, she began a course of treatment from her new base: our home. Following Dr. Masterson's advice, we scheduled counseling appointments at a local mental health center and visits to the University Outpatient Adult Psychiatry Clinic at the hospital. The idea of caring for Amber at home again was daunting, but I felt a bit better with a plan of action and coordinated efforts.

"Amber, I will drive you to your appointments," I told her at home before her first appointment. "I'll keep track of them for you for now."

"Okay, Mom. Thanks," she said as she headed to her room for a nap. The medications made her drowsy, but until the doctors found the correct combination in the proper dosage, I let her rest when she felt the need.

I accompanied Amber during her first visit to the local counselor. Apprehension filled me. The last counselor refused to visit Amber in the hospital. She left me angry and disappointed. I glanced again at the name of the new counselor on the paperwork: Connie. I was concerned Amber wouldn't like her or that Connie wouldn't understand Amber's needs. I feared that these sessions would prove ineffective in helping Amber improve.

A pleasant-looking woman entered the waiting area. "Amber?" She smiled as she scanned the room.

Amber and I stood up. We walked to her.

"Hi, I'm Connie," she said as she extended her hand to Amber. Amber took it without any reaction.

"May I come in?" I asked.

Connie looked at Amber, who shrugged, before answering me.

"I'd like to speak with Amber alone first. I'll come and get you when you can come in," Connie said, speaking directly to me.

"OK." I went to a chair in the waiting area and picked at my fingernails while I waited. Finally, Connie stepped into the waiting area and called my name. I followed her to her office.

"I've had a chance to visit with Amber," she directed her comment to me. "I think I've come up with a plan for her therapy," she said as she nodded to Amber. "Amber, let's keep your appointments brief for a while," Connie suggested. "I don't want to tire you out. I think a half-hour session would be a great place to start." She waited for Amber to answer.

"Okay."

"Let's start with every other week for a half hour. When you feel up to it, we can increase it gradually until we meet for an hour," Connie continued addressing Amber. "Does this sound okay to you?"

I sat and listened, taking note of how Connie tried to give Amber a measure of control.

I like how she makes Amber part of the process. She doesn't tell her; she asks her. Lord, I think you found us a good match.

We left her office after the half hour of our allotted time. Amber moved in her usual sluggish gait, but I felt like skipping. I tucked another hopeful event in my heart. Slowly, the jagged rips in my heart were being mended with tiny stitches of hope and healing.

As planned, Connie scheduled an appointment for Amber every two weeks. We didn't trust Amber to drive yet, so I took her each time. I knew the sedating effect of the medications she took, and I think she realized it, too. I felt more comfortable taking her, and she didn't seem to mind. She didn't ask about driving.

After the first visit, Amber went in alone. Connie had suggested I wait in the waiting room. "I want Amber to feel she can speak freely," she offered as an explanation.

I hesitated. My inclination was to go in so that I could see if Amber gave honest feedback or if her delusions still had control of her perception. I wanted to know whether or not she would open up to Connie and tell her everything.

With these musings, it didn't take me long to realize I wanted to micromanage Amber and her illness. I wrestled with this for a while but decided I needed to trust Connie and her training.

So I sat in the waiting room while Amber and Connie met. I took a book along to read. Every once in a while, I chatted with others in the waiting room, but I found I'd rather sit quietly. The atmosphere in the room emitted an aura of pain, as if we all understood the same secret sting that accompanied our loved one's illness. I pondered the events that caused my life to spin out of control and wondered if this had happened to them. The idea of spending time in a waiting room for mental illness treatment never entered my vision for the future. So I sat with a book on my lap, often unopened, as I tried to sort out all the confusing situations I had faced during the past few months.

Connie slowly increased the time Amber spent in her office until each visit lasted around fifty minutes. Amber loved pastries, so after each counseling session with Connie, we stopped at a nearby bakery. We each ordered a gooey roll or sugary donut as a treat before we left town. I knew it didn't help Amber's weight problem, but right then, it felt more important for me to give her positive reinforcement for a completed therapy session. We would deal with her extra pounds down the road.

We also made a trip every three weeks to Iowa City for an appointment with a psychiatrist and to receive her medication. I learned to be grateful for the decision Roy and I made to keep Amber's appointments at their Adult Psychiatric Outpatient Clinic. Roy and I knew the delusions still haunted Amber from our conversations at home. Amber trusted the doctors there but didn't have any faith in ones she saw earlier in our area. It didn't make sense to us to risk losing that trust.

But we faced a new challenge. Her previous insurance covered the university hospital and clinics. When we transferred her there in January, we had no concerns about her coverage for the cost. But when Amber's employer fired her on February 1, Amber no longer had health insurance. This threw her into the Social Services system in our county.

We made an appointment at the local CPC (Center Point for Coordination) office. During the interview, we learned Amber had too much money to qualify. I couldn't believe that her wise management of time and resources before she became sick now prevented her from the help she needed. We had to take her savings and apply it to her car loan so that she met the guidelines. After she qualified, the county paid for the majority of the expense of her appointments with the doctors and counselors as well as her medications. Roy and I paid the copay for her.

After Amber's release from the University of Iowa Hospital, in another county, her caseworker wanted to switch Amber back to our county for all of her care.

"We need to transfer Amber's doctor visits back to our county," I heard the voice on the phone explain.

"We'd like to discuss this with you. May we meet?" I said, determined to protect Amber's relationship with the psychiatrists at the university hospital and now at the clinic.

A few days later, Roy and I sat in a cubicle of an office while I explained Amber's paranoia, her lack of trust, and our desires for her care. As her legal guardians, we had the right to discuss and make decisions for her. Franklin, her caseworker, made notes in Amber's file. "I'll discuss this with my supervisor and let you know."

The promise was vague, and we had no assurance that our local services would cover the care outside our county. All the same, Roy and I both knew the value of supporting Amber and diminishing the paranoia. She had lost trust in her doctors before; we didn't want to travel that road again.

"We'll figure out a way to pay for these services ourselves if they refuse," Roy said to me as we left the office. "I'd rather go into debt than take the chance of her sliding backward."

Fortunately for our finances, the office granted Amber permission to receive her care in Iowa City until the paranoia ceased. Since the court order in January stated Amber must accept medication once every three weeks, she received the correct dosage by injection ordered by her psychiatrist. Initially, she fought it, but she quickly resigned herself. "I didn't like it when they held me down. Once was enough," she told me after the first injection. "They're gonna give me a shot no matter how much I fight. So what's the point of fighting each time?"

She also agreed to take tablets for the other prescriptions she needed, remembering the dystonic reaction she suffered at the university hospital after her increased Haldol injection. The medication that helped combat the reaction brought with it more side effects. So her doctor added still another one to the arsenal. Amber willingly accepted the handful of pills I gave her each day. She wanted to avoid that terrifying incident when her muscles stiffened and she lost control of her body. The memory bridged her from the refusal of medication to acceptance.

To get the injections, we traveled eighty miles each way for each appointment at the outpatient clinic. I decided to make a day of it. After her appointment, Amber chose a restaurant, and we relaxed over a meal.

"Do we have time to shop?" Amber usually asked when we finished.

A nearby mall became our next regular stop. Sometimes, we window-shopped at clothing stores, but mostly we browsed through books at the mall bookstore. I gave Amber some space to explore books on her own but never let her out of my sight. I wanted her to feel independent but didn't want her to react negatively toward anyone, so I watched her from afar.

Typically, she headed straight to the department on pregnancy. She stood by the shelf, chose books on stages of pregnancy, and thumbed through various books of baby names. As I watched her, my heart sank. It told me the delusion of pregnancy lingered, even if she never mentioned it. From there, she moved to the religious reading section and thumbed through various titles for a half hour or so.

Each trip, I relived the pain of her illness. Amber felt exhausted most of the time. Physically, she had changed rapidly since the beginning of the year, gaining weight due to the medications and the increased appetite that accompanied them. I think it contributed to the delusion about her pregnancy. Pounds piled on, almost weekly. Her breasts enlarged, her stomach protruded, and she felt lousy—all symptoms typically associated with an expectant mother. I think for her, everything pointed toward pregnancy. She overlooked the fact she had never been intimate with a man. Her brain refused to process that vital piece of information.

She slept twelve to fourteen hours a day. When awake, she sat in the front room in front of the picture window. The winter sun streamed in our large south window, filling the room with brilliant light and warmth. The combination created a welcome environment. She read her Bible for hours or just rested it on her lap. Sometimes, she wrote in a journal, but other times, she just relaxed and basked in the wonderful rays. When she wasn't sleeping or sitting, she ate. Her relentless appetite made her continually crave carbohydrates, also contributing to the pounds that appeared almost overnight.

In the past, she ate large quantities of food but didn't gain an ounce. People often commented to me about her thin physique. But the medicine she needed to manage her delusions and paranoia altered her metabolism. It made her hungry all the time and too lethargic to work off the extra food.

That bothered me—a lot—to see her body change from slender and trim to carrying too many pounds for her frame. For her first twenty-four years of life, she'd had to fight to keep every ounce she gained. Now, her body inflated with excess weight. She turned her nose up at vegetables and fruit; instead, she devoured potatoes, pasta, chips, and bread.

At first, I tried to fight it by plating her food and giving her reasonable amounts of a variety of nutritious food. She ate only what she wanted and raided the refrigerator within an hour. I tried to tell her how to eat. That particular bad idea only angered her. In the end, I relented and let her eat what she wanted.

We'll have to deal with the weight issue later, when she has improved more. Lord, help me to keep my mouth shut about this.

It still bothered me.

After reading the book *When Bad Things Happen to Good People*, I realized I needed to study to help handle the stress that arrived every day. And who, other than Jesus, knew the pain of suffering better than Job in the Old Testament? So I picked up the Bible and opened it to the Book of Job. I read the first few chapters. Job, a wealthy man with a large family, had everything he loved stripped from him, compounded with physical torment. I learned Job didn't turn his back on God; rather, he continued to praise him. *If Job did it, then surely I can follow his example.*

"Teach me, and I will be quiet."[17]

The words spoke profoundly to my spirit; they became the words I didn't know to pray. I wanted the Lord to teach me how to love Amber and care for her. I wanted his strength to bite my tongue, and I needed his comfort to quiet my fears and Amber's mind.

I promised myself to carve out some prayer time each morning. No TV, no radio; just total silence. I read, I studied, and I listened. Thoughts took root; ideas began to form.

God loved her first. She is yours as a gift. But really, she belongs to him.

One morning as I read my devotional and prayed during the quiet of the dawn, I imagined Amber and me alone. I lifted Amber high into the air with my arms stretched to full extension. I envisioned a strong presence of love above us while I prayed, *You loved her first. I give her back to you. Not my will, but yours.* And I gave her back to the Lord, who I now understood loved her first.

I felt a calm wash over me as I surrendered my parenthood to God.

Dear God, let our journey bring you glory. Heal your servants and direct my steps.

Another morning, I pondered information I had learned about mental illness since this journey began. Earlier I had read *The Quiet Room, Surviving Schizophrenia*, and *The Broken Brain*.

I came to understand schizophrenia as a brain disease, a brain disorder. Some scientists believe the chemicals in the brain aren't functioning correctly. The neurotransmitters—the substances in the brain that allow communication between cells—broke due to my daughter's illness. The correct medication enabled the brain to fire the electric impulses properly to allow the chemicals to travel millions of times per second to the correct destination. I also learned schizophrenia, left untreated, causes permanent brain damage. It destroys the gray matter in the brain. Unchecked, it moves through the brain like a forest fire, causing permanent changes in the brain's structure that can be difficult to reverse.

Amber's illness is life threatening. I forced myself to answer hard questions: *If Amber had cancer, how would I treat her? Would I let her rest? Or would I expect her to help with housework? Would I make her do her own laundry? Would a job help her get back into the world quicker?*

The answer came to me: a resounding "No." I knew she struggled to overcome a serious brain disorder. She didn't ask for this, and she certainly didn't deserve it. I decided to let her brain heal by any means necessary.

When Amber wanted to sleep, I let her sleep. If she wanted to eat, I made her a nourishing meal. I did her laundry and didn't even ask her to help fold the dry items. I just let her be. I treated her just like I would if I had brought her home from the hospital following cancer treatment. I knew Amber's brain had undergone months of trauma. We couldn't see it by her physical appearance, but her brain had broken. I wanted to give her brain every opportunity to heal.

And then I recalled an article in a magazine I had read years earlier about helping the brain make new connections. The article talked about humans as creatures of habit. We use the same hand to eat, brush our teeth, write, etc. These actions form pathways in our brain to remember how to do these tasks. As we continue to do them without any thought, the brain uses the route already formed. It doesn't challenge the brain, and the action becomes a habit. The author encouraged us, the readers, to try things in different ways: eat, write, or brush our teeth with our opposite hand; wear our watch on our other arm; anything we could do to force our brain to form new pathways. At the time, it made sense to me; I used many of the suggestions. I switched my watch to the opposite wrist and ate meals with the fork in my left hand.

As I read, prayed, and listened in the dawn, that article came to mind. *If a healthy brain continues to make new connections with new challenges, can a broken brain be encouraged to do the same? What will it hurt to try? It can't possibly hurt to try, right, Lord?*

I thought about it and lost myself in prayer. I didn't notice the darkness around me morph from deep grays to lavender through pale rose, orange, and finally brilliant yellow. Light filled the room with the promise of a new day. Words seeped into my heart and soul.

Remember how you taught your children to count, to read? Games—you played games. Play games.

I finished my morning devotions then hurried to my computer, connected to the Internet, and searched for word games. I found a site with a new word-find puzzle every day. I scrolled through the various levels until I found one I felt Amber could handle. I hit print and felt prepared for our first lesson in retraining her brain.

When she woke and came into the living room, I patted the empty spot next to me on the couch. "Amber, how about we do a word-find puzzle together? It will help pass the time."

She moved beside me, and I handed her the pencil, clipboard, and paper.

"It looks too hard," she said as she passed it all back to me.

"Let's do it together," I suggested and offered it back.

She reached for it and stared at the paper for a bit before she circled a word with the pencil.

"Hey, I saw that one, too," I said. "Try to find another one."

After a she found a few more, she chewed the pencil several times before the clipboard fell on her lap.

"I'm tired. Can I stop?" she asked.

"Sure, we can take a break if you'd like. You rest for now, and we'll finish it later."

She returned to her favorite chair. I heard a clunk as the footrest snapped up. She reclined, head back, and within a few minutes, I heard her long, relaxed breaths.

It's a start . . .

Each day, we tackled a word-find puzzle, played card games that involved counting, or played the dice game, Yahtzee.

"Can you count the numbers for me?" she sometimes asked me.

"I'd rather you do it," I said as she struggled to add the cards or spots on the dice.

I encouraged her to do it. But some days, it proved to be more difficult for her, and she got frustrated. So I took my cues from her. We stopped if I noticed her stress level climb.

Some days, I still had to remind her to shower, brush her teeth, comb her hair, or apply lotion to her dry skin. I often helped her shampoo her hair.

And still, Amber's moods were unpredictable: one minute she could be sitting and staring into nothingness, and then suddenly, without warning, she would break into a sob for a reason only her brain knew.

Then it seemed like only seconds to me when she would switch and laugh hysterically at a joke only she could hear.

One morning during my prayer time, a thought came to me: *I should let the doctor know what is going on here at home, day to day. How can she be treated correctly if she is only seen once a month for fifteen minutes? I have to let them know.*

When I finished my prayer time, I went to my office, pressed the power button for my desktop computer, and waited for the screen to come alive. I searched for the icon to my calendar program. I scrolled through the templates until I found one for weekly charts. I found one I thought would work: one page for each week, the days separated by a solid black line with lots of space along a horizontal grid. I printed four pages and then opened the graphics program. Next, I created a series of faces, each showing a different emotion, and printed out pages of round stickers.

"Amber, I want to show you this," I said that night as she got ready for bed.

"What is it?" Her forehead wrinkled and her eyes squinted.

"It's a calendar to help the doctors know how you are feeling each day."

"I don't know how I feel, Mom. I'm tired. I just want to sleep. I don't want to do it."

"I'll help you," I encouraged her. "I'm happy to do that. You just point to the face, and I'll put the sticker on the paper. Can you do that?"

"I guess so." She exhaled long and slow. She pointed to several stickers: a frown, eyes with tears, bored, and tired. I removed the emotion icons and stuck them in the row for today.

"Any others?" I asked.

She shook her head and slid under the covers, her eyes shutting simultaneously. I stood quietly, walked to the doorway, and flicked the light switch off in one motion. Her head popped up.

"Turn it on! Turn it on!" she yelled.

I slapped the light switch on and saw terror in her eyes.

chapter seventeen

February 12–28

Night brought new symptoms for Amber. Darkness petrified her, night-mares plagued her, and uncomfortable physical reactions manifested for her after she went to bed each evening. We left her light on continuously. The time of day didn't matter; the ceiling light in her bedroom stayed on. I could deal with that. If it helped her sleep better, I wanted it. But sometimes I felt like I had a toddler instead of a twenty-four-year-old. I grieved as my independent, college-educated daughter reverted to a scared, frightened little girl.

One evening after she had gone to bed, I sat with my feet up and relaxed. Suddenly, her voice pierced the quiet of the night.

"Mom, make it stop! Mom, make it stop!" she shrieked.

I bounded from the chair in the front room and dashed to her room.

"Mom, make it stop!" she wailed again. "My legs won't lay still. Make it stop. They're so itchy, Mom. I can't stand it."

She reached down and scratched her legs. Her torso twitched, and her knees jerked up and down. Her legs circled with bicycle movements, kicking and thrashing as the blankets twisted; Amber whimpered and dug at them with her fingernails. I reached out and touched her hand.

"Try not to scratch."

"I can't stop them."

She squirmed in her bed, flopped from side to side, and continued to pump her legs. She kicked the covers over and over.

"I'm gonna call the doctor on call," I said. "I'll be back as quick as I can. Then I'll rub your legs. Do you think that will help?"

"I don't know. I hate this, Mom; I hate this," she moaned.

Helpless, God; I feel helpless. When will this stop? Will she ever be well again? Help me stay calm—thy will be done.

I rushed to the phone, dialed the University of Iowa's on-call number, and explained my concerns.

"She's itchy all over and she can't settle down. Her legs keep moving as if she can't control them . . ."

He asked me a few more questions, and then there was silence as he reviewed her chart.

"It's a reaction to Haldol. Do you have any Ativan?"

"No."

I knew she needed Haldol to control her delusions, but I hated these terrible side effects. We had noticed a difference in Amber after her first injection. We observed glimpses of her former personality that her broken brain had hidden away.

What are we to do, God? Help us know what to do.

"Do you have any Benadryl?" asked the man.

I tucked the phone between my ear and left shoulder as I rummaged in the cupboard next to the kitchen sink where I stored our medicine.

"Yes, I found some."

"Give her a single dose. It will help with the itching and help her sleep. I will call in a prescription for Ativan to the pharmacy. Which one do you use?"

I gave him the information. "Thank you," I said and hung up.

I hurried to Amber, handed her the pill, passed her a glass of water, and sat on her bed. I massaged lotion on her legs and prayed silently until the sensation lessened for her. She relaxed and soon fell asleep again. I tiptoed out of her room and nestled into my favorite chair. I sighed and returned my attention to a book.

Within an hour, Amber's shriek sliced the quiet. Roy and I both jumped out of our recliners and rushed to her room. "We're here, we're right here," Roy said in a hushed, calm voice.

She sat up, still screaming, and reached out to him. He held her until she quieted.

"What happened?" he asked softly.

"I don't know, I don't know. It was just scary," she sobbed.

"Did you have a nightmare?" I asked.

"I dunno, maybe," she said.

I groaned.

Another side effect added to the list. It's just not fair, God. It's just not fair. Help me to stay faithful, to keep my focus on you.

"It was just a bad dream, honey. It wasn't real. Can you try to go back to sleep?" I said.

Amber shook her head. "I'm scared. I don't want to be alone. Will you or Dad stay with me?"

Roy pulled me to one side of the room. "You should stay with her. I don't think it'd be wise for me to stay. You never know what her mind might tell her." He glanced to the bed. "You know, about me in her room," he whispered to me.

I looked at him, confused.

"What if she thinks I touched her, you know, in a bad way?"

I slapped my hand over my mouth. "Ohhhh." I hadn't thought of that. "You're right. I'll stay with her tonight."

I crawled into Amber's double bed. I snuggled close, wrapped my arms around her, and held her tight. "I'll stay with you. Just try and relax, OK? I'm right here."

"Mom, why is God doing this to me?" she sobbed. "Why? What did I do to deserve this?"

"Oh, Amber, honey. You didn't do anything to deserve this. God is not doing this to punish you. He loves you," I whispered. "He said he would never leave us or forsake us. He's here for you, and I am guessing he is as saddened as we are by what is happening to you."

"I'm scared, Mom. I'm really scared."

"Me too, honey. Me too."

Amber tossed and turned.

"We'll do this together. Just like God, your dad and I will never leave you or forsake you. We'll get through this," I said. I reached over and gently lifted her hair off her face. I tucked it behind her ear. "We'll handle it together. I love you. You don't have to do this alone."

"You promise?"

"I promise. Now let's just try and relax."

I rubbed Amber's back gently. The mound of covers felt oppressive. I peeled back a blanket, then another, and finally a third one. Amber shivered.

"Are you cold, honey?" I asked.

"Yeah, can you keep the covers on me?"

I pulled them back over us and let my leg dangle off the bed. It helped a little to have one part of me in the cool air.

After a while, I could hear Amber's soft rhythmic breathing, but I couldn't sleep. I lay next to her and thought about the past few months. Had God abandoned us? Or had God worked through the lives of others? How many times had people arrived when we needed them? Did the Holy Spirit nudge them?

Brooke came to mind. *She must have been scared, too, Lord, but she didn't run away from us.* I thought about that phone call to her that first day while I drove. *Amber was so upset; what could've happened if she was alone for that hour?* I shuddered.

Brooke came to our house every Tuesday night, Lord, so we could attend the NAMI classes. We wouldn't have left Amber home alone then. Only one of us could've gone. I thought about visits she made to the hospitals; when she sat and held Amber; even the fluffy, brown puppy she gave to Amber. I peeked at Amber; she had Brown Puppy next to her on the pillow with her favorite teddy bear, Fathead, snuggled in her arms.

I shivered as I recalled the night Amber locked herself in the bathroom and lit candles. I almost panicked again just thinking about it. The idea that the house could light on fire had frightened me as I stood outside the bathroom door calling to Amber, "Let me in."

The doorbell had rang, so I had hurried to the door—Brooke had come. We hadn't called, but her presence defused the tense situation.

God, did you send her? I peeked at Amber, sleeping safely in her own bed. *Thank you, God, for the friend she has in Brooke.*

I also thought of how Mitchell found us the phone number for NAMI. Those classes proved invaluable. I relaxed a little. I thought of his encouragement to seek help for Amber, the way he dropped by after work just to check on us, and his role during the painful process of the committal.

Lord, if he hadn't researched the movie like he did, the judge might have ruled in her favor. His testimony, his support, and, yes, even his pressure to make Amber go to the hospital were so important. He probably felt as scared as we did. But he did the hard things—for us—for his sister. Thank you, God, for Mitchell.

I turned over, listening to Amber's deep, relaxed breaths. Aunt Josephine's face popped into my mind as I recalled our phone conversation. *Read* When Bad Things Happen to Good People, *she told me. That book changed my attitude about you, God. That was such good advice. And just at the right time. Anger became a part of me, and it interfered with my faith.* A warm feeling spread over me, but not from the heavy blankets. *Thank you, God, for Aunt Josephine.*

I tried to sleep, but thoughts and faces paraded through my head. I remembered the phone calls from my cousin Elaine. I recollected her loving advice, the book, and prayer suggestions she offered me—things that kept me afloat in my ocean of confusion.

I visualized the evening our friends brought a meal and stayed to eat supper with us. They stayed for a few hours and listened to us as we unloaded our feelings of helplessness on them. I could envision them in our front room, tears in their eyes as they quietly shared our sorrow.

Once during NAMI class, I heard someone say, "No one brings you a casserole when your child is hospitalized for mental illness." I took comfort in knowing my experience played out differently. *Our friends knew how to support us in our pain. Thank you for our prayerful friends.*

I could still picture Mom as she hugged Amber after she paced the room at the Christmas gathering. Mom held her tight for as long as Amber allowed. "Your warm face makes my ear feel good," Mom had said to her. It was her signature statement to Amber. Amber's reaction to her made that confusing night feel almost normal.

My hand smoothed the covers and rested on the quilt which covered us. *Phyllis gave her this beautiful quilt.*

Phyllis, my older sister, lived two hours away. The distance made it difficult for her to visit, so she supported Amber by using her talents. Phyllis, a talented quilter, gave her a gift of the quilt. It gave Amber a tangible object of her support. She created it using a pattern that featured Amber's favorite animal: pigs.

I smiled as I thought back to even a few weeks earlier. Amber's bedroom from childhood hadn't seen a paintbrush for too many years to count. When we moved her home following hospitalization, Roy and I suggested a bedroom mini-makeover to her, decorating it using the new pig quilt Phyllis gave her in January. It made me smile. *A young woman who loved pigs?*

During her teen years, Amber could pack food away like a husky farmhand but never gain an ounce. Once, one of her brothers remarked she could eat like a pig. Wesley called her Piggy, and the nickname stuck.

Instead of being offended, she loved and embraced it. She referred to herself as Piggy, answered to Piggy, and even signed her name Piggy. Soon, most everyone affectionately called her Piggy. Over the years, she acquired an extensive collection of stuffed pigs, figurines, and swine-adorned stationary, most of them gifts.

Amber brightened at the idea of giving her room a facelift and volunteered to help. She chose the color for the walls: a soft yellow, one of the colors in the quilt. The day we painted, Amber helped for fifteen minutes or so before she needed to rest. Roy and I finished the painting, but I expected to finish the job while she dozed in a chair.

Next, we replaced the standard, soft white light bulbs with full-spectrum daylight bulbs. It enhanced the room and provided a more natural lighting for her. It highlighted her bed, covered by the pig quilt with calico prints of light blue, soft yellow, pale peach, and baby pink.

Phyllis shared the extra fabric with me, so I created a matching dust ruffle and pillow shams. Stuffed pigs in various shades of pink, pale peach, and yellow adorned the shelves and the dresser tops and decorated her bed. Many of them exhibited signs of the years in her possession, but new ones demonstrated the love and support from many people as they brought them to the hospital mental health units to bring Amber comfort.

Amber's room looked cheerful and was filled with gifts of love—just the environment we wanted for her. It provided a quiet sanctuary as she acclimated to her new residence and routine of doctors, therapy, and medication.

As I continued to lay there, my physical presence keeping Amber's nightmares at bay, my mind wandered to the pile of boxes in the basement. They were full of things from Amber's apartment in Boone. Several of Amber's uncles and aunts, along with some of our friends, joined us to pack and move. We converged on the five-hundred-square-foot apartment with empty plastic containers. Together, we packed her things, labeled the containers, filled five pickup trucks, and then stopped for pizza. The compassionate group formed a caravan for the hour-long drive. Together, we unloaded the remnants of Amber's independent life into our basement. It took a mere five hours, but those people, willing to step in and help, threw me the lifeline of support during my time of despair.

I dwelled on the many times help had arrived in the form of friends and family. *God, these people, were they acting as your hands? Thank you for them. Oh, thank you.*

My eyes felt heavy. Peace washed over me as I gave them permission to slide shut, and I snuggled under the blanket of the love provided by my dear family and friends.

chapter eighteen

During the earlier conversation on guardianship, Mitchell had also suggested we should apply for SSDI for Amber.

"What's that, and why should we do it?" I asked, unfamiliar with the
acronym.

"It stands for Social Security Disability Income."

"Do you think she needs it?

"Mom, she's not gonna be able to work for a long time, if ever. If she
gets approved, it gives her a bit of money to live on, but most importantly,
she will get financial help with medical expenses."

"How does that work? And how come you know about it?" I sat down
at the kitchen table, tired of the legal hoops we'd already had to jump
through and the prospect of another.

"I researched it for you." Mitchell took the seat opposite me and
pushed a stack of printed papers across the table to me. "I found all the
information online. I think you should think about it. It takes a long time
to get approved, so you should start right away."

"You think it's best, huh?"

"I do. That," he said, pointing to the papers before me, "gives you the
basic information. You can apply online or go into the local office."

"Okay, I will check into it."

"Do it right away. Her benefits, if she gets approved, begin the date the
application is filed. So, the sooner the better." He paused for a bit. "Oh,

and expect to be denied the first time. I've talked with people who've told me it's almost automatic to be refused the first, second, and even the third try. So that's why it's important to start the process right away. Get an early application date on record."

When did he get to be so smart? And how does he even know how to find this stuff? Thank you, God, for Mitchell. He helps us so much.

The next morning before the rest of the household stirred, I went to my office, got on the Internet, and found a website detailing what I needed to apply. The long list included contact information for someone who knows about your medical condition; information about doctors who treated her; hospitalization records, dates, treatments, tests, and medications; work history and when/how the illness affects her ability to work; and her educational/training history. All the information needed names, addresses, etc.

How can anyone who is sick gather all this information? Especially when the disability is mental illness and the person can't concentrate or think clearly, like Amber? She could never do this; I'm not sure I can. But, thank you, God, that at least I can try. Please give me wisdom and knowledge to help Amber through this time. Help me to know what to do.

I didn't have time to sit and feel sorry for myself—although I think I would've rather done just that. Instead, I made phone calls to doctors, counselors, and hospitals to secure the required documentation of Amber's illness. At first, I heard, "I can't talk to you because of the HIPAA law." So I played my *Advance to Go* card and faxed my documentation as Amber's guardian. Then I found helpful people along the way as I talked with the various offices. Slowly, the needed forms arrived, and I felt armed with the necessary things to apply for SSDI for Amber. I filled out page after page of the application, made copies of everything, and mailed it in a big, fat manila envelope. I noted the date: February 14, 2005. *Happy Valentine's Day, Virginia.*

August 2005

Months passed before a letter came from the Social Security Department. We received word on August 3, 2005; over five months had passed since I slipped the packet in my big black mailbox. Five months of caring for Amber at home crawled by, trying to balance her needs and appointments, other family obligations, and my business. And finally, it was here. I tore the envelope open.

The first paragraph stated *denied*, but it felt like it read in big, fat letters across the top of the page. Though Mitchell had warned me that the application is rarely approved the first time, I wasn't prepared to see those ugly letters spell out another go around of paperwork, filing, and scrambling from agency to agency to secure financial help for her care.

I scanned the letter and read the information on how to file again. As quickly as I could, I contacted the doctor, counselor, and hospital again and updated the records, which took over a month. On September 25, 2005, I resent the paperwork. And waited—again.

I returned to the SSDI website and read the list of illnesses that qualified. After I read schizophrenia listed as one of the debilitating illnesses approved for the disability approval, I stomped around the house for a while.

This is so dumb. Why don't they approve her? Why put a family through this? Don't we have enough to worry about? File; refile. There's no way Amber could do this. Who does this for those who can't? I continued to stomp around the house, frustrated every time I saw the copies of application paperwork stacked on the desk or on the kitchen table.

"Do you think we should start a file cabinet for all of Amber's paperwork?" Roy said to me a few days later. Piles of paper accumulated on the desk and threatened to take his farm office in the house hostage. At least, that's how it looked to me.

"Good idea," I replied and opened a bottom drawer of one of the file cabinets in the office. In a few minutes, I had a file box filled with the contents and packed away with other stored files.

In a way, the work of organizing Amber's files comforted me. I had something concrete to do to make our situation a bit easier. I labeled new file folders: medicine, SSDI applications, hospital bills, bank statements, etc. Soon the papers resided in an orderly system instead of the flat-surface method both Roy and I typically used.

Though the new organization and cleanliness helped, I still worried over the SSDI application. It was never far from my mind. Bills addressed to Amber arrived almost daily in our mailbox. Cell phone bills from her earlier address, student loan payments, hospital invoices, and bills from doctor visits piled up.

"We need to stop some of the bills," I said to Roy. "She has no income and no way to pay them. Her savings and checking accounts are empty."

"I agree," he said. He picked up a bill and the phone receiver. "I'm gonna start with the cell phone company. She doesn't even have the phone for her apartment anymore and that's what this bill is for."

I heard him on the phone, not really arguing but stating his case to the company representative over and over. I could hear his frustration as he repeated himself. After a few minutes, he hung up.

"What a waste of my time," he said. "It's disgusting. Even though she doesn't use that line any longer, she is under a two-year contract. They said there isn't anything they can do."

"Oh, brother. That's ridiculous," I said, rolling my eyes.

"I'm gonna try again and maybe I'll get a different person, one who is more reasonable."

"You can always try."

He had the same experience the next time he tried: two-year contract—nothing they can do—pay almost two hundred dollars to break the contract.

Once again, I felt like yelling, "Thanks for nothing!"

Instead, I called the company and found the same unwavering statements.

"Let me talk to your supervisor," I said.

"You want to talk to my supervisor?"

"Yes. Now, please."

I waited a few moments before a new voice came on the line.

"How may I help you?"

I repeated my request, "We need to cancel this policy for our daughter."

"I'm sorry; she signed a contract. To break it, she must pay $175, the rest of the contract."

"Ma'am, may I level with you?" I said. There was a pause on the other end.

"I'm listening."

"Our daughter is really ill. She's been hospitalized most of the winter and she is unable to work. Right now, I don't know if she will ever be able to work again." I paused to let my words be absorbed.

"I understand your position, but she signed a contract with us," she replied.

"I understand that, and I see the reason for your policy," I continued. "But I want to tell you about our situation. May I tell you more?"

"Yes, but I don't think it will change anything."

In the next few minutes, I told the woman everything. I explained mental illness and the effect it had on our daughter. I described Amber's lack of money, her inability to care for herself, and the financial burden we hoped to avoid for her once she recovered.

I didn't spill my guts to get her sympathy; rather, I wanted empathy. Understanding Amber's broken brain helped me make better decisions. I hoped this would be the case with this supervisor. I didn't want her to shirk her responsibility, I explained; I only wanted to help my daughter.

Silence greeted me for a moment as I finished my lengthy explanation.

"Mrs. Pillars, this sounds like an extremely difficult situation. I appreciate your honesty with me," she said.

I held my breath.

"We never allow customers to break their contracts with us, but I will make an exception for you and authorize this for your daughter. I am truly sorry for her troubles."

"Oh, my. 'Thank you' doesn't seem adequate," I said. "Our family is grateful—more than words can say. Thank you so much. Thank you."

"You're welcome. And Mrs. Pillars, I wish you the best with your daughter."

I hung up the phone and let out a yell.

Next, I tackled Amber's student loans. I contacted the Direct Loans organization where Amber owed money for her college education. A fat packet of paperwork arrived. After filling in the forms, including a copy of my guardianship paper, I sent it back and waited. Eventually, they approved an economic hardship deferment for her.

Some days, it seemed all I accomplished was filling out paperwork for Amber. Hospital bills flooded the mailbox. Amber's copayments added up quickly from the local hospitals. Amber's termination from her job on February 1 left twelve days of hospitalization with no means to pay for them. I investigated the hospital policies and discovered they had a provision for hardship cases. More letters from me ensued, and eventually, the hospitals forgave her outstanding invoices.

After each letter arrived with the good news, I thanked God that we had reduced Amber's debt. But the rejection from the Social Security Disability Office from August still hung over our heads. After the rejections and seven months of waiting, I contacted our local Legal Aid office, as Katherine—from the NAMI class—suggested. They assigned us a caseworker, Hannah, a paralegal. After Amber and I met with her to fill out the needed paperwork, I put it on the back burner while we waited again.

The waiting time was filled with doctor and counselor visits, continued retraining with Amber at home, projects for my business, and continued attempts to minimize Amber's bills. One day, our local NAMI chapter held an educational day at the courthouse for the county and municipal law personnel, along with local members. There, I was able to meet with a pharmaceutical representative from one of the sponsoring companies, and he explained to me how to apply to the companies for assistance with Amber's medication. I visited websites and applied to the manufacturers for the various prescriptions. Before too long, Amber's much-needed medicine came through the mail, compliments of the companies.

Thank you, God, for NAMI and the people who give me such great advice. Without them, without you, I would be so lost.

chapter nineteen

Since the beginning of this year, I had learned so many lessons on trusting my faith in God. For the most part, I kept a positive attitude. The days usually began with devotions and prayers. Even still, some days I felt like a robot; I did the same thing each day. From March to October 2005, I kept busy with appointments for Amber, filling out paperwork for SSDI, and operating my business.

I took an additional NAMI class that spring called "Family to Family." This added to my understanding of mental illness and what Amber faced each day. Over the course, lasting twelve weeks, it was stressed that families often experience three different stages of emotions: catastrophic emotions of feeling overwhelmed, confused, lost, and in denial; learning to cope; and finally, acceptance and advocacy. When I first learned of Amber's illness, I found myself in the catastrophic stage. I felt confused, in shock; our chaotic life left me denying she had schizophrenia, and I hoped against hope that life would return to normal, to our world before December 9, 2004.

Through reading and education, I gradually accepted her diagnosis, understood the recovery process, and lowered my hopes of a quick resolution to our situation. Most days, I managed to cope, but sometimes, I wanted to explode. I wavered between anger, acceptance, resentment, guilt, grief, and back to acceptance. I also learned that jumping between the emotional stages of chaos and acceptance and advocacy is a typical reaction.

Even so, the continued rollercoaster of emotions took its toll on me. I based my daily activity schedule on the conversation with her doctor in the parking lot. I remembered his words that it can take up to two years for a patient to stabilize. Amber needs to heal, I reasoned, so I didn't ask her to assist with housework, with running my business, or watching Carter whenever he visited. If she helped around the house, it left her exhausted. So I helped her channel her focus on healing efforts: resting, learning to trust others, and retraining her mind through games and reading. Amber's social activity became more important to me than her help with household chores.

Roy resumed his normal work routine, spending long hours on the farm. Equipment to repair, crops to plant, weeds to control, bookwork, meetings, and continuing education—his to-do list resembled mine in length and urgency. It just made sense for me to manage the household and him to manage the farm work.

Each day, I woke early and put one foot in front of the other. But knowing in my head and feeling in my heart were two different things. Sometimes, I was frustrated with the routine: Roy left the house and went back to life as normal while I spent my days as a caregiver to Amber. I lived on an emotional roller coaster. At times, I felt strong, inspired, and at peace with my role in Amber's recovery process. But then I crashed to the ground like someone jumped off a teeter-totter while I sat high in the air. Jealousy and resentment crept in when I thought about those around me whose lives, in my limited view, went on as they had before.

I want to keep Amber's environment at a low-stress level, so managing everything is part of that. It's temporary; it won't be like this forever. God, I need your help to remember you. Help me to remember you here with us. And to remember to take baby steps toward her recovery—baby steps.

My glimmers of hope came as I watched Amber continue to recuperate. The feelings of constant fatigue and lethargy began to subside as she adjusted to the medication cocktail. Soon, she felt well enough to drive her car again. I have to admit, the first time she drove solo, my anxiety level flew off the chart. But after I saw her handle it as though she had never stopped, I relaxed.

Sometime in August, during one of our routine stops at a bookstore, she stopped reading books on pregnancy and baby naming. Instead, she turned her focus to inspirational reading, the study of her faith, and journals to record her thoughts. Relief washed over me as I knew another one of her delusions had been conquered.

There was another change in routine that gave me a renewed optimism. Carter, his second birthday months behind him, began to spend his days with me again. Amber improved enough for Mitchell and Melinda to feel comfortable letting Carter stay with me as his daycare provider, as before. His presence in our home brought positive energy and much laughter. I realized, like seeing the first petals of a spring flower after the months of a snow-covered ground, how much pleasure his company gave me. His mind resembled a sponge. He learned something new each day, and his sweet personality returned wonder to me each day. Reading books with him, snuggling in a chair, listening to his soft, high voice, and even cleaning up his messes, I discovered pleasure in small doses.

Because of Amber's improved health, on occasion, I left Carter playing with her in the front room while I fixed lunch in the kitchen, a few steps away. One day, I walked back into the room just in time to witness Carter stomp his foot at Amber as he declared, "You, you, you're a lobster!"

Amber and I burst out laughing. He looked confused.

"Why did he say that?" I asked Amber.

"I told him he couldn't drink his milk in the front room, that he had to sit at the table for that," she said. "I guess he thought I was a little grumpy."

We laughed even harder when we realized he meant to call her a crab. It felt so wonderful to share a joke with Amber again. At the beginning of the year, I didn't think I would ever get that back.

Brooke continued to visit Amber several times a week. She invited Amber to join the young adult Bible study she attended. Each Thursday evening, Brooke came to pick her up and bring her home. Their study group joined a sand volleyball league; Amber joined the team. This group of close-knit friends met on weekends to play games or watch videos. Brooke took Amber along whenever Amber felt up to it.

Amber's social calendar filled up with activities with people her own age. Her circle of friends and trust grew at a steady pace. This proved to be an incredibly important part of her journey toward health. Schizophrenia typically leaves people unable to enjoy the activities many of us take for granted. Often those who suffer from this brain disorder withdraw, avoiding groups of people. Roy and I couldn't provide the interaction with individuals her age. Brooke did. Bible study became an avenue to wellness for Amber. Her faith life continued to be important to her. She explored it further within the safety of a compassionate, understanding group of young professionals. I felt encouraged as more of her personality emerged from under the oppression of mental illness. Each time she had pushed another symptom into submission, a new patch of healing was applied to my frayed heart.

Fall 2005

Autumn arrived, and Amber continued with steady signs of improvement. Every few weeks, she'd decide she wanted to try some new step to independence. At one point, she became convinced she was ready to move into an apartment again. My comfort level with that thought hovered between "absolutely not" and "it's not a good idea." Roy and I talked about it and agreed that she wasn't fully ready, but we decided to let her try.

"Jennifer from our Bible study owns a house. She said she wants a roommate and will rent out the basement to me. I told her I wanted it," Amber announced the next week.

"How are you going to pay rent?" Roy asked.

"I'll get another job."

Memories of the short-lived employment with a local youth organization rolled through my head like a movie reel. I thought back to her excitement to start the job and how she gave it her all, but within three weeks, the stress of coping in a work environment left her feeling defeated. I remembered her distress:

"I can't do it. I can't handle it. I had to quit 'cause I'm just not ready," she announced after she resigned, a defeated look in her eyes.

Since I observed Amber on a daily basis, I didn't think she could handle living on her own any more now than she when she tried to enter the workforce less than a month earlier.

"We'll pay your rent for now," I said, not wanting her to take on both another job and living on her own. One such change alone could prove to be too much stress for her.

Moving day arrived—and not without apprehension on my part. I kept my mouth shut and used my stress energy to help fix up the basement room into a cute space. Since there wasn't a closet, Roy suspended a pipe from the joist and I hung fabric from it. When it was finished, we hung her clothes behind the sectioned-off part of the basement. Next, we set up her television and her stereo and arranged a small sitting area with her cream-and-rust flowered sofa and hand-me-down end tables. We used a small bookshelf to divide the living space from her bedroom area. After a quick trip to the grocery store, I stocked her cupboard shelf with easy-to-heat meals.

She waved goodbye to us when we finished and promised to call each day to check in.

Three weeks later, we moved her back home with us. Even though I saw her disappointment, frustration, and anxiety, I was proud of her progress and courageous attitude. She tried.

chapter twenty

October 2005

One Sunday afternoon, Mitchell, Melinda, and Carter stopped by.

"Is Dad around?" Mitchell asked.

"He's in the basement putting salt in the water softener. He'll be up in just a minute."

I opened the basement door. "Roy," I called down the stairs. "Mitchell, Melinda, and Carter are here."

Roy came up with a smile and two buckets of ice cream. "Anybody hungry?"

Carter broke into a big smile. "I want banilla."

"Vanilla," I heard Melinda whisper to him.

I smiled as I scooped out two small scoops into a bowl and set it in front of Carter. Then I grabbed the container of chocolate chip ice cream, ready to dish it up.

"We have an announcement," Mitchell said.

I looked at him, ice cream scoop poised midair. I glanced to Melinda and back at Mitchell.

"You're going to be grandparents again," Melinda chimed in.

"Congratulations. That is so exciting!" Roy said.

I flashed Melinda an enlightened grin. "I suspected you might be," I chided her. "I offered you a Diet Coke the other day, and you turned me down." I beamed at her. "The only time I've known you to refuse a Diet Coke was when you were expecting Carter."

"I thought you might catch on," Melinda laughed.

"When are you due?"

"Toward the end of April," she said. "I'm just past twelve weeks."

"I say we toast with ice cream." Mitchell picked up an empty bowl. "How 'bout it, Mom? Can I have some ice cream?"

"My birthday is the twenty-ninth of April, don't forget," Roy added. "Getting a grandchild on my birthday would be a great present . . ."

Mitchell and Melinda glanced at each other, laughing. "We shall see," both said in unison.

How many times did I use that line when Mitchell was little? What goes around comes around.

The rest of the afternoon, we chatted in the front room while Carter played with his toys. Amber arrived home after attending church with Brooke.

"Hey, Mitchell. Hi, Melinda. Good to see you," Amber said when she walked into the room.

It seemed like a normal Sunday afternoon, something that, less than a year ago, I felt I had lost forever. It had been over nine months since Amber's break with reality. Now we saw a steady improvement in her state of mind. She no longer believed she was pregnant, and she trusted people again. Her relationship with Melinda slowly evolved from hands-off through mutual understanding and finally back to friendship.

I admired Melinda and her reaction. Her college degree in education, with a minor in psychology, gave her the foundation to understand Amber's accusations earlier in the year: a symptom of her brain disorder, schizophrenia. She didn't take it personally.

The joy of anticipating another grandchild and watching Amber's reconnection with the world continued to grow. The next Sunday afternoon, we had a phone call from Wesley.

"Hi, Mom. Is Dad around?"

"He's in his office. Do you want me to get him?" I asked.

"I want to talk to you both."

I covered the receiver with my hand. "Roy, pick up the extension, will you?"

When we were both on the phone, Wesley didn't hesitate. "I have some good news for you," he said, his voice sounding excited. "Suzanne and I are going to be parents."

"Congratulations!" "Such great news!" Roy and I exclaimed.

"So, when are you due?" I asked.

"Early May," he replied. "About two weeks after Melinda. Suzanne just had her twelve-week check-up yesterday," he continued. "We waited to tell you until after she passed the first trimester."

A small pain stabbed my heart as I thought back to Suzanne's previous two pregnancies which ended in miscarriages in the past year. Both times, they had shared the exciting news early only to have to let us know she had lost the babies.

"I get it. I'm just so happy for you. I don't care when you tell me. Is she feeling okay?"

"Yeah, just exhausted from the pregnancy."

We chatted for a few more minutes. After we hung up, I did a happy dance around the kitchen. My spirits were uplifted, more so than they had been for the past ten months. The thought of two grandchildren coming two weeks apart brought me immense joy.

As I reveled in the exhilarated feeling, I whispered "Thank you" to God many times. The sun was shining bright on my family once again, chasing away the black cloud that had hovered for too many months.

chapter twenty-one

In early December, Melinda stopped to pick up Carter after work. "Do you have a minute?" she asked.

"Of course."

"Well, it's probably nothing, but I found a lump in my left breast last week," she stated calmly, which surprised me. I wouldn't have such a calm reaction.

"I showed my obstetrician, and he wants me to see a breast specialist in town tomorrow after work," she continued. "He didn't think it's of concern; he's just being cautious."

I listened. I didn't know how to react, so I kept quiet.

"Can you watch Carter late tomorrow while I go see him?"

"Absolutely."

"My OB said they can't do anything while I'm pregnant, but it's best to keep an eye on the lump anyway."

I just nodded.

I sure hope it's nothing. God, let it be nothing.

The following day, I watched the clock, my imagination running wild. *She's probably meeting with the doctor now. I wonder what he thinks. What happens if it is cancer?*

Relief flooded over me when Melinda bounded into my shop.

"The breast specialist thinks it is regular breast tissue. It could be a result of the pregnancy," she said. "He will check it after I deliver. He said don't worry about it."

"That's a relief," I said and exhaled louder than I intended. "How did you find it?"

"My seat belt rubbed it, and it felt tender."

"That's weird," I commented, and then smiled. "I'm so glad everything is okay."

I bundled Carter in his coat and gave him one last snuggle for the day, and they left.

Neither Melinda nor I mentioned the lump again, but my concern remained high, right next to my continued worries about Amber's brain disorder. I'm guessing Mitchell and Melinda felt it even more. But we continued on joyfully, trying to ignore the worrisome cloud far off on the horizon.

A couple of weeks later, a phone call from Wesley raised yet another red flag for me. "I've got some news, Mom," he said, his voice soft. He sounded tired.

"What's wrong?"

"Suzanne's doctor thinks there may be a problem with the baby."

"Oh, no. What?" *No, Lord. Not Suzanne's baby.*

"They're going to run some tests tomorrow. He suspects the baby may have Down Syndrome."

"Oh." I didn't know how to answer.

"Suzanne's pretty upset," he went on.

I took a moment to think before I answered. "I imagine this is quite a shock. Just know your baby is wanted and loved already. If you have a baby with Down Syndrome, it will be more of a challenge, yes, but I have confidence in you and your abilities."

"I don't know what to think," he said. "We didn't expect this."

"No one does. But I know people with handicapped children. They have said their child taught them so much about love," I said. "They say it has made them better people."

Silence.

"It's tough, I know, but let's wait and see what the tests show. Okay?" I didn't know if anything I said made any difference. "I'll keep you in my prayers."

"Thanks, Mom."

We hung up. I shared the news with Roy when he came home. He just shook his head.

What else, God? What else?

I tried to stay positive, but an upbeat attitude eluded me. Worry about Melinda's lump, Wesley and Suzanne's new baby, and Amber, always Amber. Now more than ever, I centered my morning devotion and prayers on the health of my family.

A few days later, Wesley called with the results. "We're having a boy," he said, but his voice didn't have the excitement I would have expected from a father-to-be. He continued. "The tests confirmed the doctor's suspicion; the baby has an extra set of chromosome 21." Their son, our grandson, would be born with Down Syndrome. "The doctors advised us to terminate." His voice broke, and it sounded like he choked back a sob. "Why did he even bring it up? Doesn't he think we can handle it?" He paused for a bit. "Will I be a good enough father to love and care for him? I'm so scared."

"The doctors aren't always right in their advice. I know this is hard. You'll do the right thing and you will be a great father, no matter what," I said in a calm voice, but my insides crumbled.

Oh, God, don't let the doctors talk them into that. I couldn't bear that thought.

I handled my fear the best way I knew: first, I prayed, and then I went to the Internet for information. I learned about Down Syndrome births: there are three types—trisomy 21 was the most common at ninety-five percent; it occurs in about every 691 births; heart defects often accompany trisomy 21; there may be developmental delays; people with Down Syndrome are able to lead full and happy lives. I kept reading. I felt a pain in my chest when I read the percentage of babies with Down Syndrome aborted in the United States.

Wesley had also told me the doctors would be looking for heart defects in ultrasound testing. He called a few days later.

"The baby has three problems with his heart," he said, his voice dejected. "They can repair two of them with surgery."

"That's tough, but at least there is surgery," I assured him.

He sounded so troubled, so sad, so confused. I wanted to reach through the phone and hold him.

"It's so hard, Mom." His voice cracked again.

"I'm sure it is. You know we are here to support you and Suzanne. You won't be alone. We're always here for you. Remember that."

"I know." He still sounded dejected. "We'll keep in touch." I heard the shock and fear in Wesley's voice as he doubted his ability as a father. He spoke with me about society's reaction to Down Syndrome people and his inability to cope with that. He sounded scared, confused, and in a very dark, painful place. My heart broke for them.

"I love you, Wesley. I'll keep you all in my prayers."

Our conversation ended, but I held an ongoing conversation with God. I prayed for strength, courage, and wisdom for them. And, I'll admit, I had my own doubts about me. How will I react? Will I love him as much as I love Carter? Could I support them when they needed extra help?

Through prayer, I shoved my feeling of inadequacy aside. I knew the answer.

How did I react with Amber? I loved first. I discovered that deep in my heart, I already loved this new grandson.

Still, I felt helpless as I watched my son and his wife struggle, agonizing their way through the horror no parent should ever have to face. Wesley and I had many conversations as he shared their sorrows over the unexpected turn of events. I also talked with Suzanne, pledging our support and love. She hurt, too. The impending birth of a child was supposed to be a happy time for couples, wasn't it?

I prayed about their situation constantly, adding in prayers for Amber and Melinda as well. I found it difficult to concentrate on my job. One evening, just before Christmas, Wesley called. I heard pain and self-doubt in his voice as we discussed the health of his son, still growing in the womb of Suzanne.

"Wesley, I want you to know this. I want your son in our family. I think you and Suzanne will be great parents. But, if it gets too hard for you as he grows, I will take him and raise him for you," I said. "I love you and Suzanne, and I already love your son. I'm here for you."

"Thanks, Mom," he said sadly. "I wish I felt as confident about me as you do."

We hung up. Later, I repeated my vow to Suzanne as we discussed the baby over the phone.

They're scared, God, and I don't blame them. It's a big unknown for all of us. Give them courage as they learn about their son's health. Give them grace as they face his surgeries and other obstacles. Give them strength, O Lord, give them strength.

A week or so later at our family Christmas celebration, my two daughters-in-law sat on the blue plaid sofa in the front room where they compared pregnancy notes. Carter played with his new toy near the Christmas tree. The hand-painted crèche adorned the table in the corner. Roy, Mitchell, Wesley, and Clinton gathered around the table in the next room with game pieces scattered around them. Their good-natured teasing and competitive conversation drifted to the front room. Amber sat with her feet up in the recliner, resting and absorbing the conversation around her. As I observed everyone celebrating Christmas, it seemed we had no worries or cares at all. My heart swelled. I listened to my family's sounds of Christmas as I thought about the past year of our life: Amber's health had improved significantly, and our family would increase by two in the spring. What a change from a year ago.

A few days later, my extended family converged in our home per our tradition. Mom, seven of my eight brothers, my two sisters, their spouses, and their children joined together for a celebration. We enjoyed the customary meal of oyster stew, chili, cold cuts, vegetables, and sweet treats. I watched as my family acted as if Amber's meltdown a year ago never happened. They treated her as they always had, not as someone who suffered from a mental illness. Clusters of cousins visited while they played Scrabble; the young children chased each other in an excited frenzy; the men played an intense game of poker as chips and cards flew across the table; the women caught up on the past year's events. The house was noisy, crowded, messy, and wonderfully normal. Surrounded by my family, I felt extremely grateful for their love and support; I knew they had my back. But more importantly, I came to realize over the past year that whatever came my way, my God and I would handle it together. Bring on the new year.

chapter twenty-two

January 2006

Because Amber was doing so well, one of my friends suggested I contact Vocational Rehabilitation as the next step to regaining her independence. Amber and I went to the office and met with Rita, the counselor assigned to her. After an interview and several assessment tests, Rita suggested job training.

"Where?" asked Amber.

Rita explained, "Typically, clients work at Goodwill or a similar place." Seeing the look on Amber's face, I interjected.

"We'd like to think about it," I said.

"Okay," Rita said as she opened her calendar. "Let's make an appointment for next week."

We left her office and stepped into the biting wind. We hurried to my car and both jumped in quickly. Once inside, Amber shook her head.

"I don't want to work at Goodwill. I'm a college graduate."

I nodded. "Let's give it some thought, okay?"

The following week, we again sat in Rita's office. Amber shared her thoughts with Rita, who nodded as she listened.

"What would you like to try?" she asked Amber.

"I thought about training to become a Certified Nursing Assistant. I still want to help people."

"Okay, we can definitely support you doing specialized training. We can help you get your certificate. Enroll at the local community college and let me know when you start. We'll help pay your tuition, books, uniforms, and any other expenses." I was pleased that it was as simple as that. Rita looked past Amber's illness and was willing to help her pursue a path that would give Amber satisfaction and self-esteem.

After we left Rita's office, Amber turned to me in the car.

"Did Rita say I'm a loser? Did she say I'd never complete the course?"

Only moments before, my hope had risen. Now, I felt my heart plunge back to the black hole of uncertainty as Amber's auditory hallucinations appeared again.

"No, Amber. She didn't."

"I didn't think so; that's why I asked you." *Oh, God, the hallucinations and paranoia still plague her. But thank you for helping her recognize it and be willing to ask for me to discount it. Thank you, oh, thank you!*

"I'm glad you asked me," I said out loud. "But no, Rita said only positive things to you. You know, you might want to mention this the next time you see the doctor," I suggested to her.

"I will, Mom. Thanks."

Neither Amber nor I brought it up again. At her next appointment, she told her doctor about it, who adjusted her medication. Six weeks later, Amber completed the CNA course, took the test, and passed with flying colors. My heart soared.

Thank you, God. She's doing so much better. Please continue to guide us.

With her CNA certificate in hand and Rita's permission, Amber enrolled in the Licensed Practical Nursing program. At Rita's suggestion, Amber started with two classes instead of the full load. She anticipated finishing the course in two or three years, rather than the typical one.

Amber left each morning for class and spent time studying each day; Carter came each day for Grammie Daycare, and Roy attended farm meeting after farm meeting. Life felt normal as I went about my days with a lighter step and prayers full of gratitude.

April 2006

As Melinda's due date approached in the spring, Roy teased her at every opportunity when she stopped each day to pick up Carter after work. Roy insisted she could wait to deliver until April 29, his birthday. Because Carter had been delivered by C-section almost three years earlier after thirty-six hours of unproductive labor, Melinda and Mitchell knew the day their daughter would join their family, just four days shy of Roy's birthday.

"I don't know why you won't have this baby on my birthday," he chided her.

"I just don't love you enough to wait those extra days," she retorted.

Both of them laughed as the scene repeated over and over, week by week.

Madelyn Kate arrived on April 25, right on schedule, at about 8:30 a.m. I couldn't wait to greet mom and daughter. A few hours after delivery, Roy, Amber, Carter, and I went to greet the newest member of our clan. I marveled as I watched Amber enjoy cuddling with her niece and Carter learn his first lessons as an older brother.

The next morning as I shared the news of Madelyn and a cup of coffee with my mom in her kitchen, my cell phone rang.

"Mom, you have a grandson!" Wesley exclaimed.

"What?" I asked, concern starting to rise inside me. "He wasn't due for another two weeks! Is everything okay?"

"Yes, Jack decided to come a bit early," he explained. The excitement in his voice resonated through the phone. "He is in the NICU for now, but we expected that. And Suzanne is recovering well."

"Congratulations, Daddy," I gushed, relief replacing my concern. "How is little Jack? What about his heart?"

"Right now, he's stable, but he will need heart surgery as soon as possible. The pediatric cardiologist is in Mexico doing mission work, but he will be back next week." He talked calmly, surprising me. "He will do surgery then. We will call as soon as we know the date."

"I wanna come see him right away," I said, "but I can't. I told your brother I would watch Carter while Melinda is in the hospital. That will be a few days. But then I will be right there, don't you worry."

"I get it, Mom. Don't worry about it. We can't wait to show him off."

"I can't wait. I'll see you in a few days. Congratulations again, Daddy." I smiled so hard I thought my face would break. "Tell Suzanne congratulations, too."

I flipped my phone shut. "You're a great-grandma again," I said to Mom. "That was Wesley; their little guy arrived early, but he's doing okay."

"Praise the Lord," Mom said as she threw her hands in the air. "What's his name again?"

"Jack. They named him Jack Michael. He'll be in the NICU for a while, and then he will have surgery on his heart, but they are just thrilled."

I felt elated—two grandchildren less than twenty-four hours apart. After the pain during last sixteen months and the worry over Jack, I welcomed the joy.

A few days later, Melinda and Madelyn came home as scheduled; Mitchell took a few days off work, and Carter stayed home with them.

Roy and I left early the next day for the two-hour drive to the hospital near Wesley and Suzanne's home. We had driven the route many times before when visiting them, but today the road between our home and the hospital NICU seemed longer than usual. Finally, I stood beside the enclosed plastic crib. The portals on both sides allowed hands to reach him, touch him, and caress him. Wires from monitors, intravenous lines, and oxygen were attached to his tiny body. A tiny diaper covered his bottom; a Bob the Builder quilt lay over the top of his bed, like a colorful roof.

"Volunteers make and give a quilt to every baby in the ICU," Wesley explained when I asked about the quilt. "Isn't he beautiful?" he said. Pride filled his voice as he beamed.

"Oh, he is; he is so beautiful," I said. I watched in awe as Wesley reached in through the portals and stroked Jack's back. His touch looked so soft, so gentle.

"Hey, little buddy. Daddy's here. How ya doin' today? You ready to meet Grammie and Grandpa?" he asked. His voice sounded soothing and gentle as his large hand covered Jack's entire back. Suzanne stood on the opposite side, her hands nestled around her newborn son. She linked pinkie fingers with Wesley while we all admired Jack through the clear plastic.

"Isn't he the most beautiful baby?" Suzanne asked for the umpteenth time. As she gazed at Jack, the emotions of her overfilled heart spilled out through her eyes and down her cheek.

"He *is* beautiful," I agreed. My heart swelled. I watched my son and his wife heap love and praise on the tiny new member of our family.

"He will have to have surgery on his heart," Wesley said. "As soon as Dr. Beckett gets back from Mexico, he will schedule it. It will be next week one day."

"Let me know when," I said. "I'll be here." I took my turn stroking Jack with my hands. They shook a bit as I stroked his delicate skin; he had so many tubes and lines for monitors attached to him. I had a hard time taking my eyes off him. His chest rose and fell in rhythm as he softly took each breath. He looked so fragile compared to Madelyn. But as I gazed on him, memories of Wesley's birth, twenty-seven years earlier, came to mind. I couldn't help but think how Jack looked the same size as his daddy.

"How much did you say he weighed again?" I asked Suzanne.

"Six pounds, five ounces."

I turned to Wesley. "He's almost identical to you when you were born! You weighed six pounds, five and three-fourths ounces!"

I turned and feasted my eyes on Jack again. "Your daddy started out small, too. You're gonna grow up big and strong, just like him," I whispered to him.

"How big was Madelyn?" Suzanne asked.

"She was almost eight pounds. But if Jack is anything like his daddy, he'll catch up in no time."

Suzanne's eyes looked full of questions.

I continued. "Wesley was a breech delivery, but God kept him little for that. After that, Wesley gained four pounds his first month! I don't expect Jack will gain that fast, but he's gonna grow, too. He comes from strong stock."

I smiled and turned my attention back to Jack.

"Do you want to hold him?" Suzanne asked.

"I'd be scared," I said, shaking my head. "There're so many tubes . . ."

"You can do it. I'll call the nurse to help."

Gingerly, the nurse lifted Jack and placed him in my arms. "Hello, dear one," I cooed, keeping my voice and touch soft. "We've been waiting for you. Do you know how happy you've made your mommy and daddy?" I whispered in his ear. He continued to sleep as I held him, afraid to move. I didn't want to bump the tubes that seemed to sprout from his tiny body.

We stayed about an hour before we headed home.

A week later, the hospital scheduled Jack's surgery. I returned to the hospital and found Wesley and Suzanne just before Jack's surgery. Dr. Beckett, the pediatric cardiologist, called us to a room and patiently explained the procedure to us. He planned to repair Jack's narrowed pulmonary artery during this first surgery. He commented that he often saw this heart defect among Down Syndrome children. He felt confident the surgery—one he had performed many times—would be successful. He would schedule the second surgery when Jack was a bit older, perhaps when he was four to six months old.

I held my breath as I watched nurses carefully transfer Jack to another high-tech enclosure. Once they had him settled, they paused briefly before they left the NICU. Suzanne gently laid her hand on the unit and brushed tears away. Wesley put on a brave face, but I saw the pain he tried to hide. I prayed silently as they wheeled our precious bundle down the hall.

God, be with the surgeon, the nurses, and everyone on the surgical team. Give them steady hands and clear minds. You know how much we love this little guy. Please keep him safe and help us to stay calm.

During surgery, Dr. Beckett sent a nurse to the surgical waiting room every half hour to keep us informed on the surgical progress. After several good reports, Dr. Beckett joined us in the conference room. He smiled broadly as he reported the successful outcome of Jack's surgery. "He will be in a medicine-induced coma for the rest of today to give his body a chance to heal. You will be able to see him, but no touching. His body has been through trauma; his recovery will be quicker if he has no outside stimulus."

When Jack's attending nurse allowed us in his recovery room, we surrounded his miniature bed. He lay motionless; only his chest moved.

"Our beautiful little champ—you're our little fighter," Suzanne exclaimed as she hung a pair of tiny boxing gloves on the crib.

I spent the rest of the day with them at the hospital, but once I knew everything was okay with Jack, I headed home in the evening. Within a few days, Jack returned to the NICU, where he remained for the next five weeks. At six weeks of age, he finally went home. We all echoed Wesley and Suzanne's reaction: ecstatic. During Jack's hospital stay, they learned how to care for him and his fragile health.

Over the next few months, he would endure several more surgeries: one to implant a feeding tube due to his inability to suck enough nourishment from the bottle, another for the doctor to put casts on his feet to straighten them due to severe club feet. Each time, his daddy and mommy rose to the occasion, took it in stride, and loved that little guy with every fiber of their being. I watched in awe as my son and his wife became stellar parents filled with knowledge, faith, and devotion.

May 2006

In early May, we all traveled to Dubuque, Iowa, to attend the wedding of our nephew, Jerry, and his bride, Anna. It should have been a joyful occasion, but I guess I forgot the lesson I learned the previous year in the NAMI class on grief. The emotional chart used during the class illustrated a part of the second stage of acceptance, often accompanied by grief. When Amber first became ill in late 2004, I entered the crisis stage. Feelings of denial, anxiety, and helplessness overwhelmed me. As I learned about her brain disorder and she improved with treatment, I moved from the crisis stage to one of acceptance.

By January 2006, I had edged my way toward advocacy, the third stage. I shared my experience on a retreat of high school seniors. I talked about mental illness and the role my faith played in coping with my pain.

Over the past seventeen months, Amber had improved so much, and the joy of the births of Jack and Madelyn made me forget the pain, but I neglected a major side note given during the lesson: we can jump quickly between all stages of emotions.

On May 6, 2006, grief reappeared with a vengeance. I didn't get to stay in the advocacy stage. I guess the Lord knew I needed to spend more time in acceptance and experience grief in an unexpected way.

It hit me as I watched Anna, stunning in her white gown and veil, glide up the aisle on her dad's arm. Jerry awaited her, his eyes glued to her in admiration. As I watched the scene, usually my favorite of the entire day, the unwelcome force returned, reached into my chest, clutched my heart, and squeezed.

Will this ever happen for Amber? Most of the cousins her age are in a relationship or already married. Will she ever be healthy enough to pursue her dream of being a wife and mother?

My eyes darted to Amber next to me in the church pew. I saw a single tear escape out of the corner of her hazel eyes. She lowered her head, and her dark blonde, curly hair cascaded forward. The giant hand in my chest crushed my aching heart as I realized we both must have the same thoughts. I reached out and gently touched her arm.

After the Mass ended, the crowd reassembled at a local meeting room for the dinner and dance. The lighthearted atmosphere didn't lessen my anguish. I pasted on a smile, but I inside I wanted to run away and just go home. I forced myself to chat if someone started a conversation, but I wanted to sit in a dark corner and fade into the shadows. I felt like a creep; instead of happiness for the young couple, I selfishly couldn't see past my pain.

You'll probably never get to plan a wedding with your only daughter. Schizophrenia snuffed out her vision for her life and your dream for her.

I spent the rest of the day with sobs and tears threatening to escape at any moment. But eventually, I found Marie, a kind woman, the bride's grandmother, who seemed to understand my emotional turmoil. I guess in her wisdom, she saw past my façade. We chatted about life as we shared heartaches and concluded our conversation with a promise of prayers for each other's situations.

A lesson once learned took root again: grief shared is often divided.

June 2006

Wesley was employed as manager of a fast food restaurant, and Suzanne worked as a regional manager for another fast food chain. They juggled schedules so one of them always was home to care for Jack.

Then Wesley called one day. I heard frustration as he spoke. "Mom, I just got fired from my job." He went on to explain how he had discovered an employee theft, which he reported. He felt he handled the situation properly as he followed the company's guidelines. A few days later, the company fired him. The reason: failure to supervise properly, which resulted in a theft.

"Where is justice?!" I yelled after I hung up the phone. My anger boiled over at the company, angry with the situation and frustrated because it seemed like such a low blow for him. I had watched as Wesley and Suzanne rose to meet the challenges that came with Jack's condition and so far had held everything together. Now, because of a dishonest employee, Wesley had to job hunt while maintaining care for Jack.

Later that day, Melinda dropped in for a visit. I shared my anger with her, which helped me calm down. She nodded when I finished my rant. Then Melinda asked to change the subject.

"Remember the lump I told you about in December?" she asked. "I have a biopsy scheduled for it, but the doctor isn't concerned. It's probably just a routine test," she said. "Can you watch Carter and Madelyn tomorrow?"

"Sure, just drop them off."

The following day, my time with three-year-old Carter and six-week-old Madelyn seemed too short. The buzzer for my shop door rang as Melinda walked into the work room. Carter played with plastic building blocks in the kid zone, while Madelyn snoozed nearby in a portable playpen. I looked up from putting an embroidery hoop on a shirt to catch her eye. I raised my brows.

"It will be a few days before we know anything," Melinda said, addressing my unspoken question. "I'm sure they won't find anything," She strode to her children. She bent down, gave a quick tussle to Carter's hair, and peeked at Madelyn before she hopped into the black canvas captain's chair near the work table. "How were they?"

"Adorable, as always," I replied. "He's been playing nonstop since he got here," I said, nodding toward Carter, "and Madelyn stayed awake for an hour before she fell asleep."

We chatted until Madelyn woke up. They left for home, and the wait for results began.

A few days turned into a week, which dragged into three weeks. One day, as I bustled about my shop, working on an order, the phone rang the familiar tune. I grabbed it off my hip, where I wore it so I could work, and heard Melinda's voice.

"Could you watch the kidlets if I drop them off?" she asked after a quick hello. "The doctor's office just called. They want Mitchell and me to come into the office."

"Absolutely, bring them right away," I said.

We hung up. I set the phone on the counter where I hooped shirts, laid my head next to it, and bawled.

Doctors don't call couples in together unless it's bad news. It's cancer— that's why Mitchell had to go. Oh, God, don't let it be cancer. I don't know how much more I can take.

I tried to work, but I couldn't stop crying and my mind raced with visions of her losing the battle. I loved Melinda and considered her one of my best friends. Our bond didn't feel like the typical mother-in-law/ daughter-in-law relationship. We sewed together, shopped together, and chatted about almost everything.

I don't want to lose her, God. How would Mitchell react if she died? He adores her. How would he cope as a single father of two young children?

I couldn't concentrate on the job in front of me.

Oh, God, some days I think I'm going to break. Amber is getting better, but she's not back to her old self yet, and I don't know if she will ever be. Jack is in and out of the hospital. Oh, God, don't let it be cancer. Don't let it be cancer.

A new torrent of tears cascaded down my face and my chest heaved with sobs as I gave into my grief and fears.

By the time Melinda arrived about fifteen minutes later, I had pulled myself together, washed the tears off my face, and pasted on a smile. I gave her a quick hug and took the car seat that held Madelyn as she slept. I set it down before I scooped Carter up in my arms.

"I'll see you when you get back," I said. "Good luck" seemed like a dumb thing to say. "They'll be fine, so don't worry about the time," I reassured her.

Amber came in from the living room, where she spent most of her time, and held her arms out to Carter before she spoke.

"Hey, little buddy. Want to read a book?"

Carter wiggled down from my arms to the floor. Soon the two of them sat on the couch with Carter's favorite book, *God Bless the Gargoyles*.

Thank you, God, for Amber and her help with Carter.

While Madelyn finished her nap, I quickly browned meat and added peeled potatoes and carrots before I popped it all in the oven to bake. I knew I had to take advantage of that window of sleeping and reading time to prepare our meal. Amber helped with the kids occasionally, and I'd learned that a half hour was usually her limit. She had made great strides in her management of her brain disorder but still battled fatigue and low concentration.

We spent the afternoon in the front room. Carter played with his toy barn; Amber sat in the recliner while I rocked Madelyn after she woke. My eyes flitted from Carter and Madelyn to the hands of the clock that seemed to crawl in slow motion.

Finally, the back door opened. As three sets of footsteps approached, I stood carefully, put Madelyn in her crib, and hurried to the kitchen. Roy, Mitchell, and Melinda were just sitting at the table, so I joined them. I looked from Mitchell to Melinda to Roy. For a moment, we just sat, and no one spoke.

Somebody say something! I almost screamed.

Finally, Mitchell spoke. "It's cancer."

I expected that answer; I thought I had steeled myself for those words, but I had imposed an impossible task upon myself. I jumped from my chair, went to Melinda, and threw my arms around her.

"I'm sorry, I'm so, so sorry," I said as I broke into tears.

Mitchell and Melinda put on stoic faces as I fell apart. Mitchell came to me and put his arms around me as I shook with sobs and tears streamed down my face.

As he held me, I felt even worse.

"I should be comforting you; instead you have to comfort me," I said when I finally stopped weeping and moved back to my chair.

"We've already had time to digest the news," he said. "It's okay." He took a deep breath. "There's a reason it took three weeks to get the results. The doctors around here didn't recognize it, so they sent the biopsy to Iowa City. Iowa City labs knew it wasn't normal breast tissue, but had never seen anything like it before. So they sent it to the Mayo Clinic in Rochester." He paused.

No one spoke. Melinda sat quietly, looking at Mitchell, as we digested the news. The sounds of Carter playing in the next room carried toward us, and we all glanced in that direction. Finally, Mitchell continued.

"The Mayo clinic finally diagnosed it. It's pretty rare. They've never seen it before," Mitchell said in his clinical voice that I had heard many times.

What else, God? What else can happen to our family? I don't know if I can take anymore. Please make this stop!

"We're sending the records for another opinion before we make a decision on treatment. There's M.D. Anderson in Texas and Memorial Sloan-Kettering in New York. Melinda's dad said they are some of the best cancer centers in the country," he continued. William, Melinda's dad, worked in the medical field for most of his career and frequently offered advice.

I listened as Mitchell outlined the course of action he and Melinda would take. My chest hurt as I listened, but my crying had stopped.

"Let me know what I can do to help," I offered.

Roy added, "Whatever you need from us, just let us know."

"We're probably going to need your help with the kids. Can we count on you to take care of them during treatments?"

"Whatever you need, I'm available," I said, my voice shaking.

Oh, God, help me. I'm breaking; I can feel it. I'm breaking.

chapter twenty-three

July 2006

After Wesley lost his job, he began searching for a new one. He juggled caring for Jack, now out of the NICU and at home, and online job searches. He phoned one July afternoon.

"Mom, I scheduled a job interview for tomorrow. Is there any way you can come and watch Jack while I go? Suzanne has to work." Though it was a two-hour drive, there was only one answer to give.

"Sure. I do have Carter and Madelyn, though, so I will need to bring them along," I said. "Melinda's appointment at the Mayo Clinic is tomorrow, too. Maybe I can find someone to come and help me."

"That would be great, Mom. Thanks so much."

We both hung up. I sat for a few minutes, sending my thoughts heavenward for help.

OK, God, who do I ask for help? I'm not good at this. I don't think I can do it all myself. Who should I call?

A name popped into my head: Carolyn. We had been friends for over twenty years, but as busy lives became even busier, we saw each other only a few times each year. She lived about fifteen miles away. I knew her daughter, Emily, lived in the same area as Wesley and Suzanne.

I punched the numbers on my phone. She answered after a few rings.

"Hi, Carolyn, I have to ask you for a strange favor," I said.

"Virginia, it's nice to hear your voice. What do you need?"

I quickly explained my situation. I needed to drive two hours with my young grandchildren. Amber planned to help her aunt for the day, Roy needed to cultivate corn, and neither could help me.

"Would you consider riding along to help me? Once we get to Wesley's house, I thought you could call Emily. Then you can spend the day with your grandchildren, too. I think I can manage my three grandkids once I get them settled," I stated.

"Sure. I actually have tomorrow free and would love to help you."

We confirmed the time I would pick her up, and we both hung up.

The following day, I secured Carter and Madelyn's car seats in my SUV, left home, and a short time later pulled into Carolyn's driveway. She bounded out of her house; as we drove, our chatter filled the air. About halfway to Wesley's, Madelyn wailed. I stopped, and Carolyn moved to sit in the back to calm her. It didn't help; instead, it only made it worse.

"Would you mind driving so I can quiet her?" I asked Carolyn.

"I've never driven anything like a Yukon before. It's so big, and it makes me nervous." She hesitated, but she smiled at me with her infectious smile as she reached for the door handle. "But I can try."

We switched places, and once Madelyn saw me, she settled down, sucked her bottle with loud gulps, and soon fell asleep. We switched back again, Carter joined his sister in dreamland, and we continued our conversation. The rest of our two-hour drive passed, and we pulled into Wesley's. Each of us carrying a sleeping child, we both rushed to Jack's crib in the front room.

"He looks like a little doll," she exclaimed, settling Madelyn's car seat on the floor. "He's beautiful. May I pick him up?"

Wesley grinned as he nodded, then left a short time later for the interview. Carolyn and I took turns holding Jack and Madelyn or entertaining Carter. Before long, the babies slept and Carter played with his toys.

"I think I can manage now," I said to Carolyn. "Why don't you call

Emily so you can see your grandchildren?"

"I wouldn't dream of it. I'm staying with you all day. I want to help."

"I didn't think that was the arrangement," I said, feeling a stab of guilt. She wouldn't get to see her grandchildren.

"I insist."

I knew Carolyn well enough to know to let it go, and the discussion ended. As the day wore on, though, gratitude replaced the guilt. I found joy again as my friend ministered to me while we spent the day with Carter, Madelyn, and Jack. The day went smoother than I ever dreamt possible.

Thank you, God, for the friend you gave me in Carolyn. She is so good with Jack. I will never forget her kindness. Thank you. Thank you.

Our day ended, and we returned home with contented children in the backseat. I treasured the time spent with Carolyn and knew I had been given a gift.

Within a few months, Wesley and Suzanne both secured jobs that they enjoyed and fit their lifestyle with Jack better. They gained the flexibility that they needed to care for their son that Wesley couldn't have had with his old position. Eventually, they found a daycare provider who adored Jack, which made it easier to allow someone else to care for him. But life continually challenged them as Jack underwent hospitalizations for pneumonia, a respiratory concern associated with Down Syndrome. Through it all, Wesley and Suzanne took everything in stride, calling with updates and a litany of all Jack's new accomplishments. I heard pride and love in each conversation.

About the same time, Melinda began her cancer treatments. She reacted adversely to the chemo as she battled to fight this vicious invader. Many times after a treatment, she had to be hospitalized. My prayers increased, petitioning God for Jack's health, Melinda's healing, and Amber's continued progress. Each held a special place in my heart, filling me with renewed hope when they made progress and anguish when they faltered.

But God continued to support me, and he surrounded me with the loving embrace of family and friends through their assurance of prayers and their many offers to help.

chapter twenty-four

During a routine appointment in late September, Amber and I sat in the psychiatrist's office in Iowa City. Amber and her doctor had already spent time discussing her treatment before I joined them, which I usually did at the end of each session. The doctor directed her attention to me.

"Amber feels she doesn't need the medication and wishes to try to go without it," the thin young woman stated. "We've discussed it before and have gradually cut back on her dosage of the antipsychotic medication. She is doing very well."

I stared at the resident doctor sitting across the room, her legs crossed casually. My reaction was anything but casual. *What? You want to take her off? What happens when the symptoms return? No. What are you thinking?* I swallowed hard before I spoke. "Do you think that's the right thing to do?"

"Mom," Amber said. She folded her arms across her chest. "It's already been decided."

"We will keep a close eye on her over the next few months. She's agreed to keep all her appointments, both here and with her counselor back home," the doctor said. She looked at me with confidence. "Amber really wants to try this. She'll never know if she can get along without medicine if she doesn't try. This looks like the best time to try, when she is still living in your home."

I sat mutely. I stared at the floor for a few seconds before I looked up and saw both Amber and the doctor with their eyes on me. I glanced from one to the other.

"She will continue with her antidepressant medication," the doctor added. "And you can call our office at any time, day or night. A doctor answers our phones twenty-four hours a day. You won't be alone."

"What happens if the symptoms return and you won't take the medicine?" I asked as I looked at Amber.

"She is still under court committal, so that shouldn't be a problem," the doctor spoke quickly. "Amber and I discussed the symptoms and things she must look for. I think we should let her try. Will you come on board?"

Amber looked at me. I saw hope in her eyes.

Can I deny her this chance to try—no matter how scared I am?

"I will do my best to support your decision," I said to Amber and then turned my head toward the doctor and nodded slightly.

I don't like this. I'm not comfortable with this at all. God, help us if it doesn't work. I don't know if I can go through it all again.

We all stood at the same time. The doctor reached out to me with an outstretched hand. I took a few steps toward her, and we shook.

"It'll be okay," she said. "Thank you, ladies."

She walked with Amber and me to the front desk. "Goodbye. I will see you in three weeks."

We set the next appointment and then walked in silence to the parking garage. We found my car, climbed in simultaneously, and shut the doors.

"Mom, I know you are uncomfortable with this." Amber turned to me. "But I have to try. I just have to try."

"I know, honey, I know. But honestly, it scares me."

"Me too. But I think I'll be fine."

I nodded so she knew I heard her. I put the key in the ignition, and we left the hospital. We stopped for lunch, spent an hour in the bookstore, and drove home without discussing it further.

Despite my fears, the next few months went smoothly for all of us. Amber managed the things she wanted to do, and I worked on orders for customers. I saw no symptoms, but still lived in constant fear. The NAMI class I had taken in the spring of 2005 taught me to stay alert. I remembered 50 percent of patients with schizophrenia commit suicide. It didn't happen during the lowest part of their illness; rather, the attempts happened when they felt better. During the harshest symptoms, they didn't have the strength or the thought process to carry it out. Now, since Amber felt better, the idea gnawed at me most of time.

I continued to watch for the return of any symptoms and whispered many silent prayers of gratitude each day as I didn't notice any.

Amber continued to study in a licensed practical nurse course at a local community college. She met regularly with Rita, her caseworker at Vocational Rehab, who charted her progress. Through testing, Rita determined that Amber needed extra time for test-taking and notified the school. Amber, however, shook her head at the idea.

"I don't want to be singled out for special treatment. I'll be okay."

At first, everything seemed okay, but I did notice she became agitated more quickly, had less patience, or seemed unapproachable in conversation. I chalked it up to the study load she carried and adjusting to the lessened medication, while at the same time, I scrutinized each bout for signs of paranoia, distrust, or altered thinking patterns. Thankfully, I didn't find any reason for alarm.

Even still, my spiritual state of mind took a big hit in the fall of 2006. I felt overwhelmed with the things happening around me and all the responsibilities I had taken upon myself. As Amber's conservator, I had to report all her income and expenses each year. Each month, I balanced the record books for my business and recorded all of Amber's purchases. Plus, I cared for Carter and Madelyn for Grammie Daycare when Melinda had treatments—often overnight—and helped Amber with her needs. In between, I drove to Wesley and Suzanne's numerous times to visit Jack in the hospital or to help them at home. I tried to keep my business afloat and a reasonably organized household.

Things got done as needed, but I seemed to work on autopilot. I did the necessary tasks but nothing else and fell into bed exhausted at the end of each day. Prayer, study, and daily devotions dropped to the bottom of my to-do list that summer until late October.

October 20

On October 20, I felt drawn to pick up my daily devotional book. The thought nagged me until I finally sat down for a few minutes. I opened up *Daily Guideposts 2006*[17] to the day's date. I scanned it quickly before I glanced to the opposite page, October 21.

THIS HAD NOT BEEN *a good week* was the first line on the page, echoing my personal sentiments.

So I continued to read.

THIS HAD NOT BEEN a good week. Things did not work out as I had hoped, and the last few days have brought disappointment and discouragement. No matter how mature and experienced I become, these "days in the valley" do not become easier.

Oh, my, exactly how I feel. Things are so hard.

I continued to read. It fit my life. It talked about our pilgrimage with God as a long journey with all kinds of terrain to cross. It described the valleys of weeping we encounter, but also mountaintop experiences.

We experience moments of laughter and weeping, excitement and boredom, comfort and pain, birth and death. . . . But the Bible reminds me I do not walk alone.

The author of the day's devotional, Scott Walker, reminded me of life's ups and downs, joys and sorrows. But most importantly, I held on to the idea: God will not abandon me in any circumstance.

The idea brought some comfort to me as I thought about how recently it felt like I trudged through one crisis after another; I felt like the proverbial boat, drifting away from the shore of my faith.

I closed my book and pondered what I had just read. *Is this what you want me to know, God? Keep my eyes on you?* The thought "When things get hard, depend on me; draw close to me" remained in my soul as I went about my day. I made a resolution to get back into my study of scripture and devotional materials.

October 21

The next morning, I lay on the couch in the front room. Because of restless sleep during the night, I had moved there around two a.m. The shrill ring of the telephone jolted me from my comfortable spot. I glanced at the clock as I grabbed the phone I had set near me earlier. Five thirty. *Who's calling at this hour?*

"Hello?"

"Mom." I barely recognized Wesley's strangled voice. "Jack died this morning."

As I sank into the couch, my heart crashed to the floor. What do you say to your son when he's just told you his son is dead? I caught my breath before I spoke.

"Oh, Wesley." I only could manage those two words as the horrific news settled in. After a moment, I composed myself. "Ohhh, Wesley, I am so, so sorry. Dad and I will be down as soon as we get dressed. I'm so sorry. I'm so, so sorry." The words rang hollow. Sorry just didn't cut it, but I felt helpless to say anything else.

"Don't come, Mom, don't come. The coroner is here now. You don't need to come." Wesley's voice sounded so low, so dejected, so filled with pain.

I wanted to scoop him in my arms and make it all better, but I knew there could be no fixing this. His beloved little Jack was gone. I had just snuggled him six days ago in the hospital and smelled his soft baby smell. He had just come home again two days ago. Neither of us spoke. I couldn't breathe as a pressure filled my chest and squeezed. Pain filled every cell in my body. My grief box imploded, and I felt my insides crumble.

God, give me your words. I took a deep breath before I spoke.

"Tell Suzanne she's a good mom; he didn't leave us because you are bad parents. You loved him above everything else, and he had the best parents in the world. It's not your fault," I heard words flow from my heart into the phone. "We're coming. I'm waking Dad and Amber. We'll be there as soon as we can."

I know I hurried, but it felt like I staggered along in slow motion from the couch to the hallway. Roy had evidently heard the phone ring and stepped out of our bedroom. We met just outside Amber's bedroom door. She opened her door about the same time.

"What's going on?" Roy asked.

I took one step toward him before my knees buckled. He reached out quickly and caught me as I collapsed into his arms.

"Jack's gone. That was Wesley. Jack—died—this morning—at home." The words came out broken and harsh.

Roy groaned and Amber gasped. I surrendered myself to Roy's support, unable to move or speak. Roy continued to hold me in his arms, and Amber threw hers around the two of us. The three of us held each other up in the hallway while we cried.

chapter twenty-five

Roy, Amber, and I dressed quickly, got in the car, and drove straight to Mitchell and Melinda's. We knocked softly, and Mitchell came to the door. We spoke in hushed voices as we shared our painful news.

Mitchell groaned in low tones as he looked back to the bedroom area. "I'm going wait to wake Melinda to tell her. She just had a treatment yesterday, and I want her to rest. I'll tell her when she gets up." He reached out and hugged us tightly. "Tell Wesley and Suzanne I'm really, really sorry. I know Melinda will be, too." He looked back at the bedrooms again and shook his head. "Let me know what I can do."

"Can you call the relatives for me?"

"I sure can; I'll wait a bit until I think they are up, and I'll let both sides know."

We left. The box around my heart continued to grow to a hideous, punishing size; I was sure my chest was about to split open. We decided to stop to tell our parents as well before we left town to drive to Wesley and Suzanne's home. It didn't seem right to call them on the phone with our devastating news.

First, we drove to Mom's home. I knocked softly on the door before we walked in. Mom, still in her nightgown and bathrobe, stood in the kitchen. She looked surprised as our trio walked in.

"What's going on?"

I hurried to her. "Mom, Jack died early this morning. We're heading down now, but we wanted to tell you in person."

She embraced me. "I'm so sorry. I'm so, so sorry."

Her hug absorbed a bit of the crushing feeling I had in my chest.

It doesn't matter how old I get; Mom's hugs help me know I can do this. I can do this.

We stayed for a few minutes, left, and then went to Roy's parents' home. Claudia, Roy's mom, reacted calmly, but with compassion. It shouldn't have surprised me, but it did. My mother-in-law possessed incredible strength visible to me more times than I could count. We hugged, and then we left for Wesley's home.

As Roy drove, I called a few friends on my cell phone.

"Please share this with the rest of our friends," I asked at the end of each call. I spoke with more stability than I felt. Each person assured me of their prayers. When the last of the calls were made, our car fell silent as the mile markers ticked off.

Stay close to the shore when things get hard. Stay close to the shore when things get hard. Words from the devotional I had read yesterday reverberated in my head. They were the words of comfort and direction that I desperately needed today.

Is that why the Holy Spirit wouldn't allow me to skip my reading yesterday morning? You had me in the palm of your hand; you knew what I would face. Thank you, Lord.

With that reminder and prayer, I knew I was not alone in this journey. Humility mingled with my pain. There were billions of people in this world, and still God had given me reassurance to cling to just before I faced a dark, excruciating loss in my life.

I stared out the window at the fields that whizzed by, afraid to see the pain in either Roy or Amber. Instead, I sought guidance from the Lord. *If I were to help my family be strong today, to feel God's love, I needed to be taught first.*

Oh, God, I don't know what to say to them. Please give me the words when we see Wesley and Suzanne. Oh, God, I know how I hurt—I can't even fathom their agony. This is wrong—it feels so wrong.

New thoughts rushed in, memories and images that both hurt and strengthened me.

They rose to every challenge that came with Jack. They proved their ability as the parents he needed. So why did he have to die? Lord, why did he have to die?

I continued to pray silently until a new, totally alarming thought crowded out my prayer.

How will Amber react? She's off her meds. Will this be a trigger for a relapse? Oh, God, don't let her go back there. Protect her. Protect us all.

We arrived at our painful destination. Our trio rushed into the house. Suzanne, Wesley, and Carrie, Suzanne's best friend, sat mutely in the front room with tear-streaked faces and hollow eyes. Silence hung in the air, an oppressive fog of sorrow. A desolate, empty space glared at me where Jack's Pack-n-Play usually sat. The shock of the naked spot in the room pierced me as it screamed, *He's gone!* I wrapped my arms around Wesley; next I went to Suzanne, and, finally, Carrie. I wiped my eyes and nose before I spoke, just above a whisper.

"I'm so, so sorry."

They each nodded. No one spoke. We all digested our grief in our private world of disbelief. Words were inadequate, but I longed to comfort my son and daughter-in-law.

How does heaven react to an infant's death?

"I think there are two types of tears in heaven today," I said softly.

Five heads slowly lifted, and five pairs of red, puffy eyes focused on me.

"Some of them are tears of joy because Jack's pain no longer exists for him and he came home to Jesus." I inhaled before I continued, before I said the hardest words. "But there are tears of sorrow as heaven sees our agony at having to say goodbye to him."

No one responded; we each turned back and stared at the floor in commingled agony.

Over the next few days, we shifted into autopilot. Our grieving group made funeral and burial arrangements together. As we sat with the parish priest to pick the readings and songs for the church service, Wesley turned to Roy.

"I'm going to be a pallbearer, and I want you, Mitchell, and Clinton to be pallbearers with me. Dad, will you help?"

My heart jolted. I scanned the room for other reactions. No one said a word. I saw a flash of pain in Roy's eyes.

Wesley asked again. "I'm going to carry my son into the church. Will you join me, Dad?"

"It would be an honor," Roy said.

I wanted to burst into tears but locked my eyes on the table before I looked up at Roy and Wesley.

Where did my menfolk get their strength?

Amber's voice broke the silence. "May I be the lector at the Mass?" she asked.

Wesley turned and looked at her. "You want to?"

"Yes, I've lectured lots of times before. I'd like to do this for you."

"Are you sure, Amber? The church will be full of family and friends. You don't think it will be too stressful for you?" I said.

She shook her head. "I can do this. I want to do this. Will you let me?"

Wesley glanced at me.

Apprehension filled my being, but a small, calming voice settled my mind. *Let her do it. She wants to do this for her brother. Let her go. Just let her go. I'm with her.*

I let the words seep in as I sat quietly, gave him a weak smile, and nodded.

"I would like to be a Eucharistic minister," I said. This time, I was the object of scrutiny.

"Are you sure you can do this?" Roy asked.

I tilted my chin down slightly then raised it up to look at him.

"Yes, I can, and I want to."

"Me, too. Put me down, too," Roy said.

Our family would surround Wesley and Suzanne as we each took an active role in the funeral Mass. We would say goodbye to our cherished Jack together.

The day of the visitation arrived. We stood in line for hours as family and friends offered condolences and prayers. As the multitudes filed by, I saw a reaction that I didn't expect: the profound sorrow from women who had also lost a child or grandchild. Their wounds, once scabbed over by the passage of time, ripped open, and the deeply buried anguish escaped as they reached out to me to offer sympathy. It didn't matter if their loss occurred months or decades earlier; their raw emotions resurfaced that night.

Concern for Amber's condition hovered just below my own tormented spirit, concern for how she was handling the stress. Many times, I stopped to scan the gathered crowd to find her. I usually spotted her as she stood with her cousins and friends who came. I felt a little more at ease, but not completely. I couldn't guess how she would react during Mass while off her meds. Would standing in front of everyone be too stressful for her?

The following morning, we gathered at the church an hour before the service. I had managed to control most of my emotions up until now, but couldn't hold it together any longer. I burst into tears each time new people arrived. People, tears, hugs, prayers, and more tears all blended together in one big mess. But one experience carved a memorable notch in my misery.

A distinguished gentleman strode through the crowd. I noticed him in his pristine suit, tie, and wool overcoat. He looked familiar, but I couldn't remember why. As I stood next to Wesley, he leaned over to me and whispered, "That's Jack's doctor."

I had met Dr. Beckett only once at Jack's heart surgery when he talked with us, dressed in green scrubs, so it was no wonder that I didn't recognize him. Dr. Beckett stopped to offer his sympathy to Wesley and Suzanne. Then he stepped over and stopped beside the miniature white casket. He bent his head, buried his chin in his chest, covered his eyes with one hand, and wept. I lost it. His distress as he shared our desolation burned an image in my mind. It gave me an insight into the pain that accompanies the role of healthcare professionals.

Over the course of the day, our family and friends rushed to our side to stand beside us in our bereavement, just as they did when I shared the news of Amber's illness and asked for their prayers. One family member drove six hours one way for the funeral and back home that day. Her generous gift of time let me know how much she cared.

But even though hundreds of people gathered around me during Jack's services, one person's absence left a gaping hole: Melinda's. She endured a cancer treatment the day before Jack's death. Often, the treatment forced her to stay in the hospital, and this time, fate had no mercy. She lay in a hospital several hours away, all alone, while the rest of us held on to each other. My heart broke for her. *Please, God, be with Melinda so far away. Keep her safe and help her heal.*

The only reprieve from my anguish came during the funeral Mass. I watched Amber walk with confidence to the altar, read the selected Bible verses with clarity, and return to her seat. Feelings of pride and hopefulness melded together.

She did it. Maybe she doesn't need medicine any more. Maybe . . .

The rest of the Mass and the funeral brought mingled peace and fresh grief. As we processed to the cemetery, I noticed a postal worker, with his pushcart of mail, stop. He stood at attention with his hand over his heart as we drove by. The sight brought a fresh batch of tears as I saw the respect he showed us. He couldn't have known we grieved for our precious Jack; he just showed respect.

Amber and Roy returned home after Jack's funeral. She needed to go to class the next day, and Roy needed to continue with the fall harvest. But I stayed for a few extra days offering whatever comfort I could, physically, emotionally, and spiritually.

Once home, I returned to our family's newest version of normal: Melinda continued with the cancer treatments, Amber continued with classes for her LPN degree, and I returned to my embroidery business again. But there was a taste of grief coating everything I did. Carter and Madelyn came most days, which helped me keep my mind off the pain.

The grief box in my chest, once again a constant companion, had returned with a vengeance. It squeezed my heart so hard some days I questioned if I should call a doctor. The pressure, the box in my chest, stayed with me all day. Sometimes, I stopped, leaned on a piece of furniture, and rested until it subsided.

Up to this time in my life, I had never truly understood the physical pain that accompanied profound grief. The phrase "a broken heart" took on a new meaning for me. I knew it broke on October 21, but no doctor could reset it to heal. I had pain—only pain—unrelenting physical pain.

For the past few months, when I'd been consistent, my daily prayers included pleas for my family's health, wisdom for myself, and a healing environment for our home. I'd prayed, *Dear Lord, please help Amber to understand her illness. Heal Melinda and Jack. Help Wesley and Suzanne with each new challenge.* Now, I added a new request to my list each day. *Please send a new life to Wesley and Suzanne. Their sorrow is too great. I know a new baby will never take Jack's place, but, Lord, could it lessen their grief? If so, please grant this plea. Please give them a new child soon. I ask this in Jesus's name. Thy will be done. Amen.*

A cloud of sadness hovered over me as I got ready for our Christmas celebration. Yes, I rejoiced in the reason we celebrated—the birth of Christ. I was glad to know my children would gather around me. I forced myself to write and send the annual Christmas letter. I also included a photo we had taken in our basement in early September. Roy held Madelyn, I held Jack, and Carter sat between us—a perfect picture of two proud grandparents and their grandchildren. I anguished over sending it. I worried that people would think I was morbid, sending a photo of someone after their death.

In the end, though, I decided to celebrate Jack, even if we only held him in our arms for five months and twenty-seven days. I knew I would treasure him in my heart forever. Most people on my card list never got to meet him, and sending this photo acknowledged him and his gaping absence. Reactions of those who received the card and called to express gratitude let me know I made the right decision.

But I couldn't dismiss my concerns about Wesley and Suzanne. It had been only two months since we'd lost Jack. I worried that coming to celebrate with us would be too painful for them; that Madelyn, only a day older than Jack, would serve as a constant reminder of their loss.

The day of our celebration arrived. Grief joined our gathering, uninvited. But joy managed to sneak in the door as well. After our Christmas dinner and gift exchange, Suzanne approached me and guided me into my laundry room. She leaned in before she whispered, "I'm pregnant. We're not telling anyone until I've passed the first trimester. But I wanted you to know."

She wiped a tear away before it reached her smile. In her eyes, I saw a jumble of emotions: hope for the new life she carried, sorrow from Jack's death, and a heaping dose of uncertainty. But mostly, I saw hope. I saw hope.

I hugged her tightly as I thanked God for another answered prayer.

chapter twenty-six

One morning in late December, our nephew Christopher called Roy with an invitation.

"Christopher said they had a couple back out of the company trip to the Panama Canal," Roy told me over lunch. "They paid the deposit, so we'd only have to pay the balance. It's a half-price trip for us," he said.

"When is it?"

"The end of January. Christopher said he'd like to see us come along. He said, 'You've been through a lot in your family. Paula and I want you to get a relaxing break.'"

"When is it again?"

"The end of January."

After discussion and looking at schedules, we decided to take the opportunity. "I've always wanted to see the Panama Canal," Roy commented, his face beaming as his eyes twinkled.

I haven't seen him this excited since before Amber became ill. It's good to see him excited again.

January 2007

A few weeks later, we left the cold, snowy Iowa weather to spend time in the warm, sunny weather in Panama. We went with Roy's parents, his brother and his wife, Christopher, Paula, and Roy's cousin and his wife.

We enjoyed the boat trip through the canal, and we absorbed the information in the attached museum.

During a dip in the pool, Paula and I discussed the fact we didn't have a bathtub in our rooms, only a shower.

"You can get a bath here in the spa," Paula said as she reminded me the resort had baths, massages, and various other luxuries available for guests.

"I saw the brochure in our room. It looks expensive," I said. My frugal spirit traveled with me everywhere I went.

"I'm signing up," Paula said. "It's okay with Christopher. He encouraged me to have one."

"I'll think about it."

"Do it," Christopher interrupted as he waded up to us, splashing water towards us as he came. "It's my treat."

"No, it's too much. I can't let you pay for me. You helped us take this trip," I answered without hesitation.

"I insist. You've had a rough two years. I want to do this for you. Let it be my treat."

Humbled by his generosity, I agreed.

Paula and I went to sign up. She added the optional full body massage before her hot chocolate bath. I read the description and it sounded intriguing, but when I saw the price, I hesitated to add one to my cappuccino bath.

"Add a massage for her to my room tab, please," Paula said to the receptionist, seeing my hesitation. She turned to me. "Christopher told me to add it for you before we left."

"It's too much. You paid for my bath already."

"Please, let us do this for you. We want to—really. Please?"

I felt a lump rise in the throat. I swallowed hard and blinked back my tears of gratitude.

"You guys are so kind," I said softly. "I didn't expect this."

"I know, but you deserve this."

I turned to Paula. "I appreciate this. I really do."

My first-ever massage and luxury bath did not disappoint. I totally relaxed as the bronze-skinned, beautiful young woman massaged my weary muscles, packed me in warm mud, and let the treatment soften my skin. She left the room as I rested in the darkened room while soft music played. She returned and showed me a robe hanging next to the shower with instructions to wash off the mud. Then she allowed me a generous amount of time for my refreshing shower before she led me to the bathhouse. I slipped off the fluffy white terrycloth robe before I stepped into the deep, dark liquid swirling in a porcelain tub. The aroma of hot milk and coffee surrounded me. I glanced to my right and saw a silver tray with silver coffee pot. Next to that, I saw a white china cup on a matching saucer.

"I've provided you a pot of cappuccino for you to enjoy while you bathe. Let me know if you need more," the masseuse said as she arranged towels for me on the bamboo table next to the tub.

I forgot my troubles as I soaked in the steaming, bubbling water. When I finished, the masseuse returned and gave me warm lotion. I rang my fingers lightly down my forearm.

I don't ever remember my skin feeling this soft.

The sensation of silky, smooth skin stayed with me for weeks, but the cherished feeling I received from Christopher and Paula took root, deep in an untouchable part of me. I returned home refreshed and renewed.

Months passed after Jack's death with no signs of Amber's illness coming back. She continued her studies for the LPN course, joined her friends for weekly Bible study, and attended services on Sunday morning. I began to hope that the doctor made a mistake with diagnosis in 2005 and she didn't have schizophrenia, that maybe it was in fact depression, as she had originally been diagnosed.

March 2007

Roy, Amber, and I decided to fly to North Carolina to see Clinton during Amber's spring break. Getting ready for our trip kept my mind occupied, and it seemed as if the grief, though still sharp, was starting to shift back out of every moment.

Clinton met us at the airport, dressed as a bum just to make us laugh. The last time Roy and I flew to Raleigh, he met us wearing a suit and a top hat. He had looked like a driver for a celebrity. This time, he swung the pendulum in the opposite direction, looking scruffy and destitute. I never knew what to expect with his keen sense of humor.

It's gonna be a great week; I can just tell.

We spent the first few days exploring the area, enjoying a round of disc golf, and visiting historical landmarks.

Midweek, after a day of sightseeing, we chose a local restaurant for our evening meal and piled into Clinton's car for the short drive. As we drove, Amber hijacked the conversation in the car.

"I checked my bank statement online last night and discovered Natalie from Bible study messed with my account. I called the bank just before we left."

"What? How'd ya know that?" I said.

"Well, do you remember when we went to Chicago a few weekends ago?"

"Yeah, I remember. Wasn't there a carload of you that went together?"

"Yeah," Amber agreed. "Well, Natalie went along, and we met her friend in Chicago. Her friend works at a bank, and I think the two of them are trying to get me in trouble."

My heart sank. "That's a pretty strong accusation, Amber. Do you have proof?" *Stay calm. Stay calm.* "You need evidence before you call a bank, don't you think?"

"Mom, I just know. I could tell. And I already called the bank before we left."

Roy stared at the road ahead while Clinton and I exchanged glances. No one said a word.

"I also found out in Chicago that Sean likes me," Amber continued.

I knew Sean from her Bible study, having met him on several occasions. He seemed to be a nice guy, quiet and polite.

"Oh?" I said. "Did he ask you out?"

"No, I saw it in his eyes. The way he looked at me, I could tell," she continued. "When we get back, I'm gonna talk to him and see how he wants to go ahead with our relationship."

"Are you sure he's interested?" I asked.

"I could tell, Mom. I could just tell!" she yelled.

I swallowed the words fighting to escape.

Amber continued. "And I also found out Dawn messed with my bank account, too."

This is not okay. This sounds too similar. I'm sure her cousin, Dawn, hasn't done anything to hurt Amber.

I rolled down the window and stared at the scenery as the air rushed into my face, too afraid to look at anyone in the car. My carefree enjoyment of my trip blew out the open window as we drove the stretch of road.

Oh, God, not here. Not now. Not on our vacation. We can't do anything about it here. Why now?

My heart leapt into my throat with the feeling of an impending explosion. My relentless grief box reminded me of its never-ending presence as my stomach twisted and churned and my chest compressed as if to hold my heart in place.

Clinton broke in and quickly changed the subject. "So, did I tell you about my roommate's band?"

Amber's rant ended in the face of Clinton's anecdotes. We pulled up to the restaurant, went in, and found our table. Without a word, Amber headed quickly to the bathroom. I jumped up from my chair to follow her, fearing the worst and not wanting to let her out of my sight. Once we stepped into the ladies' room, she resumed spewing venom about her friends and cousins. *Oh, God, I can't say anything here. I have to wait until we get back home.*

My chest filled with pressure. I dreaded the remaining days of our trip, the flight home, and the confrontation I knew awaited me there.

God, I know it's back. Help me through the next few days. And I really need your words when I tell Amber she needs to go back on her medicine. I closed my eyes. *Be with us, Lord. We are in trouble, again.*

For the next few days, we all stayed close to Clinton's apartment, using the excuse that we needed to rest. We watched a few movies while Clinton worked on his studies. At night, I barely slept. I kept one eye on Amber and one eye on the clock as the hands moved in slow motion around the face, ticking off time until our flight home.

The day of our departure arrived; Clinton drove us to the airport. He hugged each of us goodbye with the assurance he would be home in August. As he embraced me, he whispered, "I'm here if you need to talk. Just call."

We flew home without incident, arriving in the evening. I didn't say anything to Amber right away. It didn't make sense to set her off just before bed. But I had a hard time concentrating on anything the next morning while I waited for her to get up. I did laundry, which felt like a mindless task. I knew I could handle that but not much else.

Finally, she emerged from her room. I stood in the kitchen. I don't remember what my hands were doing, but I still recall the feeling of dread that enveloped me.

"Good morning, Amber. How'd you sleep?" I said. I willed my voice not to show my anxiety.

"Good morning, Mom. I slept alright," she answered. She came and stood next to me. "Mom, will you call the doctor this morning for me? I'm pretty sure the delusions are back."

I felt like I was about to burst with joy. The yoke of worry I had carried the past few days disintegrated. With that burden lifted, my prayer of thanksgiving ascended heavenward as I turned to face Amber. *Oh my God, thank you. Thank you. I didn't have to tell her.*

Amber continued. "I got to thinking last night after we got home. Natalie wouldn't do anything to hurt me. She's too good of a friend."

I turned and focused my eyes on her.

"I thought about it a lot and decided she wouldn't. Then I wondered if I was wrong about Sean liking me. So I called him after you went to bed last night."

"You did?"

"Mom, he is a true friend. He reacted so lovingly and with compassion. We talked for a long time. He helped me sort things out."

I took a step closer to Amber, reached out, and drew her into my arms. "I'm so proud of you. What a brave thing to do."

"Thanks. He pointed out lots of things until I realized I am imagining things again. Mom, it's back."

I pulled away from her and looked into her eyes. The relief was so great, I almost started to cry.

"I need to get back on the meds. Call the doctor and tell her. Will you?" she said. "Right away? Today? I don't want this to go on."

Thank you, God. Thank you.

"Amber, I am so proud of you. You continue to amaze me. This morning, I planned to tell you I noticed things on our trip. I dreaded telling you I thought you needed your medication," I said gently. "I'm so grateful you came to that conclusion yourself."

"Sean helped me realize it. We talked a long time last night."

"Thank God, then, for Sean."

Amber nodded before she turned back toward her room. "I'm gonna take a shower. Will you call the doctor?"

I went to the phone and dialed the number of the psychiatry clinic. I

asked for her doctor and explained the situation. She promised to phone
a new prescription to our local pharmacy. Later, I called Clinton and told
him. I heard a long, slow sigh from him.

"That's great news, Mom. Great news."

I made a quick trip to town, picked up the prescription, and headed
home. Amber waited for me and she took the pills as soon as I walked in
the door.

"I'll never be able to go without medicine again," Amber said. "My
body needs it if I want to be healthy."

Within a few hours, Amber was back on the antipsychotic, the medicine that would help combat her delusions. I knew it would take some
time to take effect, but she wanted to be on it. A prayer I had asked others
to pray so many months earlier—that Amber would understand her need
to be on medicine—had been answered. And I had my peace.

A new feeling filled my chest, different from the grief box: a feeling of
gratitude. *God, you promised never to leave us or forsake us. I know you
are here with us in our mess. Thank you for everything.*

"Amber?" I said later that day as I slid in a chair near her in the front
room.

"Yeah?"

"Do you think you can resume classes?"

"I'm going to try. I don't want to fall behind."

Spring Break ended, and the following Monday, Amber resumed her
nursing classes. I returned to my business, caring for Madelyn and Carter,
and managing our household.

Her paranoia and delusions gradually went dormant again with the
medication. Melinda finished her cancer treatments, and our family
looked forward to the new life Suzanne carried. God taught me to hope
and fortified me once more. With a renewed spirit, prayers of gratitude
became part of my daily devotion.

chapter twenty-seven

Summer 2007

Amber continued her schooling for nursing. She had a small setback when she fell down a few steps at school. She managed to hobble to her next class, but the pain and swelling in her ankle prevented her from concentrating on the instructor. Afterward, she hopped on one foot to her car and dialed me on her cell phone.

"Mom, I fell down the steps and I hurt my ankle," she spoke calmly.

"Can you drive home?"

"I don't think so. It's pretty painful and swollen to about twice its normal size."

"I'm on my way," I exclaimed as I slipped on a jacket, grabbed my purse, and headed out the door.

I drove quickly, but within the speed limits, to the school and found her sitting quietly in her car. A quick look told me she needed medical attention. Her ankle resembled an overstuffed sausage with black and purple color spreading in all directions.

Because her health insurance was paid by social services, our only options for her meant a drive to Iowa City or Des Moines. We chose Iowa City. I knew they already had access to her records. The emergency staff there took great care of her, and within a few hours, she sported a neon-purple-and-pink cast. In spite of a broken ankle, she cheerfully continued to go to her classes as scheduled.

We scheduled her follow-up appointment for her ankle to coincide with her regular meetings with the psychiatrist. On August 22, while sitting in the waiting room, I received a phone call from Wesley.

"Our little girl arrived today, Mom!" His voice was filled with pride and happiness, so similar to the tone I'd heard when he'd told me of Jack's delivery. "She's beautiful."

"Oh, my goodness! That is such wonderful news. I'm so happy for you." I think I probably squealed into the phone, as excited as a small child on Christmas morning. I turned to Amber.

"You have a new niece."

"Can we go see her as soon as we're finished?" she asked, her thoughts echoing my own.

"Wesley, we'll be there in a few hours. Both Amber and I can't wait to meet her." I grinned at Amber, who beamed. "Have you named her yet? How big was she? How's Suzanne?" Question after question spilled out.

Wesley's laughter resonated over the phone line. "Her name is Ella, Suzanne's doing great, and Ella was over eight pounds. Just come see her for yourself."

"Are you gonna let Dad know or should I?"

"I'll call him myself," Wesley said. "And I want to call Mitchell and Clinton, too."

"Okay, I'll let you take care of letting the rest of the gang know, and we'll see you later today."

The hour and forty minutes on Interstate 80 seemed to take forever. Once we pulled in the parking lot of the hospital, I couldn't get to Suzanne's room quick enough. We hurried through the parking lot and hospital lobby. I had to consciously slow my progress and knocked softly on her door before Amber and I padded in.

Roy sat holding Ella with an "I beat you here" smirk on his face. I raised my eyebrows at him, totally surprised.

"Remember I had a meeting in Ames today? I came straight here after Wes called," he said as he winked at Amber.

I rushed to them to snatch Ella, and he reluctantly transferred her to my arms. I admired Ella's porcelain skin, with a hint of rose on her round cheeks, and her tufts of auburn hair that circled her round face. She had Roy's coloring. Her hair was the exact color as his in younger years.

"She's so beautiful. She's just perfect," I gushed as I beamed at Wesley and Suzanne.

"Isn't she the most beautiful baby in the world?" Wesley and Suzanne chimed in together. I sat back and basked in their excitement as I studied this tiny member of our family. She had a sweet, innocent smell as she opened her eyes and gazed at mine.

Amber held out her arms. "Do I get a turn?"

I stood, leaned over Amber seated in a chair, and placed Ella in her outstretched arms. Amber's face radiated joy as she gazed at her newborn niece.

Ella let out a wail.

"It's time for her bottle," Suzanne suggested.

Wesley reached out to Amber, took Ella, and snuggled her before he nudged her cheek with the bottle nipple. Ella's tiny mouth opened like a little bird as she turned to the nipple and latched on.

"Look at her go after her bottle," Wesley exclaimed. "Isn't she wonderful?"

"Did you hear her cry? She's so strong already," Suzanne added.

I remembered Jack's soft cries and how drinking a bottle challenged him.

Thank you, God, for another answer to prayer. I see joy once again. I love watching them exclaim over every little thing Ella does. Most parents take these things for granted—drinking a bottle, a healthy cry—but they don't. Thank you for the gift of Ella.

After Ella finished her bottle, Amber held her again. I snapped photo after photo and sat in awe as Amber cradled Ella.

God, we've come a long way. Thank you for never leaving us, for catching me when I stumbled, for showing me your presence. Thank you.

chapter twenty-eight

Earlier in May, Amber had had a hearing with the Social Security Disability Income board. After three denials for benefits, Amber, with the help from Legal Aid and the paralegal, Hannah, had requested the hearing. Now, on September 26, Amber finally received a letter from Social Security. After three denials, her application was approved.

I felt so grateful to Legal Aid and to Mitchell. We followed his suggestion to apply immediately. He prepared us for multiple denials and encouraged us when discouragement held me in a vise. With legal support, Amber finally had the financial support she needed for her living expenses.

We scanned the letter which stated Amber would receive benefits back to the date of application—thirty-two months earlier. With SSDI benefits, Amber now qualified for Medicare. She still battled the symptoms of schizophrenia, but we were all relieved of the burden of financial worry and could focus on moving forward.

During one of Amber's visits to the University of Iowa Psychiatry Clinic, a young man approached her in the waiting area.

"Would you be interested in helping with a study?" he asked.

"What's it about?" she questioned him.

"We're looking for volunteers for a study on schizophrenia. We pay mileage and a small stipend for participants."

Amber shook her head, and he moved on to the next patient. I was sorry to see him leave. The study could have been interesting, and I truly believed that Amber would benefit in the long run from understanding more about her condition.

Several months later, a young woman dressed in a white lab jacket visited with patients in the reception area. I watched her flit from one person to another, clipboard in hand. I knew we'd be next.

She sat next to Amber. "Are you interested in a study?"

"What's it about?"

"I am student involved in research here at the hospital. We are looking for a genetic link in schizophrenia," the attractive young woman explained. "It involves blood draws and an interview."

Amber turned to me. "I'd like to try it. What do ya think, Mom?"

I gave her a nod and a smile. "Studies help doctors find answers. If you want to, I'd say go for it."

Our eyes met briefly before she spoke. "Okay." Amber reached out her hand to the young gal in the white jacket.

The young woman smiled broadly as she handed her the clipboard. "Are your parents available, too?"

"Yes, I would love to be a part of the study," I said. "I think my husband will, too."

Amber signed her name and phone number. With that, her journey into the world of research participation had begun.

After we met with the doctor, stopped at the bookstore, and then stopped for lunch, Amber brought the study up.

"What do you think, Mom?" she asked. "Do you think it's okay for me to do the study?"

"I'm glad you said yes. And I'm glad the parents are part of it."

Her hazel eyes looked into mine. "I don't like what I've been through these last few years. But if I take part in a study and it helps someone down the road benefit, then maybe good can come from my challenges."

Her reaction to research humbled me. I looked at her with amazement. I had watched her struggle for months trying to make sense of what happened to her, yet she still cared about people she would never know. I saw her ambition to help make the world into a better place resurface, something I didn't think I would see again.

Thank you, Lord, for her generous heart and her thoughtfulness. I begged you once for my daughter to come back. This is a part of her I cherished. Thank you for leading her back to herself.

It took several weeks for all the paperwork to get filed. The study accepted Amber, Roy, and I. But by this time, Roy had entered the fall harvest season. During a phone conversation, I let the researchers know we couldn't get away to give a blood sample and complete the interview.

"No worries," the cheerful voice on the other end of the line told me. "We'll come to you."

Within a week, a worker came to our home to draw my blood and take a family history. Because Roy spent most of his time in the combine, he couldn't join us. So we went to him. I drove the kind gentleman to the field and watched him climb into the combine. He wiped Roy's arm with antiseptic, poked him with the syringe, and filled several tubes with blood.

Roy rolled the worn, oil-stained work shirt sleeve back in place and buttoned the cuff as though nothing out of the ordinary had happened. The combine took off across the field with the researcher sitting beside Roy in the cab. The interview continued as the combine chewed the stalks of corn, stripped the kernels from the cob, and deposited them in the combine hopper. The researcher impressed me with his dedication to the project and his willingness to come to us for his research.

As this first study ran its tests, Amber continued to sign up for research studies at the University of Iowa. One study lasted ten years and beyond. The researchers wanted to track long-term outcomes for schizophrenia. She was determined to make a difference. I remembered her words in my mind and heart: "I want to help others. If I can prevent others from going through what I went through, it may help make some sense of all of this."

Her words reminded me of the words I had read in *When Bad Things Happen to Good People*. In it, Kushner stated, "We can redeem these tragedies from senselessness by imposing meaning on them." Amber knew that. It was as if she had also read the book, but I didn't think she had. She just knew. She planned to live with the attitude Kushner suggested:

> "The question we should be asking is not 'Why did this happen to me? What did I do to deserve this?' That is really an unanswerable, pointless question. A better question would be 'Now that this has happened to me, what am I going to do about it?'"[18]

As I saw her embrace the challenge of making a change for the better, my admiration for my daughter grew.

One day in early December, I picked up the latest copy of my NAMI quarterly magazine, *Advocate*. I noticed an article about a nationwide research project. I showed it to Amber. After she read it, she commented, "It looks interesting . . ."

Christmas 2007

Our family gathered a few weeks later to celebrate Christmas. The eleven of us filled the familiar oak table in the dining room: Mitchell, Melinda, Carter, Madelyn, Wesley, Suzanne, Amber, Clinton, Roy, and I. Ella sat in her high chair next to us. My mom and brother joined us as well. We feasted on our traditional dinner of prime rib, twice-baked potatoes, green beans, homemade rolls, and butter. The chatter and good-natured banter throughout the meal made a noisy but delightful commotion. I felt full from my favorite foods but also from the affection that surrounded me. Too stuffed to have room for pumpkin pie, we decided to open gifts and eat dessert later.

We all converged in the family room in the basement. The decorated

Christmas tree, with its branches heavy from my Coca-Cola ornament collection, sat in the corner with piles of brightly wrapped packages spilling from beneath. My treasured coordinating Christmas village was assembled on the table along the wall.

All my loved ones settled down, filling every seat from the black leather chairs to the old van seats I tried to pass off as authentic chairs scattered around the room. The electricity of excitement lit the room from corner to corner. I looked around the room; pride and affection filled me as Carter and Madelyn scampered to the gifts under the tree. Mitchell and Melinda sat near them. Wesley slid next to Suzanne, snuggling with Ella, on the couch. Mom and my brother, Vince, Clinton, Amber, Roy, and I rested comfortably in the recliners and nearby chairs.

I couldn't stop smiling. There was no crisis this December—so different from the past three years: Amber's fears in 2004, Jack's future in 2005, Jack's death and Melinda's cancer last year. *And now this year—Melinda beat cancer, Amber improves more each month, and we have Ella, another answer to prayer. Thank you, God. Our family faced some major battles, and we've made it through. Thank you, God, for my family and their health.*

We took turns opening gifts, beginning with the youngest, Ella. Suzanne held her and the package as Ella's pudgy hands fumbled with the paper. Wesley reached over and gave a loose piece a tug, and Ella took over. Next, Carter and Madelyn squealed as they tore open packages and laughter filled the air. After the boys tossed the last shreds of gift wrap in the garbage, Amber stood up.

"I have a question for you guys," she said to her brothers.

Everyone stopped talking, and nine pairs of eyes turned in Amber's direction.

"There's a study on schizophrenia at the National Institute of Mental Health. They want families to take part. I'd like to do it." She took a breath and looked at each of her three brothers in turn. "Would you consider joining me?"

"Where'd you hear about it? What does it involve?" all her brothers asked simultaneously, as if on cue.

"It means a trip to Washington, DC. And I read about it in a magazine." She held a copy of *Advocate*, along with three sets of papers. "I printed out all the information. I knew you'd want to know about it before you'd give me an answer." She handed the stacks of papers to her brothers.

Silence filled the room as Melinda and Suzanne leaned over Mitchell and Wesley's shoulders and read along. Amber returned to her spot in a chair and chewed on her fingernails as she watched her brothers and their wives.

"Yup. Yes. Absolutely," Mitchell, Wesley, and Clinton responded.

Amber's hands came out of her mouth as her shoulders relaxed. "Thanks! You guys are the best." She stood up, walked to each of them, and threw her arms around them. Mitchell pretended to back away, his reaction back to the one he typically uses, but she caught him. They both laughed as she grabbed him and squeezed. It did my heart good to see the playful interaction between them return as if Amber had never been sick.

"What about our wives?" Mitchell asked, glancing at Wesley.

"I wouldn't be able to go," Melinda spoke up. "A fast trip with two kids under the age of four doesn't sound like a fun time."

Suzanne chimed in. "Not with a baby; I'll stay home." But each of my daughters-in-law urged their husbands to go; they'd be fine.

And I knew they would be; they had both demonstrated their inner strength over the past two years.

My boys married understanding women. Thank you, God.

The boys grabbed pens and filled out the application forms included in the pack of papers Amber had given them. As they finished, each handed their papers back to her. The following Monday, she slipped the manila envelope, addressed to the study, in the mailbox.

Within a week, Amber received a phone call with her acceptance notification from the National Institute of Mental Health (NIMH). It took a bit of schedule shuffling and telephone calls between siblings and NIMH before everyone's plans fit together for July, like pieces of a large puzzle.

The study, held in Bethesda, Maryland, involved spending two days testing two siblings at a time. The study paid for travel and lodging for the four siblings, but Roy and I only needed to give blood samples. We could have them drawn at a local hospital, which would send them to NIMH.

Roy and I discussed the possibility of a family trip. Our last trip together took place in 1993. "It's a great chance to spend some time together. Let's drive to Washington, DC, and meet with the kids. We can sightsee in the evening after we finish each day," he said.

"Let's go for it."

A nurse from the NIMH called to schedule them for testing. I took the call.

"Is it possible to schedule two of them for Thursday and Friday and the other two for Monday and Tuesday?" I asked. "My husband and I plan to join them. We'd like to spend time, the six of us, together in Washington, D.C."

"You understand we don't pay for your transportation or motel, don't you?"

"Oh, yes. We plan to pay for our own transportation and room. But we'd like to plan on having our blood drawn there instead of at a local hospital."

"We are excited to have an entire family unit for this study. Let me see what I can do to help you out."

A few days later, she called again.

"I've worked out the details to make it work for your family. We have your family's testing scheduled for mid-July. I've scheduled Mitchell and Clinton for Thursday and Friday. The following Monday and Tuesday, we'll test Amber and Wesley. I've made arrangements for their motel rooms."

"Fantastic," I said. "I appreciate your time and effort."

She continued. "I reserved one room for Mitchell and Clinton for Wednesday, Thursday, and Friday nights. Reservations for Amber and Wesley are for Saturday, Sunday, and Monday. They can check out Tuesday morning, and I'll schedule their flight home for Tuesday evening, after the testing is complete. Can your family share two rooms on Saturday night? Can you make this work?"

"We sure can," I exclaimed. "The boys can share one room and Amber can share ours. Do you need us to pay for the rooms on Saturday? What about their return flights home?"

"Mitchell and Clinton fly home on Sunday evening; Amber and Wesley's flights are Tuesday, after their testing is over. And no, don't worry about the cost of Saturday night."

"That's perfect. I really appreciate this."

"It's our pleasure. We appreciate having all four siblings and both parents."

It seemed like only a few days later when Melinda received bad news during a routine check-up. Her cancer had returned. She and Mitchell made a trip to the Mayo Clinic for a consultation. Doctors decided on six weeks of radiation. She would live in Rochester during the week, receive a treatment each day, and return home for the weekend. Melinda's treatments began in early February. They coincided with the beginning of Lent and would last through entire the Lenten season.

What a way to focus on sacrifice for these six weeks, enduring radiation away from your family. God, see her sacrifice and heal her, please.

As the treatments started, Carter and Madelyn spent extra time with us while Mitchell juggled his practice, his children, and his wife's health. Carter made me laugh one day as he counted his overnight visits.

"Ten days overnight at Grammie and Papa's," he exclaimed as he bounced up and down.

I felt grateful they looked at overnight stays as a treat, not as time away from their mommy.

We all waited patiently for the results of Melinda's treatments. Amber continued with nursing school, Bible study, and socializing with her friends. Roy planted the crops in the spring, as he had every year since he was a young man still at home with his parents. Life went on.

Summer 2008

In early July, Roy and I left early for the study at the National Institute of Mental Health, planning to make it a two-week trip. We drove north through Michigan to Canada and on to Niagara Falls. Though Roy had visited there as a young teenager, he had forgotten much of the trip. We became like teenagers as we explored the area. We laughed as the spray from the falls drenched us on the boat. Standing under a section in the yellow cellophane rain ponchos, we laughed as we caught our breath.

"I never knew paying money to get sprayed with cold water would be so fun," I giggled during one of the excursions.

From Niagara Falls, we traveled to Maine and spent a few days with Roy's brother and his family, and then to Boston, and then to Cape Cod for visit with a cousin of mine. We finally landed in Washington, DC, just ahead of Mitchell and Clinton.

The following morning, the four of us navigated our way on the Metro and arrived at the National Institute of Mental Health. The staff whisked the boys off to the first test and escorted Roy and I into an office. An efficient nurse met with us.

"I'd like to ask you some questions for a family history. Typically, we mail this form to the parents, but this is so much better to have you here with us. We rarely get a complete family for this study." She smiled warmly and picked up her pen. "Shall we begin? Since it's so many questions, we'll do half of them today and finish tomorrow, if that works for you?"

"Sure."

After an hour or so of asking and answering questions, she stopped and looked at me. "Your family endured so much in the past few years.

Your story is amazing. You should write a book."

Her comment startled me. "What?"

"You should write your family's journey in a book. You could help others understand that a family can face crisis after crisis and come out okay on the other side."

I dismissed her idea but felt pleased with her comment. *That's an odd thing to say. Me, write a book?*

As we left her office, I saw Clinton and Mitchell in the waiting area. I heard their laughter before I entered the room.

"What's so funny?"

"Oh, we had the staff laughing just a minute ago. After Clinton came out of his MRI, I commented to the staff, 'I'll bet you've never seen such low blood flow to the brain before,'" Mitchell said with a grin.

"And I fired back, 'Wait until they see yours, brother,'" Clinton retorted with a smirk.

"The staff member roared before he said, 'I've never heard trash talk at an MRI before.'"

"Leave it to you two to cause a ruckus in the hospital," Roy chimed in.

A staff member called the boys for another round of tests, so Roy and I left for a day of sightseeing. Once the study ended for the day, we met the boys back at the motel. The following morning, we went for the rest of the interview for our family history and they disappeared for their part in the study.

When we finished, the same young nurse closed the file before she repeated her words from the day before. "You really should consider writing a book. Will you give it some thought?"

"Okay, I'll think about it," I said as Roy and I left.

We spent the second day exploring our nation's capital before the boys joined us in the evening. On Saturday morning, Wesley and Amber arrived at the motel. We all took the Metro for a day of sightseeing. Amber tired quickly but did her best to keep up.

"I don't want to hold anyone back," she whispered to me.

"We can go back if you need to," I answered.

"No, I want to be with everyone."

I kept a close eye on her stress level for the rest of the day, making sure we took breaks for her to rest. She went to bed early after we returned to the motel, but the boys and Roy went to a local pub. On Sunday, we found the National Cathedral, attended a service, and then made our way to the Holocaust museum.

I wanted to spend the entire day there, but after an hour or so, Amber came to me.

"I need to leave. Can we leave?"

"Is this too stressful for you?"

She nodded. "It bothers me to see the displays. Can we just leave?"

I told Roy, and Amber and I went outside. Roy, Mitchell, Wesley, and Clinton stayed until Mitchell and Clinton needed to catch their flights home. After Mitchell and Clinton left, Roy, Amber, Wesley, and I relaxed in the motel for the evening.

In the morning, after accompanying Wesley and Amber to the hospital, Roy and I spent the day visiting other monuments (there were lots to see in DC). On Tuesday morning, after breakfast, we said goodbye to them. They planned to go directly to the airport from the hospital, and we knew we wouldn't see them all day.

"We'll see you at home. Safe travels, and I hope the day goes well for you," I said as I hugged them.

We left the DC area and drove toward Ohio, where we planned to attend a trade show for my business. As we made our way from booth to booth, I visited with the vendors. One woman went beyond the customary business chatter, and I found myself sharing my personal story about Amber, Melinda, and Jack. She listened intently, as if we stood alone in a quiet room.

"You should write a book," she said, looking me in the eyes.

"What?"

"You should write a book. People need to hear your story," she repeated.

Two times in less than a week, a stranger suggested I write a book. How odd.

The thought didn't really stick—I couldn't write a book. I'm not a writer—but I was flattered nonetheless. We finished our trip, settled back in at home, and submerged ourselves in our day-to-day routines: Amber studied, Roy farmed, and I embroidered and cared for Carter and Madelyn.

Amber continued to live with us but by now had moved to the basement space once used as bedrooms for the boys. She joked that she lived in our halfway house. Every time she mentioned it, I smiled—though not far from us, it gave her a feeling of some renewed independence.

Melinda received a clean bill of health after her treatments finished; Mitchell kept busier than ever expanding his business. Wesley and Suzanne doted on Ella and worked hard. Clinton focused on his studies for his master's degree as he worked full time at an advertising agency. And Amber continued to study and grow and heal.

One day, when Amber returned home from class, she was excited about a notice she had read on the bulletin board at school:

"Mom, there's an ad for a helper for a shut-in woman. It said Certified Nursing Certificate a plus but not required."

Amber applied, and soon she scheduled an interview. The disabled woman hired Amber immediately. Amber helped her several days after school, fetching groceries and needed supplies.

"She's lonely, Mom," Amber remarked one evening. "And so needy. I'm feeling stressed when I'm there. I'm not sure I'm qualified or even doing her any good."

She continued to work for her, despite her reservations. But as time wore on, school, studies, and a job became harder and harder for her. She cut back on the hours she took each semester, but her fatigue and stress hung on like two stubborn dogs fighting over a bone. These two symptoms from the nasty brain disorder, schizophrenia, refused to let go of my motivated daughter, despite how determined she was to resume a life similar to that of other young women.

We continued to meet with Vocational Rehabilitation services on a regular schedule. Her counselor encouraged her to keep working toward graduation. She had only one more semester to go.

Amber came to me one afternoon after class. Part of the course involved working with the instructor in a hospital setting. I could see by the look in her eyes that her stress level had taken too much of a toll.

"Mom, I'm thinking of not finishing my LPN degree."

"Really? Why? You're so close. It's just a few more classes."

"I get so tired, and I'm afraid I can't do the job correctly once I'm finished," she shared.

"But you're so close to graduation."

"I know, Mom, but when I get so tired, I have a hard time thinking clearly. As a nurse, I would work with sick people."

"Yeah. Go on."

"Mom, I don't want someone's life in my hands. I've realized how I think when I'm tired during our clinical rotations. What if I get too tired and make a mistake? I don't want to risk it."

Her face fell.

"I never thought of that," I said as I thought about her reasoning. "I think I understand what you are saying. You're worried you'll make a mistake that could hurt someone if you feel tired or stressed?"

"Yup, I've thought about it a lot. I'm not going to finish. I don't want to take the chance and risk someone's life."

I couldn't argue with her. I felt proud of her and respected her for the concern she expressed for others. It was a hard decision, and I knew it hurt her to quit, but Amber had grown to understand herself better and was learning what she needed to do to cope. With a doctor's note, she withdrew from the Licensed Practical Nursing degree.

"I'm a failure," she confided to me when it was all done. "I didn't finish, and I let everyone down."

"You are not a failure," I exclaimed. "You tried as hard as you could, and anyone who works hard can never be a failure in my book."

I stopped and let her think about that before I continued.

"Did you do the best you could?"

She nodded.

"That's all God asks of us, you and me both. To do the best we can."

"But what about the money for the classes, the books, and the shoes—everything?"

"Try not to worry about that. I think going back to school was part of your recovery, Amber. It got you up in the morning, it helped you focus, it helped your brain build new connections, and it got you out socially. I think it was money well spent."

"Do you really think so?"

"I do."

The conversation ended, but we revisited it many times. Each time, I did my best to reassure her that money spent on education is never wasted, especially for her recovery. I saw it as a vital part of the equation.

Since she didn't have school anymore, Amber worked several part-time jobs. With each new position, she stretched herself a little further. And in each new job, she surpassed what she had done at the previous one. As she learned to balance the responsibility of employment, continued to keep appointments with Connie, her counselor, and continued seeing doctors at the adult psychiatry clinic in Iowa City, I saw improvement come at a steady rate.

chapter twenty-nine

August 2009

"Mom, a couple of girls from church want to share an apartment. I told them I would move in with them."

"Are you sure you're ready?"

"Mom, don't worry."

"I can't help it. I'm your mom. It's hard not to worry."

Amber rolled her eyes. "I already told them yes."

I swallowed my words and turned back to the sink. There was no point in saying more; all it would do is make her mad. *You've got to let go more. Just let her go.*

I grabbed a potato, scrubbed it, turned it over, and scrubbed it again, all the while asking God to guide us both as we took the first steps on this new, unfamiliar path.

Later that week, I sat at my desk. I kept my eyes focused on the computer screen, my right hand on the mouse. *Click, click, click.* The patterns duplicated the logo as I digitized the design for my customer.

Bang. The back door slammed and the house shook slightly. The sound of rushed footsteps bounced off the walls.

Amber bounded into the room. "We found a great place, Mom. It's brand new and has three bedrooms."

I saved my work and spun around in my office chair. I raised my eyebrows when I saw her eyes dancing with excitement and a broad grin.

"Really?"

Will she be able to handle the problems that come with roommates, God? What happens when she needs downtime and she can't find a quiet place? Can she cope with working and keeping an apartment and still manage her health?

I buried my reservations.

Be supportive. Keep calm. Watch what you say.

"Where's it located? You said it's new? You'll be the first renters?"

"It's near the college. Yes, it's brand new, so we'll be the first people to move in," Amber said. "We looked at it this afternoon. It has a nice big living room, a cute kitchen, a master bedroom with a private bath, and two other bedrooms. Amanda gets the big room with the bath; Alicia and I will take the smaller rooms and share a bathroom."

"Are you okay with that? Why does Amanda get the master suite?"

"Yeah, I'm okay with it, and why isn't important to me," Amber fired back.

"Okay."

Don't say anything. Just let it go. It's a step for her independence, so don't upset her. Keep your negative thoughts to yourself. God, help me to know the right words to say.

"So is the moving day set?"

"September 1," Amber said. She brushed her hair back from her face and smiled at me. "Finally, I get to leave my halfway house. Nothing against you and Dad, but it will feel so good to be in my own apartment." She giggled.

I laughed. "That always makes me laugh when you call home your halfway house. And I bet you're excited. I would be, too, if I were you. It's a big step."

Amber turned and bounded out of my office. I heard the basement door creak open followed by her footsteps thumping down the stairs. I gave my chair a slight spin and turned back to my keyboard. Instead of returning to work, though, my thoughts drifted back to setting up her mini-apartment in our basement.

Years earlier, when all four of the kids still lived at home, we had re-purposed a storage area in the basement into extra bedroom space. My brother built a wall of shelves to divide it in two. The older boys, Mitchell and Wesley, moved their beds and belongings down there and enjoyed their personal space. Amber and Clinton claimed the two main-floor bedrooms near Roy's and mine. It served us well; each teenager in our home claimed a bedroom of their own. When Mitchell moved out for college, Clinton happily moved his things down into the now vacant room. One by one, each of our children grew and moved out of the house for school. By the fall of 2000, our bedroom became the only one used in our home.

When Amber first moved home in late 2004, she used her old bedroom on the main floor. It made me feel secure having her close to Roy and me. As her health improved, the need to be near me lessoned for both of us. So the basement bedroom became a mini-apartment for Amber. She put her bed on one side of the shelving wall and used the other half for a sitting room. A desk sat under the window, and a television, stereo, and VCR sat in the opposite corner. There was an older, overstuffed chair and a small end table. I think it gave her a feeling of making progress toward independence.

Now, in 2009, four years after her diagnosis, Amber regained her independence. She was working full-time, ready to share an apartment with friends, and led a single lifestyle similar to many in her generation.

September came, and we helped her move to her shared apartment. I felt more comfortable about the move because of the pact Amber and I made before she left.

"Amber, your brain can play tricks on you. It can tell you things that are not correct." She nodded. "Your brain disorder is a sneaky one. It can weave back into your thoughts without you even realizing it."

"I know, Mom."

"I think you should have someone you talk with every day, either in person or on the phone. They can help you watch for those subtle changes and alert you if they notice things going the wrong direction."

Amber looked up at me, and I saw her independent nature that I had always loved mingled with her trust in me and a minute dose of uncertainty. "Would you be that person, Mom?" Amber asked. "Can I call you every day, just to chat?"

"I would love that."

Amber moved out, and her road to complete independence began.

Our mother-daughter relationship grew stronger because of our decision. Our phone calls gave me peace of mind. There were several times when Amber confided to me that she needed to talk to her doctor. "Things just don't feel quite right," she'd say and get the help she needed.

I thought back to the three prayers I had asked others to pray for me when Amber first became ill: for the doctors to find the correct medicine to help her; for Amber to understand her illness; and for wisdom and understanding for me. Now, as she shared with me that she went back to the doctor because she didn't feel quite right, I found that the words to express the gratitude in my heart seemed inadequate. In addition, knowing that Amber could recognize for herself that things were changing and could seek out the medical help she needed brought an added measure of reassurance to me. I could release the grip I had clung to for so many years. I knew her growth and awareness came about because we learned to rely on the strength we received from God. I prayed to the Lord, and he answered me. I knew he fortified her, and he fortified me.

Since the fall of 2009, my life has become more like my friends'. Our four children held jobs, lived on their own, and had their own friends and activities. Melinda fought valiantly against her cancer from 2006 to 2008 and won the battle. She and Mitchell kept busy with their jobs and raising Carter and Madelyn; Wesley and Suzanne worked in secure jobs and enjoyed their time with Ella; Amber lived in an apartment and worked full time; and Clinton worked to pay his way through his master's degree. I poured energy back into my business, and soon it ran on full steam once more.

Over the next few years, Amber held various jobs and moved to several different homes. She moved home briefly in between jobs but kept her positive attitude. Every time she moved to a new town, she found a psychiatrist and a counselor. "I need to always have a good doctor and counselor and be able to work with them," she told me during one of our daily conversations.

2013

Amber experienced a brief setback in February 2013. In the summer of 2011, she took another job as a youth minister, her first passion. During a retreat with fellow employees, she shared a few of her struggles with her brain disorder. Shortly after that, her boss began to micromanage her work. Frustrated, she still did her best, but I could tell during our phone conversation that the job lost the joy she initially felt. Discouraged, she continued for over a year, but problems outside her parish and within the diocese piled up. All of it affected her. I heard her frustration during our daily chats, but she still continued to give the job her all.

On Valentine's Day 2013, her boss called her into his office and demanded her resignation—immediately. He announced to the parish the following Sunday she left because of illness. I was infuriated. Every part of me wanted to walk into the office to yell and scream. After cooling down (slightly), I decided I couldn't put Amber through the stress of a confrontation, so I chalked it off to stigma and a petty, little man's lack of education. The following weekend, we moved Amber home again.

I saw a change this time, though. Instead of becoming paralyzed by a state of depression, she immediately searched for a new job. Within a few months, she started a new job a couple of hours away from our home. We packed up her things and moved her to a new town. She loved her new job and thrived there. The stress she felt in the previous job dissipated, and she has stayed in her new employment for over two years. Each year at the yearly review, she received outstanding evaluations from her employer as well as her coworkers.

There was one unexpected benefit of her new job—more physical movement. She found herself up and down all day long, lifting and carrying. The extra movement worked as exercise and she began to lose weight. This served as a catalyst for Amber to want to go one step further: take off the extra poundage she had gained since she became ill.

"Medicine made me gain this weight, so I decided to try some medicine to take it off," Amber declared to me during one of our daily phone chats. "Hopefully, it will suppress my appetite."

I applauded her decision. From the beginning of her treatment, I had read the statistics about the shortened life span for people with brain disorders due to excess weight. The extra poundage led to other health issues, such as heart disease and diabetes. I felt grateful to God, once again, for her insight into her body's needs.

Amber started to work toward a healthier lifestyle. She ate smaller portions and tried to make better choices for her meals. She made an effort to incorporate walks outside in her weekly routine.

The dietary change, along with her resolve to eat healthier food, began to pay off. Slowly, the excess weight came off. Within eighteen months, she lost sixty pounds.

"I haven't reached my goal yet," she told me when I congratulated her.

"You'll get there. You've made a lot of progress. I'm so proud of you."

Fully employed, she no longer needs SSDI or Medicare or any public assistance. She manages her finances, her job, and her social life and even reminds Roy when it's time to change the oil in her car.

Amber's journey from the debilitating symptoms of schizophrenia to full independence arrived at a place called success. Through our struggles, I learned that God will never abandon us. Since Amber's illness began, I've been reminded often to listen to the wisdom that has always been available. I just needed to ask. My faith deepened as I dealt with the heartache and hardship of mental illness. I came to realize God worked through the people around me as well as the scriptures and readings I did. With them, he held me up when I was too weak to stand. I gained the assurance that I was not alone. I knew in my heart that God took my hand and Amber's throughout every trial; he saw her broken brain and my broken heart; he mended us; he fortified us.

He made us whole.

epilogue

In December 2004, mental illness entered my daughter's life. It snuck in and took root before I knew what had happened. Confusion, anger, frustration, and guilt quickly followed. I felt helpless, hopeless, and terribly alone. Nothing we tried helped her. I had a choice to make: I could wallow in my misery or I could learn all I could. If I educated myself, I could do more to help my daughter on her journey to recovery.

I chose the latter, although at times, self-pity took over. But mostly, I threw myself into education. I read books on mental health and schizophrenia, as well as books that fed my soul. I wanted to feed the mental part of me as well as the spiritual part of me that felt like it was starving. I knew those two parts of me worked together.

As I strove for knowledge, it helped with some of the choices Roy and I made on her behalf. These decisions took place after an excruciating discernment process. Now, as I look at Amber and where she is today, I know the decisions proved correct for our situation. I see how they benefited her.

Even still, I did feel like a traitor to my child when we committed her and forced her to take medication. I felt we had no choice; I watched helplessly as she entered a world where her reality no longer matched mine. Roy and I couldn't reach that place, no matter how hard we tried. Also, I couldn't allow her illness to affect and threaten the rest of my family any longer. I agonized over the issue, but in the end, I knew forced medication was the best option she had to recover the life I felt she wanted for herself.

At the time, Roy and I were taking the NAMI class, and we learned the difference early intervention can make for first-time psychosis. It scared me when I learned how the gray matter in the brain is slowly destroyed when left unchecked. If we hadn't forced Amber to take the antipsychotic medication, would she have ever recovered?

During the classes, I also learned about the four stages of schizophrenia: prodromal (beginning symptoms), active, recovery, and remission. As I learned about the prodromal stage, guilt set in. I kicked myself around, disgusted, for not realizing sooner what Amber faced. I did notice Amber seemed anxious and/or depressed a few times during high school and then later in college. She always assured me she had it under control. I had no reason to doubt her, so I dismissed my concerns.

Why didn't I recognize the big change in her personality in 2004? Roy and I commented how it seemed odd she let her car run out of oil in early November that year. The previous year, she had shown us her ability to take care of the car. She had trouble with it when she lived about four hours away, volunteering for a year of mission work. It continually overheated. Since Roy had taught her the basics of car maintenance during her high school years, she kept an eye on her antifreeze and coolant levels, refilling them almost daily, until he could check it out. Yet we overlooked it when she ruined the engine in her car by running it without oil. We also noticed her quiet demeanor at Thanksgiving, but again, it didn't click for either of us. Even when she came home in December, we overlooked her odd behavior and hoped the situation would just go away.

Should I have done something then? Had I ignored the motherly instinct that something was wrong or had I just hoped it would pass those last few weeks before we moved her home? Could the acute stage have been avoided? Guilt consumed me.

As the NAMI course progressed, it taught me the prodromal stage is often hard to detect. Often disguised as depression or anxiety or odd behavior, it gets overlooked, as we had done. When I learned it is rarely diagnosed in this stage, I began to forgive myself. The class also gave me a quote, which helped me understand why I didn't see these changes in Amber. The phrase "You can't know what no one has told you" comforted me. I didn't know the signs because, to put it simply, we just didn't know.

I found I needed to learn to let go of the things I couldn't change and focus on the things I could do to help her. I couldn't move forward if I only looked back with regret.

For our family, it meant moving her home and working with her doctors, therapists, social workers, and friends to create a healing environment.

Part of the environment meant letting her sleep when she wanted, eating at odd times of the day, working with her by playing games that required thinking, and not requiring her to cook, clean, or do laundry. It also included continual communication with her doctors and therapists. Even when the doctors couldn't speak to me, I could tell them what I felt they needed to know. The awareness of how things went for Amber on a day-to-day basis, I believe, led to a better understanding for all of us. I think about those years as a hand-up, not a handout.

Yes, some days I felt sorry for myself. So many things went wrong in a short amount of time for us. I refer to late 2004 through 2006 as the hard years—the years of the three biggies: mental illness, cancer, and death of a loved one. At times, I felt angry. I looked at people whose lives resumed to what I perceived as normal, while my family's health seemed to fall apart at an alarming rate.

Some days, I felt so tired and overwhelmed I didn't think I could cope any longer.

Yet even in my frustrated and sorrowful state, I came to rely on a power greater than my own. I realized I couldn't control the exact path of my life. Bad things happened to our family that changed the trajectory I had always envisioned for our future. Bad things happen. They just do, and it's nobody's fault. Through my spiritual studies, I discovered Jesus never promised his followers an easy go in life, only that He would never leave them or forsake them. He promised us we would never be alone.

I found the strength to move forward because I cried out for help during my anguish. I turned to God for my strength, and as a result, my faith became my anchor. I learned to trust God with all parts of my life as I realized I couldn't fix Amber's broken brain. I've heard people refer to God as the Great Physician or Healer. I realized I needed his healing. So I prayed for wisdom and understanding and that I could learn about the problems she faced. On the morning I mentally gave her back to God, I realized who loved her first. If he loved her first and more than I could, then I could trust his will. I found peace, which helped override my paralyzing fear. My four favorite words of prayer became "Thy will be done."

I also came to the understanding that if I was alone, it was by my choice. When I finally cried out to my family and friends, they let me know that I was not alone in this journey. Sharing my struggles with them helped lighten my load. When I felt life treated me unfairly, they reached out to hold my hand as I cried or wrapped an arm around my shoulders.

There is a saying that shared grief is divided and shared joy is multiplied. It didn't matter what my loved ones said to me during the lowest points of my life. At times, there was nothing that could be said that would take away the sting. But their presence made it easier to handle. It comforted me and held me up when I didn't think I could stand alone. Letting them into my painful world was an important road for me to take. I found courage in the parade of countless people who visited Amber in the hospital. These acts that maybe seemed small to them enlightened me. I saw the hand of God working in all of them and knew I wasn't alone.

When I talk about Amber's recovery, I often hear the remark, "She's doing so well because of you and your husband." I don't agree with that statement. In my opinion, we were one part of a recovery equation for Amber. We didn't do it alone. I like to think of it as more of a village approach.

We gave her a stable and calm environment with the hope she could recover. But there's a long list of others whose roles were vital: doctors, hospital staff, counselors, therapists, social workers, family, and friends. But most importantly, Amber herself became part of the solution. Her drive to set her goals high and work hard to reach them took her beyond what I ever imagined.

The RAISE (Recovery After an Initial Schizophrenia Episode)[19] study, which began in July 2009 by the National Institute of Mental Health, tested an integrated approach for treatment. It studied a team approach for recovery. Its multifaceted care model involved medications, therapies, psychosocial treatments (such as group or individual therapy and rehabilitation), family education, and supported employment. Scientists questioned if this integrated team approach would enable the patient to recover and integrate back into society.

I look back on the last ten years and can see similarities between the RAISE approach and how our family dealt with Amber's broken brain.

The study emphasized early intervention during first-time psychosis, and our family forced Amber into treatment when we realized her brain had broken. Amber didn't have a recovery team that met regularly, as in the study, but I kept her psychiatrists and her counselor informed. We kept a journal that detailed Amber's emotional state and faxed it to them before each of her scheduled appointments. We wanted the doctors and counselors to peek into her day-to-day life; a few minutes once or twice a month couldn't give them a real view of her health. Amber and I filled out the daily log together because I wanted her involved in the process.

I think Vocational Rehabilitation provided another aspect in the equation for her recovery: rehabilitation. Her caseworker, Rita, helped ease her back into the mainstream by enabling her to go to a Certified Nursing

Assistant program and later pursue her Licensed Practical Nursing degree. The classes, the assignments, and even the time among her classmates all gave her experiences which integrated her back into society.

Antisocial behavior and withdrawal from society—two of the negative and residual effects of schizophrenia—often cause people with schizophrenia to lose friends. Her friend, Brooke, provided a piece of the puzzle for her recovery that Roy and I could not. She took her into social situations with her peers by involving Amber in Bible study, church services, and the volleyball league. Within the confines of a faith-filled environment, Amber's friendships swelled. Instead of isolation, she found acceptance.

Our families and friends also contributed to her socialization. They treated Amber with a compassion I couldn't have envisioned. I remember how nervous I felt at a bridal shower shortly after Amber's release from the university hospital.

How will her cousins treat her? I wondered. *Will they be afraid of her? Will they be uncomfortable? Will Amber feel like she doesn't fit in?*

I shouldn't have concerned myself. I watched in awe as her cousins treated her exactly as they always had. "Hey, Piggy," "Hi, Cheesy Potatoes," (a silly nickname used by one of them) and "Glad you could make it, Amber," were followed by endless chatter as the young women shared snippets of their lives since the last gathering. Love and acceptance met my fears head on.

Part of the recommended action plan in the RAISE study is educating the family about mental illness. I feel thankful that Roy and I learned about Amber's broken brain through the NAMI organization at the same time we had to make some difficult decisions on her behalf. I felt supported by my instructor and classmates as we made the excruciating choices. I learned about the biology of the brain, medications and the accompanying side effects, and treatment options, along with suggestions for self-care and coping skills. I devoured books about mental illness and tucked the lessons learned by others deep in my heart. This equipped me with an understanding of her situation. The discovery of facts and information about mental illness armed me with the tools I needed to cope as schizophrenia dumped many nasty symptoms on my daughter. And Amber's brothers also read books about schizophrenia at the onset of her illness. Their support supported me.

Education was my first step in becoming armed against the challenges and heartbreaks of mental illness. I learned about the organization The Brain and Behavior Research Foundation. It funnels money into research for brain disorders and publishes results of new brain health discoveries through a weekly newsletter. In addition, I set up a Google account which compiles all news on the web about schizophrenia and sends it to my email account. It seems as though there are always new tools and remedies to try, like taking fish oil to help brain function or an app that provides games and puzzles to reform neural connections (similar to what Amber and I tried alone).

I feel God guided me along the way on my journey with Amber as she battled schizophrenia. Time and time again, I prayed for guidance as I vented my frustrations to God and asked for specific needs. Ideas came to me during my morning devotions or while I prayed during my workday. I shut off the television and radio and meditated as I embroidered, stitched items, or washed dishes. I also received inspiration and guidance from others who shared with me their own similar paths. If I hadn't opened up to others, I would have missed this integral part of my own support team.

And I have to share with you that as I studied about the various mental illnesses and leaned on the stories and experiences of others, my perceptions changed. I came to the awareness that they are biological illnesses. They are not a character flaw. They are disorders of one of our organs: the brain. I understood this was not deserved nor wanted by those affected. They didn't ask to have this any more than a person who has diabetes wants a limited diet or the need to take injections. Both are malfunctions of a chemical process happening in the body. In diabetes, it's the pancreas that can't produce the needed levels of insulin. In mental illness, it's the brain, the most miraculous organ we have. With mental illness, some of the billions of connections in the brain are broken and need medication to work properly again.

The medication Amber needs to take assists her brain with the chemicals needed for the processes to work correctly. I look at her medication the same way I view insulin for the diabetic or pills to treat a person's blood pressure or the countless other medicines taken each day by millions of people. The body requires them to live a life similar to others around them.

With proper treatment, I believe that there is hope for recovery. Today, Amber lives two hours from us with a friend in a townhouse. She works full-time and manages all her affairs and finances. Her determination for independence with no help from social services served as a catalyst for employment. She expressed to me over and over her dislike of others supporting her. She understood that once she started working more, she would no longer qualify for Social Security Disability Income, so she worked diligently toward a full-time position. When that day arrived, I saw her self-confidence blossom. Today, she is careful to find employment with health insurance benefits; she knows her need for medication along with doctor and counselor appointments.

I had another lesson to learn. Amber's insight into herself and what she needs to be healthy was visible to others sooner than it was to me. Amber had been living on her own for several months when her counselor, Connie, called me. She wanted to let me know she planned to advise the court that Amber no longer needed the order for medication. I panicked. Fear entered with a vengeance. I remembered that relapses typically happen in the first ten years. We hadn't reached that benchmark yet. I worried Amber would think she didn't need the medication and go off it. I knew that this often happened to those affected with schizophrenia.

I voiced my concerns to Connie, who reassured me she felt Amber was ready. I still remember her words: "She has come a long, long way. I honestly feel she doesn't need the court order. She understands her illness. I highly recommend it."

So I buried my objections in "Thy will be done" and listened to the voice of an experienced professional. Connie was right. Amber proved to me, and to everyone around her, that she didn't need the court to tell her she needed medicine. God had answered the prayer I prayed so many years before—that Amber would understand her illness.

Our control over her finances and decision-making ended when we didn't renew the conservator and guardianship court order in 2014. Each year, I needed to give a financial report to the court and refile the petition. Amber wanted us to release it years earlier. That spring, Roy and I finally realized Amber no longer needed this from us. She could and had proved to us that her ability to manage her affairs had returned. Amber had held jobs almost continually since 2009, she handled her money with almost the same ability she did before her illness began, and she faithfully took her medication. We felt our family had overcome the worst symptoms schizophrenia inflicted. The time had come to end our control and conservatorship.

Sometimes I wonder: *Why?* Not why this happened to our family, but why did everything work as it did to enable Amber to move into recovery? But I discovered that if I spend my energy trying to find out the answers to the "why"s, I lose the ability to move forward.

Instead, I share our journey in the hopes our story will allow others facing similar circumstances to glean a nugget from my experience to help them along their way. I tell Amber often how proud I am of her, of the incredible courage it took to work hard and overcome the symptoms she endured.

Still, when I read of yet another tragedy due to an untreated or ineffective treatment of schizophrenia and other mental illnesses, my grief box clutches at my heart with renewed vigor. I grieve for the people: the families of both the victims and the person with mental illness. I've mourned the loss of another life as I attended funerals for members of my family and for friends who lost their battle with mental illness and took their own life. I weep for them, for their family, and for all those who must face the pain of such loss.

I know how easily that could have been us, mourning the loss of someone who we loved with all of our hearts.

Sometimes, as I mourn for another, I still can't help but ask why. I question what happened differently for them to block their recovery. Gratitude for our situation usually follows, along with a resolve to reach out.

I feel frustrated by the inadequacy of our mental health care. A shortage of trained and competent physicians, counselors, psychiatrists, psychologists, and effective treatment facilities has resulted in too many lost or broken lives. But I live with the hope that one day, doctors and researchers will discover new treatments which lead to full recovery for all those affected by broken brains. I cling to the idea; neuroscience will progress to understanding all the causes and lead to prevention.

Until then, I will hold myself accountable to the promise I made to myself years ago. The people who surrounded me in NAMI classes helped changed my attitude toward my daughter's broken brain. My fractured faith—repaired through the many tentacles of support and the grace I received from God—catapults me to share our journey at every opportunity. When Amber didn't need my entire focus, I'd decided I would remember the benefits I received from the classes I took that first year. I vowed I would pay it forward by volunteering for the organization. Within my heart, I signed an invisible contract to write and speak to people in their distress. I feel honored when asked to speak to groups about mental illness.

Each time I reach out to other families during the series of classes or the bimonthly support group, I learn more about mental illness, the resiliency of dedicated family members, and their deep yearning to help their loved ones. I also gain insight into the lives of those who battle mental illness and their journeys to achieve wellness.

I pray that my actions allow God to work through me. I also pray and study his ways to stay close to the shore at all times. I want my faith anchored in all ways of life, not just the difficult parts. The lesson "I'm not immune from life's difficulties" and the phrase "Thy will be done" became ingrained in me.

A quote by C. S. Lewis expresses my goals for the rest of my life here on earth and my reason for telling you my story: "Don't shine so others can see you. Shine so that through you others see him."

endnotes

1. Andreasen, Nancy C. *The Broken Brain: The Biological Revolution in Psychiatry.* New York: Harper & Row, Publishers, 1985.

2. Williamson, Marianne. *Illuminata: A Return to Prayer.* New York: Riverhead Books, 1995.

3. Torrey, E. Fuller. *Surviving Schizophrenia: A Manual for Families, Consumers, and Providers, 4th Edition.* New York: HarperCollins, 2001.

4. Kushner, Harold. *When Bad Things Happen to Good People.* New York: Schocken Books, 1981. Pg. 190.

5. Ibid.

6. Ibid.

7. Ibid.

8. Ibid.

9. Ibid, 180.

10. Ibid.

11. Ibid, 182.

12. Ibid.

13. Ibid, 183.

14. Williamson, *Illuminata.*

15. Isaiah 65:24, King James Bible.

16. Job 6:24, New International Version.

17. *Daily Guideposts 2006: Spirit-Lifting Thoughts for Every Day of the Year*. Grand Rapids, MI: Guideposts, 2006.

18. Kushner, *When Bad Things Happen to Good People*, 182.

19. "Recovery After an Initial Schizophrenia Episode (RAISE)." The National Institute of Mental Health. http://www.nimh.nih.gov/health/topics/schizophrenia/raise/index.shtml.

resources

Once I understood the issues Amber faced, I was able to assist her on her road to recovery. I found the following resources valuable in my quest for understanding.

Books on Mental Illness

The Quiet Room: A Journey out of the Torment of Madness by Lori Schiller and Amanda Bennett
This book gave me an insight into the thoughts and actions of someone with schizophrenia. Lori Schiller wrote an honest memoir of her experience as she suffered for many years with this illness. It also offered me hope as she detailed her recovery.

The Broken Brain: The Biological Revolution in Psychiatry by Nancy C. Andreasen
Published in 1983, this book challenged me as I strove to understand the biology of the brain and the processes affected during mental illness. It discussed the biological processes of both normal and disturbed brain functions. I realized mental illness is a biological illness, not a character flaw.

Surviving Schizophrenia: A Manual for Families, Consumers, and Providers, 4th Edition by E. Fuller Torrey
E. Fuller Torrey's 2001 book explains the natural cause of schizophrenia along with symptoms and treatments. It gave me an additional

understanding of the illness my daughter faced. In 2013, the 6th edition was published.

Books I Read As Part of My Faith Journey

Illuminata: A Return to Prayer by Marianne Williamson
The prayers in this book helped me center myself as I prayed for my home, my daughter, and myself. I carried this with me in my purse as I went to the hospitals.

Daily Guideposts 2006: Spirit-Lifting Thoughts for Every Day of the Year
This book had 365 devotionals, one for each day of the year. On the days I took time, I read a scripture, a reflection, and a prayer starter. I liked it because it gave me a focus each day, something away from my daily routine. Guideposts publishes a new daily devotional each year, as well as several magazines and other books.

When Bad Things Happen to Good People **by Harold Kushner**
As I read this book, I gradually came to accept the hand I had been dealt. I decided to learn to play that hand to the best of my ability and try to bring good out of the bad things that happened to us. I still like to refer back to it on occasion. It helps me keep life's challenges in perspective.

Other Reading I Used on the Internet

St. Charles Borromeo Catholic Church Prayers: http://www.scborromeo.org/prayers.htm
This website has links to many of the prayers I used and referred to during my faith journey. I used some of these to create my own book of prayers.

NAMI (National Alliance on Mental Illness): http://www.nami.org
This site has links to local affiliates across the nation, educational materials on the various disorders associated with mental illness, phone numbers, information on classes offered, recovery stories, updates on legislative issues, and online support groups.

NIMH (National Institute of Mental Health): http://www.nimh.nih. gov/index.shtml
This site has links for health and education, including free publications either online or to order; involvement in study opportunities; and research discoveries.

RAISE (Recovery After an Initial Schizophrenia Episode): http:// www.nimh.nih.gov/health/topics/schizophrenia/raise
The RAISE study discussed in the book was initiated by the National Institute of Mental Health in 2008. This large-scale research began in earnest across the United States in 2009. It examined a coordinated treatment approach for people experiencing psychosis for the first time, along with ways for clinics to set up this treatment plan geared toward recovery.

Brain and Behavior Research Foundation: https://bbrfoundation.org
The Brain and Behavior Research Foundation is an organization that publishes information on mental illness, funds research for scientists exploring causes and treatments for various mental illnesses, and publishes new discoveries and recovery stories.

Mayo Clinic: http://www.mayoclinic.org/diseases-conditions/index
Mayo Clinic's website offers current information on diseases, including mental illness. There is a section for a symptom checker, as well as information on each illness. These can be found in the index using the first letter.

Mental Health First Aid USA: http://www.mentalhealthfirstaid.org/cs/
Mental Health First Aid USA is a nationwide organization that offers a course on how to help people developing a mental illness or in a crisis. It is managed, operated, and dispersed by the National Council on Behavioral Health and the Missouri Department of Mental Health. I took this course in 2014 and learned more about recognizing warning signs of addiction and mental illness, the impact of substance abuse disorders, a five-step action plan for identifying a crisis and taking action, and where to find help.

Phone Numbers

NAMI (National Alliance on Mental Illness): 703-524-7600

NAMI HelpLine: 800-950-6264

Mental Health First Aid USA: 202-684-7457

National Suicide Prevention Lifeline: 1-800-273-8255 (Available 24/7)

acknowledgments

Many people have believed in me, which gave me the courage to write my memories of my journey. A heartfelt thank you to Mary, whose friendship and experience encouraged me to share our story; to the many experienced authors at writing conferences, whose knowledge taught me the process; to Sue, Jean, and the members of my local Christian writing group who gave me direction as I worked on various skills; to my editor, Lindsay Sandberg, who guided me as I finished *Broken Brain, Fortified Faith*; and to all those who have played a role in my faith formation, which kept has kept me grounded.

about the author

Virginia Pillars has owned and operated a business since 1994. She volunteers for the National Alliance on Mental Illness organization as an instructor for the Family to Family educational program and leads support groups. Certified in First Aid for Mental Health, she speaks on mental illness, operating a small business, and quilting for organizations, workshops, and faith retreats. She's had two pieces published in devotionals, four essays in various anthologies, including two in *Chicken Soup for the Soul*, and other works of nonfiction. Virginia, a mother of four adult children, lives on an Iowa farm with her husband.

about familius

Welcome to a place where mothers are celebrated, not compared. Where heart is at the center of our families, and family at the center of our homes. Where boo boos are still kissed, cake beaters are still licked, and mistakes are still okay. Welcome to a place where books—and family— are beautiful. Familius: a book publisher dedicated to helping families be happy.

Visit Our Website: www.familius.com

Our website is a different kind of place. Get inspired, read articles, discover books, watch videos, connect with our family experts, download books and apps and audiobooks, and along the way, discover how values and happy family life go together.

Join Our Family

There are lots of ways to connect with us! Subscribe to our newsletters at www.familius.com to receive uplifting daily inspiration, essays from our Pater Familius, a free ebook every month, and the first word on special discounts and Familius news.

Become an Expert

Familius authors and other established writers interested in helping families be happy are invited to join our family and contribute online content. If you have something important to say on the family, join our expert community by applying at:

www.familius.com/apply-to-become-a-familius-expert

Get Bulk Discounts

If you feel a few friends and family might benefit from what you've read, let us know and we'll be happy to provide you with quantity discounts. Simply email us at specialorders@familius.com.

Website: www.familius.com

Facebook: www.facebook.com/paterfamilius

Twitter: @familiustalk, @paterfamilius1

Pinterest: www.pinterest.com/familius

The most important work you ever do will be within the walls of your own home.

CPSIA information can be obtained at www.ICGtesting.com
Printed in the USA
LVOW08s2059141016

508840LV00001B/9/P